following our bliss

ALSO BY DON LATTIN

Shopping for Faith: American Religion in the New Millennium
with Richard Cimino

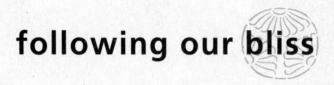

following our bliss

How the Spiritual Ideals of
the Sixties Shape Our Lives Today

DON LATTIN

HarperSanFrancisco
A Division of HarperCollins*Publishers*

HarperCollins books may be purchased for educational, business, or sales promotional use. For information please write: Special Markets Department, HarperCollins Publishers, Inc., 10 East 53rd Street, New York, NY 10022.

HarperCollins Web site: http://www.harpercollins.com

HarperCollins®, 📖 ®, and HarperSanFrancisco™ are trademarks of HarperCollins Publishers, Inc.

Book design by M. Blegen

FIRST HARPERCOLLINS PAPERBACK EDITION PUBLISHED IN 2004

Library of Congress Cataloging-in-Publication Data has been ordered and is available upon request.

ISBN 0–06–073063–3 (pbk.)

04 05 06 07 08 RRD-H ❖ 10 9 8 7 6 5 4 3 2 1

In memory of my brother, Alan

CONTENTS

For the past two decades I've covered the religion beat for daily newspapers in San Francisco, a city where the dominant religious preference seems to be "none of the above" or perhaps "all of the above." I've met Mother Teresa, held hands with the Dalai Lama and Thich Nhat Hanh, interviewed Billy Graham and Krishnamurti, cracked jokes with the Mormon prophet, and flown on the pope's plane. Oh, the messiahs I have known! Once I chased an American guru all the way out to his own private island in Fiji, where he was on retreat with a former Playboy playmate (Miss September 1976) and his eight other wives. I've investigated so many spiritual teachers, self-help swamis, and cult leaders that I've completely forgotten some of them. There have been many more memorable and compassionate souls, but too much corruption alongside all that compassion. Occupational hazard, I guess, hanging out in the dim alley where cynicism meets skepticism, looking for a little light.

This book began with the stories of children born into the Sixties counterculture—cults, communes, meditation centers, and other alternative spiritual groups. The idea was to look at the Sixties through their eyes and hear the lessons learned by their parents. Along the way, it grew into a larger look at the spiritual legacy of the Sixties—at how feminism, the drug culture, the sexual revolution, rock 'n' roll, and the gay rights movement have challenged the religious establishment and shaped our lives. These are not "only in San Francisco" stories. They are drawn from scores of interviews with people living in Texas, Tennessee, Montana, New York, South Carolina, Oregon, Arizona, and elsewhere. This is an American story.

It could not have been told without the friendship and critical assistance of Aimee Chitayat, Mitch Clogg, George Csicsery, Antonia Lattin, Susan Rock, and Cheryl Daniels Shohan. Many thanks to Wendy Miller and my colleagues at the *San Francisco Chronicle* for giving me a leave of absence to work on the manuscript; to the wise counsel of my agent, Amy Rennert, for getting it to the publisher; to the sharp eye of my editor, John Loudon, and his able assistant, Kris Ashley, for getting it into print; and to my wife, Laura, and the girls, for putting up with me through "all of the above."

INTRODUCTION

Are you experienced?
Have you ever been experienced?
Well, I have.

"ARE YOU EXPERIENCED"
JIMI HENDRIX, 1968

We were a restless bunch, helplessly hoping, endlessly searching for ecstasy and enlightenment. We didn't want to believe it. We wanted to *feel* it. We wanted to *experience* something beyond doctrine, dogma, and denominationalism—whether through Jesus, peyote, or a charismatic swami from the East. We were, famously, into spirituality, not religion.

What began with a call for what we could do for our country ended for many with a search for ourselves. Along the way a generation came of age, embracing the values, and the antivalues, of the era. Old forms of faith and family collapsed, and the search was on for something new. Parents acted like children and children like parents. We were a generation that was not content to stay in the suburbs and pray to God on Sunday morning. Many of us wanted to see God, to be God, or to at least recapture the ecstasy and revelation of that eye-opening acid trip we couldn't get out of our system.

In his memoir, *Sleeping Where I Fall*, actor Peter Coyote describes his life in the Sixties as "the pursuit of absolute freedom." He wanted to live in the "perpetual present." Coyote rolled out to the West Coast in 1964 and soon fell in with the Diggers and the San Francisco Mime Troop, two guerrilla theater groups that mixed radical politics with prehippie antics. "From our point of view," he writes, "freedom involved first liberating the imagination from economic assumptions of profit and private property that demanded existence at the expense of personal truthfulness and honor, then living according to personal authenticity and fidelity to inner directives and impulses."[1] Does that sound high-minded? Don't worry. Coyote goes on to confess that the Digger philosophy was also a great way to get high and get laid.

In more ways than one, the Sixties were a riot. It seemed like the highs were higher and the lows were lower. We felt alive. "There was a kind of wistfulness," recalls poet David Whyte. "We actually experienced life. Everything is so strained now. My son is sixteen, and it seems like he's missing something. There's a tremendous feeling of constraint. We were one of the last generations that were just let go to play when we were young. Now they are ferried from place to place and everything has to be scheduled. I think this has a huge effect. It's molding our society in ways we haven't comprehended."

Perhaps every generation thinks their youth was an extraordinary time. It's easy to romanticize the Sixties. It's also easy to parody those times, and I've tried to do neither in this book. If you're looking for a rant against the baby boomers, check out *Balsamic Dreams* or, for a more nuanced attack on the "bourgeois bohemians," *Bobos in Paradise.*[2] Both books are entertaining, but they focus on only the upper crust of the boomer pie—the yuppies, the sellouts, the radical chic, the costume hippies. Those are easy targets. This book looks at the real spiritual activists of the Sixties counterculture, idealists who were trying to save the world or at least transform themselves. They were the yeast in the dough of our generation, the lively culture that made it rise.

We will spend a lot of time looking at these times through the eyes of the *real* children of the Sixties—kids born and raised amid some of the era's wildest social, spiritual, and sexual experimentation. As we'll see, the Sixties were a mixed blessing for the actual children of that generation's counterculture. To many of them, it was an era of shattered institutions and broken homes, a time that saw the rise of no-fault divorce and no-fault religion. No unequivocal moral can be drawn from their experiences, but the stories are amazing—tales of two generations that forever altered America's spiritual landscape.

Many of their parents were converts to Buddhism, spiritualism, or other latter-day revelations. Having rejected the faith of their fathers, they were hesitant to impose their newly formed beliefs on their children. They didn't want to lay their trip on the kids as their parents had with them. Other families profiled in this book provide a counterpoint to that kind of laissez-faire religious education. They practiced extreme religion, and the kids had no choice but to follow their parents down a predetermined spiritual path. These families fully embraced the era's burst of idealism and naïveté, joining utopian movements and religious cults that promised to save the world through Krishna consciousness, Jesus Christ, or the messianic message of Sun Myung Moon. While their parents were out spreading a counterculture gospel, the kids were often left behind at nurseries, boarding schools, and communal farms. Some were abandoned and abused and left the fold as soon as they could. Others kept the faith and even passed it on to a third generation.

Many of us have our own definition of the Sixties—not only what it was but *when* it was. January 1, 1960, to December 31, 1969, is technically the decade of the 1960s, but the Sixties is more a state of mind than a frame of time. Some scholars of the decade, focusing more on politics than religion, see the birth of the Sixties at the Greensboro lunch counter sit-ins on February 1, 1960, and pronounce it dead on May 4, 1970, when National Guardsmen shot and killed four students at Kent State University. Others argue that the Sixties began in the fifties, with the rise of the Beat movement, and ended with Watergate and the resignation of Richard Nixon on August 9, 1974. There are lots of markers we could pick, but the bookends we'll use for the Sixties encompass nearly two decades—from January 20, 1961, to November 18, 1978. Our "decade" begins with the inaugural speech of John F. Kennedy, a short but powerful address that set the stage for the idealism, religious activism, and social commitment that defined the best of the Sixties. For our purposes, the era ends in 1978 with the murder and mass suicide of more than nine hundred members of Peoples Temple. They were loyal followers of the Reverend Jim Jones, an activist San Francisco preacher who took his flock to South America to establish a socialist commune and escape escalating investigations by the federal government and the news media. There, amid piles of bloated bodies in the Guyana jungle, the spiritual and political dreams of the Sixties collapsed in a collective nightmare. Jonestown forever changed the way we look at cults and communes. For those of us close to the Peoples Temple tragedy, the carnage left us sad, shocked, and wondering what went wrong.

In this book the broader Sixties state of mind is spelled with a capital *S* while the actual decade of the sixties gets a lowercase letter. That means our Sixties takes us through most of the 1970s and what writer Tom Wolfe spotted early as "the Me Decade," when the underlying inspiration for so many of our meditations, group therapies, and consciousness-raising techniques could be summed up in four little words: "Let's talk about Me!"[3]

Much of Sixties spirituality was a reaction to the fifties—a decade of prosperity, rapid church growth, and McCarthyism. The words *under God* were inserted into the Pledge of Allegiance, and going to church was right up there with Mom and apple pie. But something happened between 1961 and 1978, from the hope of Kennedy to the horror of Jonestown. Trust in the nation's institutions, including its religious institutions, went into free fall. New institutions, like the Peace Corps, the civil rights movement, and other organizations of liberation, rose to take their place, but the common bonds were broken.

There were battles in the streets and battles in the home. This was a revolution of faith and family. "Growing up in the fifties, starved for stimulation, connection, and meaning, activists and hippies turned their backs on the cautious lives of their parents," writes Alice Echols. "Nothing defines the generation that came of age in the sixties better than its determination to live outside the parameters of reasonable behavior, which, after all, seemed at the very root of the problem, the cause of America's terrible adventure shortage."[4]

We overcame America's adventure shortage with gusto, and with the help of two little pills. LSD and the birth control pill altered our ideas about sexual morality and reality itself. Mysticism and feminism were on the rise. Women entered the workplace and won the right to lead many churches and synagogues. Single mothers, gays, and lesbians forced us to redefine the family. Despite the Pill, lots of babies were born too soon, right in the middle of the great adventure. Most of them were loved, but sometimes they just got in the way.

Sixties spirituality is expressed not only through the freewheeling lives of those of us who left organized religion to follow our bliss. It also inspired changes in the churches and synagogues those spiritual seekers—and disaffected clergy—left behind. In the Catholic church, thousands of priests and nuns abandoned vows of celibacy to marry or left a church they saw as stagnant and oppressive. Their exodus only strengthened the hand of conservative, traditionalist forces in the Roman church. In mainline Protestant denominations such as the United Methodist Church and the Presbyterian Church (U.S.A.), a progressive political agenda and a new openness to gay rights chased conservative clergy and congregants from the fold. Many went straight into the arms of an emboldened conservative evangelical movement, which reset the political agenda to focus on issues such as abortion, school prayer, and "traditional family values."

Where did all the baby boomers go? Many returned to church once they had their own babies and traditional religious values no longer looked so oppressive. Some retreated to the certainty of the conservative evangelical movement; others discovered that neither Christianity nor Judaism are monolithic institutions. They found religious congregations that were more tolerant of diverse lifestyles and open to spirituality than those of their childhood. Millions never returned to organized religion but remain highly active seekers, preferring to identify themselves as "spiritual" rather than "religious."

How many millions? Tens of millions. In a national survey conducted in January 2002, pollster George Gallup Jr. found that one-third of Americans now describe themselves as "spiritual but not religious."[5] These are not just spiritual seekers and baby boomers stuck in the Sixties. Other recent surveys have found personalized spirituality even more common among those in Generation X, Americans born between 1965 and 1980. Jackson W. Carroll and Wade Clark Roof surveyed more than a thousand Americans and found rising religious individualism in Generation X. For example, nearly 73 percent of the younger generation agreed with the statement "An individual should arrive at religious beliefs independent of church groups." That compared to 65 percent for the baby boomers (those born from 1945 to 1965) and 60 percent for older Americans.[6] Look at the numbers, and the trend is clear: in the new millennium, the children of the baby boomers are also following their own spiritual path.

What do we find at the end of this path? What are spiritual seekers actually seeking?

"People say that what we're all seeking is the meaning of life," replied mythologist Joseph Campbell. "I don't think that's what we're really seeking. I think that what we're seeking is an experience of being alive."[7]

Shortly before his death in 1987, Campbell spoke at length with journalist Bill Moyers in the hugely popular PBS series *The Power of Myth*. It was an enlightening, far-ranging conversation. It gave millions of Americans a new way of looking at the mythic literature of the world's religions. But many of us remember only three words from the long series of Moyers-Campbell interviews: "Follow your bliss."

It came up when Campbell was talking about the last page in the Sinclair Lewis novel *Babbitt*, when the main character laments, "I have never done a single thing I've wanted to in my whole life!"

"That is a man who never followed his bliss," Campbell said. "The religious people tell us we really won't experience bliss until we die and go to heaven. But I believe in having as much as you can of the experience while you are still alive."

Campbell, who was raised in the Catholic church, was not recommending a life of secular hedonism. Listen to what he said when Moyers, a Baptist, asked a follow-up question: "Do you ever have this sense when you are following your bliss, as I have at moments, of being helped by hidden hands?"

"All the time," Campbell replied. "It is miraculous. . . . If you follow your bliss you put yourself on a kind of track that has been there all the while, waiting for you, and the life that you ought to be living is the one you are living. When you can see that, you begin to meet people who are in the field of your bliss, and they open the doors to you. I say, follow your bliss and don't be afraid, and the doors will open where you didn't know they were going to be."[8]

What do we find on the other side of the door? What *do* we find at the end of the path? We find our lives. There is no end. It's a circular route back to us. We are on a spiritual path that seeks the development of human potential. We are not fearfully looking to a judgmental God for approval or to Messiah for eternal salvation. We are spiritual, not religious.

Critics—secular and religious—are quick to lampoon spiritual seekers, accusing them of simplistic, narcissistic, magical thinking that acknowledges neither the power of evil nor the complexity of the real world. There's some truth to that critique, but Christians and other orthodox believers can be just as prone to magical thinking as those written off as "New Agers." In fact, many people who call themselves "spiritual but not religious" are more tolerant, thoughtful, and open to science and the modern world. They're often less likely to accept easy answers to the mysteries of life. And their eclectic philosophy is often fueled not by fear of God but by an inclusive vision of a world living in harmony. You may say they are dreamers, but compare their dream to the future vision in so many evangelical churches—an apocalyptic horror visited upon those who do not follow the one true faith.

"Is God Dead?" *Time* magazine asked that question in giant red letters on its black-bordered cover of April 8, 1966. Those who answered yes were seminary professors, intellectuals, and others unable to see over the walls of their own ideas and small circle of friends. Those believers in the march of secularism mistook the anemia of the mainline Protestant religious establishment—Methodists, Presbyterians, Episcopalians—for a broader atheism that just wasn't there. New expressions of God were breaking out all around them—Pentecostal Christians, New Age seekers, Mormon missionaries, and a resurgent Islam. Wes "Scoop" Nisker, the Buddhist comic and social commentator, gets closer to the truth when he quips: "If God wasn't dead, he at least was having a midlife crisis."[9]

If God didn't change, the way we approached her certainly did. But what do we mean when we call ourselves "spiritual"? And how do we raise our children to be "spiritual"? How do we pass on a religious tradition that seems to defy tradition?

Looking back at American religious history, we see that these are not new questions. From old-time religion to the New Age movement, American faith has always been a blend of individualism, communal spirit, and social experimentation. One of the religious traditions of the United States is having no religious tradition. Forget what the Reverends Jerry Falwell and Pat Robertson tell you about "traditional family values" and our history as a "Christian nation." According to one estimate, less than 15 percent of those living in the American colonies in the 1770s belonged to any church.[10] Astrology, divination, and other occult practices were not just the province of witches in Salem; they enjoyed widespread appeal.

At the same time, the Enlightenment inspired many of our founding fathers to seek out "rational" or "reasonable" religion and to view the established churches and Christian orthodoxy with great suspicion. One scholar of that era offers an intriguing summary of how our founding fathers saw God. It sounds more like the vision of New Agers than conservative evangelicals: "Images of God as a personal being who craves admiration, worship and obedience could be summarily dismissed as inconsistent with the goal of enhancing human agency. Picking and choosing among competing religious ideas was not only possible, it was a necessary step toward full intellectual integrity." Robert Fuller goes on to note that fifty-two of the fifty-six signers of the Declaration of Independence were Masons. "Masons viewed God in impersonal terms, as the Grand Architect of the natural order. They neither approved nor condemned Christianity, but rather viewed it as one manifestation in a long series of historical religions—a series that would culminate in the emergence of a universal faith."[11]

So America's embrace of religious alternatives and our tradition of spiritual individualism go back a long way. If you think the New Age movement started in 1965, remember that William James found that countless nineteenth-century Americans engaged in "systematic exercise in passive relaxation, concentration, and meditation, and have even invoked something like hypnotic practice."[12]

Freedom of religion—and from religion—is one of the foundations upon which our nation stands. But in the 1960s and 1970s, freedom rang like never before. We became a mobile nation, tearing up our religious roots as we moved along. Relaxed immigration laws allowed the arrival of Buddhist teachers, Hindu swamis, Sufi mystics, and others with new varieties of religious experience. Today the spirituality born of the Sixties not only helps define our religious and family life but also shapes the way we work, the kind of health care we seek, and the food we eat.

This new spirituality takes many forms. Part 1 of this book looks at three varieties—the human potential movement, the revisioning of American Catholicism, and the longing for an entirely new kind of revelation. Part 2 explores the lives of those who turned to the East, to the mysticism and meditative practices of India, China, and Japan, and the difficulties they have passing on such culturally different traditions to a new generation.

Some say the Sixties were really about three things—sex, drugs, and rock 'n' roll. They see that unholy trinity and point to our former president, William Jefferson Clinton, as a poster child of the Sixties. But the real story of sex, drugs, rock 'n' roll, and religion is very different, and you'll find it in part 3 of this book. Finally, in part 4, we'll look at paradise lost—at what happened to some of the messianic movements and utopian dreams of the Sixties. We'll end with a visit to the most infamous hippie commune in America, where a few unrepentant dreamers are still following their bliss.

Searching for the Sixties

We start the search at Esalen Institute in Big Sur, the birthplace of the human potential movement and the spot where Sixties spirituality took root on the California coast. Esalen is a retreat center based upon the belief that our human consciousness and capabilities are evolving, in the broader culture and in ourselves. Through a variety of spiritual disciplines, physical training, and psychological therapies, we can transform our consciousness, improve our communication, and deepen our compassion for other people. There are many levels of reality, but most of us barely scratch the surface.

There is no doctrine, no exclusive claim to sacred truth. Sixties spirituality is like a course in comparative religion, a search for the mystical center in all major faiths. Esalen and Sixties spirituality are not about believing in God.

They're about *experiencing God.*

At Esalen we meet David Price, born in 1963 to the institute's cofounder, the late Richard Price. A literal child of the Sixties, David was born at ground zero of the Dionysian decade and shares the mixed memories of many kids raised amid the wonder and the craziness of that extraordinary era.

While Esalen blossomed during the early 1960s, another spiritual revival was happening on the other side of the world. In Rome the Second Vatican Council opened up Catholicism to the modern world, redefined the church as the "people of God," and began (albeit briefly) a new openness toward other ideas and theologies. Like Esalen, Vatican II inspired a feeling of hope and sense of possibility. It also unleashed a new wave of social activism in the church that became an important part of the broader peace and justice movements of the 1960s, 1970s, and, mostly recently, in a revived antiwar movement.

In the late 1970s and 1980s there was reaction against this newfound freedom in the Catholic church and among evangelicals on the religious right. Pope Paul VI refused to reconsider church teachings against birth control, married priests, and the ordination of women. Pope John Paul II tightened the doctrinal reins, appointing bishops who would continue the campaign against perceived excesses of Vatican II. Thousands of priests and nuns left the fold, and we'll meet some of them in chapter 2.

Millions of Catholics, Protestants, and Jews in the baby boomer generation left organized religion in the Sixties and embarked on a new spiritual search. There was no shortage of gurus, self-help groups, and new revelations to explore. In chapter 3 we look at one of them. A Course in Miracles envisions a loving and accepting God, not a deity who rules with fear and judgment. Like many other New Age philosophies that blossomed in the sixties and seventies, the goal here was not to trust Jesus but to "know thyself."

The Baths at Esalen

Woodstock, 1969

CHAPTER I

Esalen Institute and the First Child of the Sixties

And so, become yourself
because the past is just a "good-bye."
Don't you ever ask them why.
If they told you, you would die.
So just look at them and sigh
and know they love you.

"TEACH YOUR CHILDREN"
CROSBY, STILLS, NASH, AND YOUNG, 1970

Every story needs a beginning and every religion its Garden of Eden. Ours begins on a green shelf perched above the rugged splendor of the central California coast. Blue and orange wildflowers dazzle in the noonday sun. Steaming hot springs bubble up from the ground, forming pools with a pungent smell but a sensuous, silky feel. Sixty feet below, the cold Pacific crashes ashore. This is a place of pilgrimage, but not just for humans. Monarch butterflies rest here during their annual migration. They make the round-trip only once, but somehow their progeny find the way back. In coastal canyons cool with morning fog, these noble insects annually blanket the landscape with wings of orange and black.

Big Sur is wild and full of wonder. It's danger and delight. You feel the seasons. Rain and wind lash the coast in winter, sending mud and rock sliding down the hillsides. But those same storms nourish this dry landscape, inspiring green grasses, poppies, and lupine to shoot up in the spring. Summers are cold and foggy, but the salt air warms in early fall, drying the spring grass and fueling wildfires that blacken the land.

Big Sur opens you up, but it can tear at your soul, leaving emptiness inside. It's the end of the line for those of us who wandered across the continent, running from the past or toward an uncertain future. There's nowhere to go but off the cliff or into yourself. At the edge lies the serpent, coiled and ready to help you find the truth. Take this knowledge, drink this potion, shed your skin, find yourself, find God, find something, but be careful not to lose it because you can't go back.

David Price was conceived here. It happened in the Waterfall House, a little cabin built atop some of the rocks that channel Hot Springs Creek. The creek tumbles to the sea through one of those butterfly-covered canyons, past the shack where sperm met egg in 1963. His parents, Richard and Eileen, met at a resort called Big Sur Hot Springs. It would soon be known as Esalen Institute—ground zero for a revolution in consciousness, a place where the young and the hip would soon take off their clothes, drop their defenses, and revel, wail, whine, and dance around whatever came forth from the psyche, spirit, or soul. It would be silly, serious, spiritual, sensuous, self-indulgent—all at the same time. It would be religion, California style, and would spread across the country and around the world. It was about workshops, not worship, seeking your true self, not eternal salvation. It was experiential, not theological. What would happen at Big Sur during the next few years would be nothing less than the birth pangs of a new religion, a new kind of spirituality. But for young David, it was not the Garden of Eden. It was paradise lost.

His mother, Eileen, had come to Big Sur in 1958. She stayed for a while at the home of Emil White, an old friend of Henry Miller, who moved here in the 1940s. Miller attracted an enclave of artists, freethinkers, and hangers-on. His sexually explicit books, *Tropic of Cancer* and *Tropic of Capricorn,* were still banned in the United States, and the author had become the folk hero of the fringe literati. Their Big Sur hangout had been notorious since 1947 when it was described in an article in *Harper's* magazine titled "The New Cult of Sex and Anarchy." Author Mildred Edie Brady found a new kind of religion percolating along the coast, an erotic, sentimental mysticism that traded a wrathful Jehovah for a subtler "life force."[1] Its sages were Miller, D. H. Lawrence, and William Blake; its philosophers, the mystics G. I. Gurdjieff and P. D. Ouspensky, along with the crazed genius Wilhelm Reich.

David's father, Richard, came to California to attend Stanford University. Richard earned an undergraduate degree in psychology in 1952 then headed back east to Harvard for graduate studies. Richard Price had no interest in the business world of his father, a corporate leader with Sears, Roebuck & Company back in Chicago, nor was he taken by mainstream academia. He soon left Harvard, returned to San Francisco, and signed up for classes at the Academy of Asian Studies. Price was drawn to Eastern mysticism and the emerging Beat scene in North Beach, but there were demons. A strange euphoria was building up inside him. One spring night he started acting out in a North Beach bar and was tossed into a paddy wagon by six San Francisco cops. According to the authorities, and his father, Price had gone nuts. He was now in the system, sent through a string of mental hospitals, ending with nearly a year at a private psychiatric center in New England called the Institute for Living. They pioneered shock treatment there, and they tried it out on Price. Later he'd refer to this as his "incarceration." His brain was zapped dozens of times with insulin and electric shock. They beat him down but didn't knock him out. Price returned to California in the spring of 1960, this time with a vision that there must be another road to mental health for those struggling with emotional and spiritual turmoil.

Eileen's relationship with Richard lasted only a few months after David's birth. She was living a few miles up Highway One from Big Sur Hot Springs, and Richard wasn't around much. "My father was not very available when I was growing up," David recalls. "He was still going in and out of his psychotic breaks. That finally went away by the seventies. He was around, but not that much. He was focused on the 'I' stuff then. He was a brilliant man. Brilliance and craziness can go together."

His mother also had problems. She'd taken LSD several times and had amazing mystical journeys. It opened her up to the spirit world. She could hear the music of the spheres. Then one day the music sounded weird. She didn't come down from the drug as she had before. It was a bad trip, Eileen was frightened, and she had an eighteen-month-old child on her hands. One of her LSD guides at Big Sur was a man named Richard Alpert, later known as Ram

Dass. He sent her up to San Francisco to see a psychiatrist. The shrink wanted to give her more pills. She didn't want more pills, but she didn't know what to do. Then she wandered into a metaphysical bookstore where an Indian guru, Swami Chinmayananda, was speaking. Eileen was already interested in Indian philosophy. She'd read Krishnamurti and visited the Vedanta Temple in Hollywood, but this was different. Chinmayananda was the real thing: smart, dynamic, funny, and apparently without ego—an embodiment of his teachings. At her new guru's direction, Eileen changed her name to Nalini. She and David left Big Sur and moved up to the northern California town of Napa to be closer to other devotees. There she married another vegetarian and student of Indian philosophy.

It was not easy for David. "My mother got into Hinduism very heavily, which I still rebel against. 'Mom's going off to India. Who's taking care of you?' Well, that was a problem. There was my stepfather. This is where I have a lot of issues with my mother. She was New York Italian—a very Catholic family. She substituted one orthodoxy for another. But she was on the leading edge even if she wasn't aware of it. The Beat scene. India. Hindu stuff in '64 and '65, before George Harrison was into it. She took acid with Richard Alpert at Big Sur, before he was Ram Dass. Joan Baez lived next door when I was a kid. My father was in a relationship with Jane Fonda. Crosby, Stills, Nash, and Young were here. Bob Dylan. I was too young to get it. Bob Dylan didn't mean anything to me as a kid."

David Price did not want pop stars and instant enlightenment. He wanted a mom and dad like they had on TV, stores to go to, and other kids to play with. Forty years later, when he spoke to me about his childhood, David and I were sitting on the Esalen grounds, just up the hill from the cabin where he was conceived. "People wax nostalgic about the good old days and how everything was so perfect in the past, and details like this get overlooked. The sexuality was so free, I think people didn't want to be reminded about kids—that there was some consequence to their activity."

Oh, yeah, consequences. The real world. At Esalen, it's easy to forget about the real world—at least for a day or two. It had been a year since I had first met David at Esalen, and I was back. On that day, I woke up in a private room next to a workshop space called "Maslow." Some seminarians, as Esalen calls its customers, had passed the night in there on the floor, curled up in sleeping bags. Their home for the night is named after Abraham Maslow, one of the founding fathers of humanistic psychology. Maslow was fascinated by "peak experiences," intense moments when we suddenly feel a sense of ecstasy, empathy, and awe. These are the seeds of all religion, but most churches merely hint at this ineffable wonder. That was something for Jesus or the saints, but not for us. It's different here. People come to Esalen to have peak experiences, and they often do.

It's one of those mornings at Esalen when all things seem possible. From my deck at sunrise, I see a solitary man practicing t'ai chi on the deck next to the swimming pool, right on the edge of the cliff. His arms rise with the tides and a lazy bed of kelp floating near shore. The ocean is murky green in the morning light but soon brightens to a serene blue. Garden of Eden, indeed.

Over in the dining room, a few early risers seek out caffeine. Before long, the first seminarians arrive for a morning yoga class, mostly women wearing tights and sensible shoes. The early morning buzz of self-improvement fills the air. The budding yogis stretch their arms and legs as a line of Tibetan prayer flags—green, yellow, blue, and white—flap in a soft breeze. Others are already in the yoga room, which is named after Aldous Huxley, the novelist and providential explorer of mystical states, and they are singing and swaying to mellow music. "It's Yoouuuu. . . . it's yoouuu," they chant, sounding like a chorus of offbeat owls.

Other sounds arise. Beyond the shelter of a giant Monterey pine, the swish of powerful sprinklers can be heard over the waves. Long streams of water shoot over a flower garden, an enlivening quilt of pink, white, maroon, and blue. A path winds through the garden, down the side of a small canyon, and onto a bridge that crosses the creek at Waterfall House—now expanded and remodeled into a charming little *zendo*, a circular meditation room with black cushions.

Esalen always seems on the verge of going upscale. There are lots of expensive cars and sport utility vehicles in the parking lot. There's a giant Ford Expedition XLT, painted a tasteful forest green, gleaming as though it's right off the showroom floor. There's a metallic gray BMW Z3 convertible that's so new it doesn't even have license plates. You can almost hear the proud owners: "Let's drive the car down to Esalen this weekend and do a workshop." But on the northern end of the property, where the Esalen staff lives, it still looks like the funky sixties. There's a woman living in a ragged tepee. There's an old pickup truck with a large yin-yang symbol on the hood and a Compost Happens bumper sticker on the rear fender. You can almost feel how it was back then in the Sixties, when young David was playing by himself down in the creek.

Back in those days, raising kids was not what was happening. The baby boom had turned to bust. It was the dawn of a new decade, high time to act out a grand vision.

ACT ONE

It's 1960. Richard Price meets Michael Murphy in San Francisco at an old brick house near Golden Gate Park. It's full of seekers and followers of an Indian guru named Sri Aurobindo. It turns out that Price and Murphy were both born in 1930, graduated from Stanford in 1952 with psychology degrees, but never met at the university. They both come from successful, hardworking American families—one in the Midwest and one from central California. They start talking and realize that they both learned about Aurobindo, a Bengal-born, Western-educated yogi, back in the comparative religion class of Professor Frederic Spiegelberg. Murphy has just gotten back from India, where he studied at Aurobindo's ashram. The guru died back in 1950, but his ideas planted a seed in Michael's soul that will later blossom into Esalen Institute and the human potential movement. "Man lives mostly in his surface mind, life, and body," Aurobindo wrote, "but there is an inner being within him, with greater possibilities to which he has to awake—to greater beauty, harmony, power, and knowledge."

ACT TWO

Flash back fifty years to 1910. Michael Murphy's grandfather, Henry Murphy, a successful doctor from the small California farming town of Salinas, stands on a cliff at Big Sur. He's just bought 375 acres of magnificent coastal property from the original homesteader, Tom Slate, and dreams of building a European-style health spa at what was then known as Slate's Hot Springs. But little can be done until Highway 1 connects Big Sur to the rest of the world in the 1930s. "Then the war comes," Michael Murphy recalls in a voice offstage. "They black out the highway. You can't drive down Highway 1. All my grandfather's dreams end right there with Pearl Harbor." Henry Murphy dies after the war, but Michael's grandmother keeps his dream alive.

ACT THREE

It's 1961. Michael Murphy and Richard Price have come down to reclaim the family property at Big Sur and play out their version of Grandpa Murphy's dream. They are greeted by a strange assortment of bikers, gay bathers, fundamentalist Christians, and other locals hanging out at the Murphy family hot springs. Henry Miller, the famous novelist and bohemian, still lives nearby and comes down for daily soaks. Joan Baez lives in one of the old cabins. Murphy's grandmother has hired a young guy from Kentucky to guard the place. His name is Hunter Thompson, and he has shown up on the heels of Henry Miller. Neither the folksinger nor the gonzo journalist are famous yet, but it's quite a mix. "It's really wild," Murphy recalls. "Hunter Thompson is the caretaker, and he is fully armed. My grandmother has retained an evangelical lady, Mrs. Webb, who holds prayer meetings. Henry Miller and his crowd are down during the day, and at night the Hells Angels appear. It took Dick and me awhile to establish law and order."

ACT FOUR

It's 1964, and Fritz Perls, the cofounder of Gestalt therapy, enters stage right. Esalen Institute is just a few years old, and Perls stalks the grounds like an Old Testament prophet. He will spend the next seven years there, until his death in 1970. Onstage, a spotlight illuminates the "hot seat." Perls is holding one of his famous Gestalt sessions before a live audience in the rustic Esalen lodge. A brave female volunteer sits down and is asked to recount a dream. Fritz pays close attention to her words but also to her mannerisms. He lets her ramble on, allowing her to make a fool of herself. Then he goes silent, smoking a cigarette while the poor girl squirms.

"Without a doubt, the sessions were good theater," writes Esalen historian Walter Truett Anderson. "The people were real, the problems were real, and the emotions were real."[2]

Perls hated the hand-holding of most therapists, who allowed patients to wallow in the past, hand over money, and never really change. Some felt Perls was a genius. Others thought he was a psychopath. But Perls had quite a history. He'd met Freud and was a patient of Wilhelm Reich back in the 1930s. Reich was an Austrian psychologist and biophysicist who believed that there was something called "orgone energy" and that it must be released through sexual activity. Otherwise, sexual inhibitions led to neurotic behavior, individually and as a society. Later, living in the United States, he developed an "orgone box" to help release that energy. The government didn't believe his claims, convicted him of fraud, and sentenced him to two years in prison, where he died in 1957. But many of his ideas were embraced by Perls and brought to Esalen. "Reich had the idea (novel at the time, though it would become central to Gestalt therapy) that it was more productive to pay attention to the patient's present action and attitudes than to embark on archaeological expeditions through the past," Anderson writes. "And he always insisted that neurosis took up residence in the body as well as the mind. He had his patients do breathing exercises, and even—unthinkable for a Freudian—touched them with his hands to massage tense and twisted areas of the body."[3]

Esalen's first event had been in January 1962, when Alan Watts, the brilliant writer, prodigious drinker, and great popularizer of Eastern religion, held a seminar at Big Sur Hot Springs. Maslow and his peak experiences came later that year. In the late sixties and early seventies, Will Schutz, the author of the best-selling book *Joy,* ran encounter groups and helped spark a wave of interest in group therapy. Journalist Tom Wolfe, the ruthless chronicler of the seventies scene, gives us a taste of that period:

> *Encounter sessions, particularly of the Schutz variety, were often wild events. Such aggression! Such sobs! tears! moans, hysteria, vile recriminations, shocking revelations, and such explosions of hostility between husbands and wives, such mudballs of profanity from previously mousy mommies and workadaddies, such red-mad attacks.*[4]

Forty years later the workshops have been dialed down a few notches. Gestalt sessions and encounter groups are still available in the broader Esalen mix. When I'm there I just like to hang out. On this visit, it's a bright spring day and the Pacific Ocean is the color of blue jeans. Seminar attendees sit on the large green lawn that gently slopes down from the dining room to the edge of the cliff. Esalen is booked solid, and it's the usual five-ring circus. There's a workshop on dreams, one about dance, and another called "Lasting Love: Real or Just a Fairy Tale?" There was a workshop promising "Transformation: From Facade to Self," and a fifth and final one on "Authenticity, Intuition, and Creativity: A Workshop for Gay and Bisexual Men."

salen remains a refuge for people in transition. You constantly hear them talking about life's little dramas, but especially in the silky radiance of the baths. That night, two women talk about a workshop they're taking on keeping the spark alive in intimate relationships. One woman had talked her boyfriend out of coming with her to Esalen. "It didn't seem right to have him here," she says. "I came here to reinvent myself."

Her friend sighs and lowers herself a little deeper into the steaming water. "You know, I didn't have one serious relationship in my thirties. Actually, I'm not sure if I ever had one. It's hard to believe the kind of guys I used to go out with in my twenties. I wouldn't walk across a room to meet one of those guys now."

In another large tub, four older women are talking about dying, about going to a hospice. "Often it's the children who refuse to let go," one of them says.

"Look at those stars," another woman says, pointing.

Extraordinary things happen in the baths at Esalen, some of them historic. According to Esalen lore, this hot water helped end the Cold War. During the 1980s, when President Ronald Reagan was condemning the Soviet Union as the "evil empire," Esalen was doing its bit to improve Russian relations. "We had Russian Politburo members and their State Department counterparts here—guys who are used to wearing suits and ties and talking to each other across big tables," said David Price. "First we had them sitting on the floor of the Big House with pillows, meeting as people rather than adversaries. Then we threw them, naked, into the hot tubs together."

Michael Murphy, the man who made this place famous, hates hot tubs and social nudity. Back in the 1980s, when Esalen was celebrating its twenty-fifth birthday, I had lunch with Michael at the hillside home in Marin County he shared with his wife, Dulce, and their two-year-old son, MacKensie. They were about to move into a new house in Marin, and the first thing Murphy was going to do was tear out the hot tub. "We have a wide range of friends, and this mixed nudity makes some people very uncomfortable. I'm sorry Esalen contributed to this whole hot tub thing," said Murphy, who once considered becoming an Episcopal priest. "People down there at Esalen think I'm very puritanical. I've slowly tried to restrain a lot of the nudity. We've had to make some tougher rules because of these characters who want to show their enlightenment by walking nude into the dining room."[5]

Murphy's vision for Esalen is a place for serious study and analysis of the body and the mind, an experiential think tank where scientists and mystics come together to unlock the mysteries of higher consciousness and paranormal phenomena. Murphy wants Esalen to be famous for its Soviet-American Exchange Program, its collection of studies on exceptional human functioning, and its program of "Revisioning Philosophy." But it's famous for the baths, which were there before Murphy or his grandfather ever heard of the place.

Nothing bothers him or his longtime Esalen associate, George Leonard, more than people using *Esalen* and *hot tub* in the same sentence. Leonard, who originally met Murphy as a journalist working for *Look* magazine, remembers sitting in the living room of his San Francisco home with Murphy one afternoon in 1964, writing ideas on little pieces of paper and arranging them on the floor. One of the slips of paper read "human potential movement." They weren't sure they liked the sound of it, but they decided to go with that name. "Our original idea had more to do with the civil rights movement. It was about unused human capacities. It had a lot to do with education. One aspect of it was learning to feel and to be open, but it had nothing to do with hot tubs," recalled Leonard, who went on to become a popular author and martial arts instructor. "The media discovered Esalen in 1968, and they couldn't figure it out. They saw people nude in the baths, and they thought it must be about sex. They didn't understand about multiple levels of consciousness, one of the basic ideas of Esalen—the idea that Western objective consciousness is only one form of consciousness."

But most people don't come to Esalen to think. They come to feel. For years, there's been a gentle tug-of-war at Esalen between workers on the body, seekers of the spirit, and explorers of the mind—a perennial irony for a place designed to bring mind, body, and spirit together.

"When Dick and I took it over, the idea was to do these seminars. For me, the mission is the same today," Murphy told me fifteen years later. "This was an experiment. Nobody got paid much. The spirit of the Sixties and the idealism was the thing. It's been forty years now, and the place has matured. We've tried to not let anyone capture the flag. We were not like est, which had a viewpoint and was for profit. We conceived ourselves as a mini-university. Now we're getting a more mature staff. There's an evolution under way from accounting to everything else. It's still a work in progress, but the best it's ever been."

It was the spring of 2002, and Michael Murphy was seventy-two years old. He looked to be in good shape and fine spirit. We were having lunch at a waterfront restaurant in Sausalito, watching sailboats glide across the bay. San Francisco dazzled in the distance like the city of Oz. Our waitress walked up, and Murphy greeted her with a wide smile. She offered us a cappuccino, but Michael was transfixed by the vision standing before him.

"Are you wearing contacts?" he asked. "Those are the biggest, bluest eyes I've ever seen."

"Really? No, it's all me," she replied, smiling back.

"My God," Murphy exclaimed, "unbelievable! You could hypnotize me right here. You *are* hypnotizing me right here."

Like I said, Murphy is in fine shape at seventy-two. The waitress walked away, and we got back to the interview. Murphy takes issue with my breezy description of Esalen as the birthplace of religion, California style. "Esalen is not a religion. It's a forum for divergent ideas," he said. "People bring their religious aspirations to Esalen, but I hope we cultivate a more complex sensibility. We've never had any pretension about being the way and the light."

That's true. If Esalen is anything, it is eclectic. But so is the religious philosophy of millions of baby boomers who came of age in the sixties and seventies. Of course, the individual traditions that comprise the Esalen faith were not revealed at Big Sur. What was cooked up here is a mix of Eastern mysticism, American spiritualism, and Western humanism, along with a healthy pinch of hedonism. Esalen provided the mixing bowl and has been serving it up for more than forty years.

If there is a dominant dogma or doctrine at Esalen, it's Murphy's undying faith in the imminent transformation of human consciousness and the evolution of humanity into nothing less than God. Murphy looks to this transformation with the hopeful surety of a Christian fundamentalist awaiting the Second Coming. His is a serenely optimistic philosophy. "Through the actualization of our latent capacities," he writes in this latest book, "we both share and further the progressive manifestation of divinity that comprises the evolving universe."[6]

There's a timeless quality to Murphy's thinking. He seems both ahead of the curve and behind the times. He sounds like a philosophy professor one moment, a New Age seeker the next. He cares deeply about the reconciliation of science and mysticism, a concern that predates by several decades the latest wave of fuzzy thinking on that subject. Murphy sees a stubborn prejudice in the media and the university when it dismisses mystical and paranormal experience—everything from communicating with dead relatives to spiritual healing to bending spoons.

We spent one afternoon in the early 1990s talking about his beliefs and my skepticism. We were in the kitchen of the Big House at Esalen, part of the old family estate where Murphy spent many summers as a child. He'd just published his magnum opus on the paranormal, *The Future of the Body,* where he employs the tools of ethnology and natural history to collect, categorize, and chart thousands of accounts of metanormal human experience. But it took some prodding to get Murphy to talk about his own religious beliefs and experiences.

"There are armies of scientists and philosophers who deny mystical truth claims. Many of them have come here to Esalen to teach," he said. "Many people think these experiences are just about us—that they are just an extension of the self. They say this is just a fancy way of saying you feel good, and you say to them, 'No! I am saying God is real. God is there whether I know him or not.' But I'm a realist, not an idealist. I am also an empiricist. To understand what is happening you have to work as a synoptic empiricist, and you must have the experience. You must pray, or meditate, and when you have these experiences it is overwhelmingly apparent. There is no longer any doubt these domains exist."7

Back in the 1970s Esalen was alive, cutting edge, liberating. And all that meant absolutely nothing to young David Price. Neither did the Indian philosophy his mother embraced. "They were trying to make the world a better place, but it's the family that suffered most. I felt my mother put the interest of society as a whole over me and the family. It was an issue for me with my father, too. People visiting Esalen were 'in process,' and that would take precedence over everything else. It felt like people outside the family got treated better than those inside the family." David pauses, then says, "Remember, this is a child speaking. They were saving strangers rather than focusing on what was happening at home. I hope I handle that differently with my child."

David Price was back at Esalen with that child, Aleksander, in his arms. It was the summer of 2002, forty years since his father and Michael Murphy founded their institute. David had been away for years—studying, working as a musician—but returned in the late 1990s to work as operations manager. "In the Sixties there was a much less child-friendly atmosphere around here. There was no preschool. In the early seventies there was a period when children weren't allowed in the lodge after 6:30 in the evening."

Things weren't much better in Napa, where David and his mom had moved so Nalini could be closer to her fellow devotees. Today Napa is a tourist town in the heart of the northern California wine country, but it wasn't so sophisticated back then. When David and his half sister, Anjali, grew up there in the 1970s, few parents were devout disciples of Indian gurus, and two hippie kids stood out. David had long hair when the other kids had crew cuts. There was never any meat in the sandwiches Mom put in his lunch box, just avocados and tomatoes. People worried that his weird vegetarian mother was starving the poor child.

Anjali Browning is David's half sister, born in 1970. I called her to get another perspective on what it was like growing up as a hippie kid in Napa. She remembers being embarrassed when the school bus picked them up, and their classmates would see strange people in the backyard wearing white saris and doing morning meditations. "It wasn't the cool thing to do in that place," Anjali recalled. "Napa was a Podunk town. We were the only people who weren't Christian. We were freakish. We were in a regular school and were teased a lot.

"It wasn't a terrible upbringing," she continued. "We were loved. Our parents treated us with respect. We'd go to summer camps—actually they were spiritual camps for the parents—and there we would kind of fit in. But even there, we weren't Indian and a lot of the kids were Indian. There was always this feeling of not fitting in anywhere. I never thought of my parents as hippies, but maybe they were. They were just looking for something."

Anjali said there's some truth to David's feeling that his parents were more concerned about saving the world than caring for him. "As kids, we felt second fiddle. They wanted to be involved in something larger. And, you know, there was a lot to change about the world, and here was this man [Chinmayananda] trying to make a difference. But it's easy to resent the lifestyle."

Their mother and father/stepfather were still together when I tracked them down. They were living in Garberville, up in the marijuana-growing region in the northern California redwoods. They'd worked with Chinmayananda for decades, helping him get his movement established in the United States. Their swami died in the late 1990s, but they still see him as their teacher. "My kids sacrificed a lot," Nalini told me. "I couldn't give them as much attention as I wanted. I was at the core of this movement, and there was just a handful of people. If I didn't do it, it wouldn't happen. At least that was the way I felt."

On the Sunday I talked to Nalini, David had driven up and was visiting his mom with his wife and young child. It was a long time coming, but Nalini was a grandmother now. Anjali and her husband had also come up for a visit, so the whole tribe was back together again.

"We weren't raised with the mentality that you have to go to college and start a career," Anjali said. "My parents had this free-floating, go-with-the-flow attitude. It was selfish to have goals. If it's meant to be, it's meant to be. That's good in a lot of ways, but I was kind of a dreamer—not realistic about how the world worked. I didn't really know how the world worked."

David reconciled with his father in the late 1970s and early 1980s. "By then my father had another child. He *was* ready to be a father, and other people at Esalen were having kids. There was more support. There were more committed couples. We'd been separate so much when I was younger, but were able to meet as equals. My relationship with him in my adolescence was good. Later, as a teenager, I liked being here. There were times when I wasn't treated as a child when I was a child. The age barriers didn't matter much."

What about all the free sex, nudity, and drugs? "I wasn't that aware of the free sex, and the nudity wasn't a big deal. As for the drug stuff, frankly, I did my share but never really had a problem with it. I smoked a lot of pot and did a fair amount of psychedelics, including some with my father, which was really very valuable. When I was going through adolescence, I could call him in the middle of the night if he wasn't there. When he died, I was at a good place with him."

Dick Price died in the summer of 1985. It happened just up the creek from the Waterfall House. According to one version of the story, Price was meditating in the canyon when a giant crystal came down upon him, killing him instantly. "It's been turned into a story right up there with Muhammad ascending from the rock, but what happened was very different," the son explained. "There'd been a fire in July and it had rained for a few days. The silt clogs up the filters at the water source. 'The source'—that adds greatly to the myth. Anyway, he was working on the water system when this rock the size of a Volkswagen bus came tumbling down. It was white crystalline. It broke into three pieces, one of which hit him in the head." David Price had hiked up that canyon enough times with his dad to have an idea about how he died. "He was very aware of the danger up there. He might have been running for his life and turned back to look when the rock hit him."

David came back to Esalen and worked his way up to the job of operations manager. He came back, in part, because he'd been thinking about his father's legacy. "Esalen was resting on its laurels and backsliding," he said over dinner in the Esalen lodge. "There were always a lot of people down here just trying to hang out and get laid and get stoned. And there were people who really wanted to learn or had something to offer. The people with a lot to offer were leaving, and those who stayed were just pulling the place down."

These days David Price is thinking about how to make Esalen relevant to a new generation of seekers. It's time, he says, to finally put the "Me Decade" behind. "Esalen has put so much emphasis on the 'I,' on the individual's experience. It placed it above all else. We need to be more integrated, part of something larger than ourselves. Why are we here? What do we represent? How do we evolve?"

Reinventing Esalen is no easy task. Running this place is like herding cats. Part of the institutional ethos at Esalen is an anti-institutional ethos. "It's an irony," Price says, "that a place predicated on personal transformation can be so ambivalent about change."

As operations manager, Price plays the mediator between Michael Murphy and the staff who till the fields, clean the toilets, massage the muscles, and soothe the souls of the paying customers. Price appreciates that there has always been a wild side to Esalen, a dance between the outlaw, the hedonist, the intellectual, and the spiritual being. Nevertheless, the petty rebellions can be maddening.

Price met his Polish-born wife, Kasia, at Esalen, and having a newborn son has him thinking about his childhood. "A big part of having my son is wanting to do it better. I guess that's the same with every father. I don't want to criticize my parents. It's not like I would even want to trade my experience, but I don't want to be absent from him too much. I don't want to fall into other things that distract me too much so I replicate the stuff with my parents, where I resented that they put other things over what I saw as the responsibilities of a parent. It puts life and metaphysics and spirituality in an entirely different perspective."

David is more worried about being with Aleksander than raising him in any religious tradition. His father's family was Jewish and his mother's Catholic. They turned to Hinduism and Buddhism, but David wants none of the above.

"I feel quite pessimistic, not about spirituality, but about religion—the Muslim-Judeo-Christian religion," he says. "Of the people I know, I can't think of any that go to church on a regular basis. I'm pretty reactive against organized religion."

For Murphy, Sixties spirituality remains a work in progress. His vision of the coming transformation of human consciousness—that old dawning of the New Age—may seem like a pipe dream from a past life, hazy and idealistic. But not to Michael.

"For me, the Sixties is not a determinate event," he says. "This won't happen overnight. These changes can take centuries. It's up to us, as always, as to what kind of life we create for the culture and ourselves. It's up to us."

Forty years into it, Esalen's legacy can be seen in the continued popularity of the paranormal, Eastern philosophy, yoga, massage, alternative forms of psychotherapy, and a new appreciation for the mind-body connection in mainstream medicine. At Esalen they were waxing poetic about psychoneuroimmunology decades before it made the cover of *Time*. The people who lived and played in this enlivening enclave were always more interested in transforming themselves than shaping society. Yet in many ways they did just that—one midlife crisis at a time. Esalen gave people permission to feel their pain and follow their bliss. It helped them rediscover their bodies and redefine the soul. The spirituality sent out from Esalen was a nondogmatic, personal, and experiential faith. It's what so many of us—including David Price—are talking about today when we say, "I'm into spirituality not organized religion."

Of course, Esalen was just one campaign in the spiritual revolution of the Sixties. Its workshops were available only to an influential elite. Yet the spirit of innovation was omnipresent. Just as Richard Price and Michael Murphy were establishing an alternative path, a dramatic shift was under way in mainstream religious traditions, even those as resistant to change as the Roman Catholic Church.

CHAPTER 2

People of God:
Keeping Hope Alive

It'll soon shake your windows and rattle your walls,
for the times they are a-changin'.

"THE TIMES THEY ARE A-CHANGIN'"
BOB DYLAN, 1962

To be a young American in 1961 was to have hope. No one knew what the Sixties would bring, but there was a sense of possibilities and a feeling of empowerment. There was a new decade and a young new president to lead the way. There was fear—the terror of instant nuclear annihilation—but there was a feeling that we had a choice. We had the power to do good. We believed America *was* good.

President Kennedy set the tone in a short and powerful inaugural address delivered in Washington on January 20, 1961:

> Let the word go forth from this time and place, to friend and foe alike,
> that the torch has been passed to a new generation of Americans—born
> in this century, tempered by war, disciplined by a hard and bitter
> peace, proud of our ancient heritage—and unwilling to witness or per-
> mit the slow undoing of those human rights to which this nation has
> always been committed, and to which we are committed today at home
> and around the world.

Toward the end of the speech Kennedy again addressed his own generation and the next—the one coming of age and setting the stage for a social drama that still unfolds.

> *I do not believe that any of us would exchange places with any other people or any other generation. The energy, the faith, the devotion which we bring to this endeavor will light our country and all who serve it—and the glow from that fire can truly light the world. And so, my fellow Americans: ask not what your country can do for you—ask what you can do for your country.*

Those last seventeen words have become so familiar that we have to stop and remember what happened next. Millions of Americans didn't just watch Kennedy's speech on TV and change the channel. They joined the Peace Corps and took that light around the world. They marched for civil rights in Alabama and Mississippi and Washington. They worked for nuclear disarmament and against the escalating war in Vietnam. They struggled for economic justice. They did what their president asked of them:

> *Now the trumpet summons us again—not as a call to bear arms, though arms we need—not as a call to battle, though embattled we are—but a call to bear the burden of a long twilight struggle, year in and year out, "rejoicing in hope, patient in tribulation"—a struggle against the common enemies of man: tyranny, poverty, disease, and war itself.*

On the day after Kennedy delivered his inaugural address, on January 21, 1961, a Trappist monk in Kentucky opened his diary and wrote:

> *You can make your life what you want. There are various ways of being happy. Why do we drive ourselves on with illusory demands? Happy only when we conform to something that is said to be legitimate happiness? An approved happiness?*[8]

Like Kennedy, Father Thomas Merton would inspire thousands of Americans with his vision of another way. When the Sixties began, Merton was already famous for *The Seven Storey Mountain*, a 1948 memoir about his journey

to Our Lady of Gethsemani monastery in rural Kentucky. His was a call to contemplation, and Merton's later exploration of Eastern mysticism—cut short by
his accidental death in Thailand in 1968—helped bring to the national consciousness Buddhist ideas about nonattachment and the illusory nature of the
material world.

Thousands of Americans answered Kennedy and Merton's call, basing their
social commitment on the traditions of their Judeo-Christian faith. Theirs was
not just a struggle against poverty, but a repudiation of the twin towers of consumerism and conformity, two forces that took hold of the nation in the 1950s
and refused to let go. Theirs was a growing awareness that there was more to
life than a two-car garage and a new Frigidaire.

For American Catholics, the early 1960s were an especially hopeful time.
Kennedy was the first Roman Catholic president of the United States, and his
election was a symbol of their faith's growing influence in American life.
Catholics were no longer marginalized immigrants from Ireland or Italy and
could no longer be written off as "papists" holding divided loyalties. Their
church had evolved from a religious minority to the largest Christian communion in the United States. And in the early sixties that communion underwent
a thorough examination.

In Rome the Second Vatican Council, convened in 1962 by Pope John XXIII
and adjourned by Paul VI in 1965, began an era of liberal reform unparalleled
in modern church history. In the aftermath of the proceedings, the ancient
Latin Mass was translated into the vernacular. Centuries of officially sanc-
tioned distrust of Protestants, Jews, and other non-Catholics gave way to new
ecumenical openness. Thousands of priests and nuns, inspired by a new vision
of Christian ministry, embarked on a crusade for peace and social justice.
Laypeople assumed a greater role in a hierarchical church redefined as "the
people of God."

Unfortunately, the four decades following Vatican II have often seemed
like an era of lost possibilities and unrealized hope for the American Catholic
church. Thousands of activist clergy and nuns left the institutional church.
Most lay Catholics simply ignored the church's intransigent teachings on
birth control, then began to question ecclesiastical authority in other areas. A
seemingly endless scandal over clergy sexual abuse further eroded the faithful's confidence in church leaders and exposed a hypocritical church hierarchy. While the bishops had preached "traditional family values," they had
covered up the sex crimes of pedophile priests. Thousands of homosexual

clergy stayed in the rectory closet while the church condemned gays and lesbians as "disordered."9

Meanwhile, Pope John Paul II and his bishops refuse to acknowledge a growing consensus among the Catholic laity that priests should be allowed to marry and that women have a right to ordination. The Second Vatican Council ushered in a new era of theological openness, albeit a brief one. It was said that the Vatican had "opened its windows to the world." But the current papacy of John Paul, and the reign of his chief doctrinal watchdog, Cardinal Joseph Ratzinger, has sought to clamp down on many perceived excesses born of Sixties freedom. Yet new ideas are stubborn. Once you open the windows and let them in, ideas have a way of hanging around the house—even the house that Peter built. Like Dylan said, they will soon shake your windows and rattle your walls.

Some of the church's most socially active, compassionate, and forward-thinking clergy left the fold in the 1960s and 1970s, but they nevertheless have left a lasting legacy of spiritual innovation. Consider the ministry of Thomas Moore. Back in the 1950s, when he was entering adolescence, Moore left home to begin the years of study required for ordination as a Roman Catholic priest in a religious order. Thirteen years later, just six months before he was to take his final vows, Moore opted out of the clerical life. It was 1967, and Moore was twenty-six years old.

Moore left not because of the vow to celibacy or poverty but because of the vow of obedience. "The reason I left was I'd been reading some avant-garde writers for the time and was becoming interested in theological ideas that were not really Catholic," Moore told me. "I remember thinking that I don't want anyone telling me what I can read or what I can think or say publicly. A lot of it was the spirit of the times. Change was in the air. Vatican II hadn't really showed itself at that time. I didn't see any change in the average church. I was excited about new ideas, but people in the church didn't want to hear what I had to say."

Moore looks on all this with great irony, especially when he's standing behind the pulpit of a packed church saying what he wants to say. That's because Thomas Moore, writer, has influenced far more American Catholics than he would have as Thomas Moore, priest. His 1992 book, *Care of the Soul*, was a mega-seller that refused to give up its spot on the best-seller lists for a year and then inspired a wave of self-help books with *soul* in the title.

"I'm still a monk at heart, and the writing of these books is my spiritual practice. It's not just a job. I realize how much of my Catholicism is involved in my life, but it's not the Catholicism that the church advocates. I don't care if I follow all the rules, but I have the spirit of it. In my own way I do practice the faith. My Catholicism is part of my nature. It's part of me. It's a cultural thing, and it makes no sense to me to disown it. So the alternative is to redefine it."

That redefinition began while Moore was still in seminary and reading the works of such influential writers as Pierre Teilhard de Chardin (1881–1955). Born near Clermont in central France, Teilhard de Chardin entered the Jesuits and was ordained a priest in 1911. He was known during his life for his work as a geologist and paleontologist, and his theological works were published only after his death. As Moore feared for himself if he stayed in the priesthood, Teilhard couldn't get permission from the church to publish his theological ideas. His best-known book, *The Phenomenon of Man*, was published in 1959. Teilhard believed that human consciousness, like the natural world, was evolving and had leaped forward at several critical points. The emergence of rational self-consciousness in humanity was an important threshold because humans now had a part in directing evolution in a godly manner. His ideas were not unlike the philosophy that inspired Michael Murphy to begin Esalen Institute. The other writer who prompted Moore to question his Catholic orthodoxy was Paul Tillich (1886–1965), an outspoken Protestant theologian who was born in Germany but came to the United States in the 1930s to escape certain death at the hands of the Nazis. Tillich sought to reconcile Christian faith and modern culture—to respond thoughtfully to existentialism and other new ideas about the nature of being. Again, there's an Esalen connection. During the last year of his life, Tillich spent a weekend at Esalen, talking about the synthesis of East and West and the relationship between self-transcendence and self-actualization.

Thomas Moore was perhaps most influenced by the psychology of Carl Jung and James Hillman, whose ideas form the basis of Moore's popular books. As an author and psychotherapist, Moore has continued Jung's attempts to blend psychology and spirituality. "Psychology is a secular science, while the care of the soul is a sacred art," he writes in his breakout book. "This new paradigm suggests the end of psychology as we have known it altogether because it is essentially modern, secular, and ego-centered." Moore was equally dismissive of the Christian religion in which he was raised. "Dropping the salvational fantasy frees us up to the possibility of self-knowledge and self-acceptance, which are the very foundations of soul."[10]

Moore has written a string of books over the last ten years, but none of them has come close to the phenomenal success of *Care of the Soul*. When we met at a Berkeley café, he was in town to promote his latest work, *The Soul's Religion*. At the time, the newspapers were full of stories about the latest pedophilia scandal to rock the Catholic church. Having tried the celibate life himself, Moore wasn't surprised that the church was in trouble. "For a lot of Catholic people in the Sixties there was a great desire to serve, to have a life of service, and the ticket for it was celibacy. It wasn't that they chose the celibate life, but if you wanted this life, you had to be celibate. It was the price you paid. That's a situation that's going to cause trouble."

When Moore left the church at twenty-six, he soon realized that he'd skipped right over his adolescence. He knew a lot of philosophy and theology but not much about human sexuality, including his own. "It's unnatural for someone not to have an adolescence, a sexual awakening," he told me. "I never had any counseling, education, or help on that. None. Zero. Some warnings and threats, but no help whatsoever. The church has never really dealt with sexuality."

Moore married—the first time—just eighteen months after he left the seminary. "Even then I didn't have much experience. After eight years of marriage, I got divorced. Then I had my sexual adolescence. You have to have it sometime. If I'd stayed in that order [the Servites], I don't know what would have happened."

In recent years Moore has reconnected with his Catholic identity. "You don't go through all that without being affected by it—in a constructive way. But right now I don't have an iota of concern about the authority of that church. They could excommunicate me a million times, and it wouldn't mean anything to me. But I reserve the right to say my Catholicism is more active in my life now than it ever has been."

Sounds good, but I sensed there was something else behind Moore's decision to reclaim his Catholicism. He'd mentioned that he and his second wife have two children, ages ten and thirteen, and I know from experience that people with children that age often rediscover religion when the kids start asking about God. It turns out I was right. For a few years Moore and his family had attended services held by Catholic monks at a hermitage not far from their home. "My wife and I thought it was good for the children, but then they closed the place down."

"Have you had your children baptized in the church?" I asked.

"I didn't feel a need, but my parents and extended family did. It means a great deal to them that our children are baptized and confirmed, so they are. We lived in Ireland last year, and it coincided with the children's first communion. There they just automatically do it in the schools."

Back in the States, Moore put on a home service for his family and a few neighbors. "When I was in the monastery I was very involved in music and liturgy. My wife is Catholic and has studied Eastern methods of meditation very seriously. But she wants more of a Catholic church experience. I don't feel much need for community. I'm more of a hermit. We tried Episcopal churches, but they were all unsatisfying. Then we thought, 'Let's do a couple of services ourselves.' I know all that stuff, although I don't think you have to be in a long line of priests to have effective rituals. Our neighbors come over once a month, and we do what used to be called a paraliturgical service. It's based on the Mass. We do readings, including some from the Gnostic gospels or from another traditions or secular writers. And people are blown away by it. But it's just for my family and my community. I'm not trying to start a movement."

At the same time, Moore *does* want to reclaim the word *religion.* In some circles today *religion* is synonymous with oppression or intolerance or hypocrisy. The user-friendly term is *spirituality.* I know what Moore means. At parties, I'm often introduced as the "religion writer" at the *San Francisco Chronicle,* and I see folks take two mental steps back. I usually have to say something irreverent to let them know I'm not a Methodist minister. They relax when I tell them I just wrote a piece on the rise of Buddhism in California or an article about some other nonthreatening spiritual practice.

Moore concurs: "I want to reclaim religion because I don't trust the thing many people call spirituality. It's not sufficiently grounded and does not go beyond the self. If people are going to be spiritual, it's important that they find in that spirituality a way of taking care of the environment or working for justice."

That's starting to sound like something you'd hear in the Sixties, so I asked Moore what he sees as the spiritual legacy of that era. "For me, the positive legacy comes from the sense of possibility—just the possibility of imagining a different culture than the one we're surrounded by. In the Sixties, the flower children and everyone else caught up in it created a different set of values—relating to each other and the broader world. It was wonderful. It was naive, but it was great. It was the archetype of innocence, a more childlike view, but that was its strength—to keep that vision and show that it's possible to shift. Today, people may want to have another world, but they can't imagine it can change. That's resigning oneself to an evolution of culture and saying there is nothing we can do. *That* is contradicted by the Sixties. People said you don't have to buy in to the culture around you. It's like in the movie *The Graduate.* You don't have to be in plastics. You can do other things. That's an important legacy."

When we spoke, in the spring of 2002, some Americans, including Moore, were starting to question the ongoing war on terrorism. Within a year, hundreds of thousands of people were marching in the streets. It was starting to look like the antiwar movement of the Sixties. Many churches, including the Roman Catholic Church, opposed the Bush administration's invasion of Iraq, saying it did not pass the ethical test for a "just war." Moore acknowledges that one of the drawbacks of personalized spirituality is a lack of a common social ethic. On what do you base ethical decisions regarding having sex, doing business, or going to war if you don't buy in to the whole Roman Catholic program on social ethics and personal morality?

"That's a good question," Moore replies. "The motivation for living an ethical life is not just intellectual or someone frightening you. It can be based emotionally on your sense of compassion and empathy. That's where soul and spirit come together. That's very important in an ethical life. You realize that we're all in this together. We live in a diverse world and need to have empathy for people with diverse views and lifestyles. The church has tried to use fear, but it doesn't work."

Rome may not approve of them all, but a vast diversity of views and lifestyles does exist in the American Catholic church. That's the Catholic church at its best, but the bishops are rapidly losing control over the hearts and minds of this flock. For example, recent surveys by four respected Catholic sociologists show that fewer and fewer Catholics are listening to the traditionalist view of the hierarchy. This is especially true when it comes to pelvic issues like contraception, abortion, nonmarital sex, divorce, remarriage, and homosexuality. The bishops are losing authority among individual believers over time and with each new generation. "By 1999," the sociologists report, "no more than one in seven of the Gen X Catholics would look to church leaders as the locus of moral authority on these issues."[11]

Unfortunately, this declining adherence to traditional moral teachings in the new generation is also seen in younger people's attitudes about religion and the poor. In their survey, the four sociologists asked American Catholics if they agree with the following statement: "You can be a good Catholic without donating time or money to help the poor." Less than half of the Vatican II generation (48 percent) agreed. But more than three out of five members of the post–Vatican II generation (63 percent) thought you can ignore the poor and still be a "good" Catholic.

That's troubling but not surprising. After all, this later generation were raised in the "Me Decade" and the "Greed Decade." But there's more to it than that. Many of the priests who left the institutional church in the seventies and eighties were the more socially and politically progressive members of the Catholic clergy. They had great hope in Vatican II and great disappointment that the church reforms didn't go further.

Back in the early 1990s I tried to find out what happened to the fifteen men ordained in the 1970 class at St. Patrick's Seminary in Menlo Park, the major Roman Catholic seminary for northern California. They were a young, idealistic group who rode the wave of social activism in the 1960s and the sweeping reforms of Vatican II. They went forth to preach the gospel, to change the world. But twenty years later, only five of the fifteen men ordained by the San Francisco Archdiocese in the class of 1970 were active priests.[12]

Some traded clerical collars for wedding rings. Others left after years of frustration with what they saw as a repressive church hierarchy. Their stories were a telling testimony to the turmoil that has rocked the Roman Catholic Church during the past four decades and showed how the church has failed to channel much of the positive social idealism of the Sixties. Leaving the priesthood was often about sex, love, and marriage. But it was also about a deeper dysfunction and disillusionment in the church. These priests left because the church was becoming too conservative, authoritarian, and out of touch with today's world. Although two-thirds of the class of 1970 had left the institutional church, many of them were still in ministry through social welfare work.

Gene Quinones, who left the priesthood in 1976, became frustrated with the mundane realities of parish life. "I was very interested in political change and social change, of awakening and empowering adults to change society. But I was told that wasn't my job. It was more about the priorities of the parish—raising money, supporting the school, and not talking about controversial subjects."

Bob Johnson, who left the priesthood after spending a decade working in Bay Area parishes, ran the Senior Friendship Line, a small mental health information and referral service for the elderly.

Larry Purcell, a San Francisco native who left the priesthood in 1980, still helped out in a Catholic Worker house that fed, sheltered, and assisted street alcoholics and other poor people. "When I decided to live outside the flow of normal parish life and live a resistance lifestyle in the peace movement, I stopped having a lot in common with other priests," he said. In 1979 Purcell and a group of demonstrators broke into the Lockheed Missiles and Space Company in Sunnyvale, California, with a bucket of blood and wrote the word DEATH on the casing of a nuclear missile destined for a Trident submarine. "I remember sitting in jail when, for the first time in my life, the thought crossed my mind that I might not be a priest. I figured that if I was going to have to find nurturing with other young Catholic men and women, I'd probably end up marrying one." Since his marriage, Purcell and his wife had lived and worked in a home for battered children, drug-addicted babies, and other fragile infants.

Clarence Liu, a native of Hawaii who came to the San Francisco Bay Area to complete his seminary education, rose through the church ranks to become vicar general of the Diocese of Honolulu—second in command to the bishop—then left the church in 1989. When we spoke, Liu was running a statewide agency for the homeless. "The world we live in today is a lot different than the world we were prepared for," he told me. "That was a world of unquestioning obedience, submerging your own personality, going along with the basic hierarchical line. The opposite is being stressed today—things like developing your own gifts and being creative and intuitive. After twenty years, I just saw it was impossible to change the church. It's too fossilized. We are living through the death of that institution, out of which something new needs to be born."

One of the few priests from the class of 1970 who remained in the fold, Father John Boll of Sacramento, shook his head when he thought about what happened to his fellow seminarians. "My classmates are very talented, dedicated people. If this were a corporation, I'd give the church an 'F.' Thousands of priests have left active ministry. The church is needlessly losing out."

It's not just the class of 1970 that had the high dropout rate. More than a decade after my 1990 interviews, when sex abuse scandals rocked the Catholic church to its very foundations, the issue of married priests got another thorough airing. That's when I interviewed another former priest, Bud Andre, who directed a county office that supports victims of violent crime. Back in the early 1960s, seventeen men were ordained in his class at St. Patrick's. Again, only five remained active Roman Catholic priests in the new millennium.

Like Thomas Moore back in New England, Bud Andre grew up in a devout Roman Catholic family and entered high school seminary at fourteen. "How you choose anything at that age, I don't know," he says today. "It was just understood that I would go. It was not like my parents forced me, but there was just such an expectation."[13]

At first seminary was terrifying. "You get in there, you don't know anybody. You're fourteen, your hormones are raging, and they ask you questions like, 'Do you have normal wet dreams like everyone else?' They want you to say yes, but you don't really know what they are talking about."

By the late 1950s Andre was finishing up his studies at St. Patrick's Seminary. Just up El Camino Real, the old mission road in California, San Francisco was going through a tempting cultural renaissance. There was the Beat scene in North Beach, hot jazz in the Fillmore, and women wearing tight black sweaters. "I'd just spent eight years of my life in seminary," he said. "It's hard to chuck it and become a Beatnik."

Andre was ordained in 1962, the same year the bishops of the world gathered in Rome to begin the Second Vatican Council. Finally, he thought, the church was opening to the modern world. Andre's first assignment was San Francisco's premier parish—Mission Dolores—where Franciscan missionaries established the Catholic church in 1776. It was now the 1960s, and it seemed like everything was changing in the church and society. Andre was having second thoughts about his vow of lifelong celibacy. "It was incredible the way things were changing, and there was quite a lot of speculation that the church would soon allow married priests."

Andre had already met his wife-to-be, but they'd put off a date for his leaving the priesthood. "My goal was not to leave but to stay a priest and marry." By 1970 Andre got tired of waiting. Andre and his wife married and had a son. They're still married.

These stories of priestly exodus can be heard in Catholic communities across America. Robert Charpentier, executive director of the Center for Ministry, a counseling service for Protestant and Catholic clergy, estimates there are now between five and ten thousand "married Catholic priests" in the United States. By that he means men like himself, who left active Roman Catholic ministry to live openly with their wives. He said about 10 percent of those men have expressed an interest in continuing to have an official position as priests if the church changes its celibacy rule. In 2002, when hundreds of accused and suspected priests left active ministry in the child sex scandal, Pope John Paul II still refused to even talk about letting any of those married Catholic priests return to ordained ministry.

Today Catholic commentators disagree about the seriousness of the priest shortage. That's partly because there's a new clerical class in the Roman Catholic Church—ordained married deacons—along with an empowered Catholic laity performing many tasks once handled by priests. Compared to the number of Catholic laypeople, there are now fewer priests in the United States than in 1900. But there are also an estimated thirty thousand lay ministers working in parishes and diocesan offices across the country, and the vast majority of them are women.[14]

One of my favorite stories about the rise of women leaders in the Roman church happened at St. Mary of the Angels parish in Ukiah, California, way up in northern California's Redwood Empire. The parish is part of the Diocese of Santa Rosa, which stretches along the Pacific Coast north of San Francisco to the Oregon border. In 1999 the diocese seemed to finally be recovering from a series of revelations involving pedophile priests and alleged church cover-ups of those crimes. Then Bishop G. Patrick Ziemann, the spiritual leader of the diocese, admitted that he'd had a longtime sexual liaison with a Costa Rican priest he'd brought up to California. Ziemann resigned after the priest, the Reverend Jorge Hume Salas, filed a lawsuit charging that the bishop demanded sexual favors in exchange for keeping quiet about money Salas had stolen from St. Mary of the Angels parish. Both charged the other with using sex as a tool of extortion. It was an incredibly seedy story but one that illustrates how the sex scandals in the Catholic church are often as much about power and control as they are about love or sex.

After the scandal subsided, the pastor of St. Mary of the Angels left on a six-month sabbatical, citing "the stresses of the last several years." That forced San Francisco archbishop William Levada to put a married woman in charge of the parish.

Yes, a *woman*. Mary Leittem-Thomas, a mother of four and parish member for twenty-four years, had quietly served for seven years as pastoral associate. Those are code words for Catholic women around the country who are really the associate pastor of their parishes but can't be called that because women can't be priests, so they can't be "pastors." But after her unexpected promotion, Leittem-Thomas *was* running the parish. She *was* the pastor. Priests could be brought in when needed to perform the sacraments, but she was piloting the ship. And with Mary at the helm, collections were up and people were coming back to Mass. "People feel they are being heard in a way they weren't in the past," she told me. "We have to get past the anger."

It was a wonderful illustration of how the church really changes—not from the top down, but from the grassroots. Finally, the old boys' club was breaking down. Priests were sleeping with bishops and extorting money from each other. The church wasn't changing from the top down; it was rotting from the top down. But when it all started collapsing, the hierarchical church had nowhere to turn but to faithful women like Mary Leittem-Thomas.

Three years later the clergy sex scandal surfaced again, this time in Boston. After a year of intense national media coverage, another bishop would resign in disgrace. Cardinal Bernard Law admitted he had covered up the sex crimes of his priests, and by the time he finally left the chancery, the public's confidence in the Roman Catholic Church had plummeted. By December 2002, pollster George Gallup reported, 40 percent of American Catholics were less likely to put money in the collection plate. But the church was in trouble even before the twenty-year-old sex scandal resurfaced in Boston, Los Angeles, and other cities. According to the National Opinion Research Center, the number of American Catholics reporting weekly Mass attendance had dropped from 55 percent in 1972 to 30 percent in the year 2000. And since Americans tell pollsters they go to church more than they really do, researchers estimated that by 2001 the actual percentage was down to 20 percent—and that's before another sex scandal erupted in the Catholic church.[15]

Of course, the Roman Catholic Church will weather this crisis. It always does. But it will take women such as Mary Leittem-Thomas and priests such as Father Mark Watson, who was born in 1961 and calls himself "a real child of the Sixties."

From his earliest years Mark remembers his Catholic parents engaged in both charity and social justice work. "They were very involved with the St. Vincent de Paul Society. My father would give food and clothes to the poor but would insist that we always sit down and get to know the people we were helping."

His mother, Gwen, was a strong supporter of the United Farm Workers movement in California's Central Valley. As Mark was growing up, his heroes were not Superman or Batman but Cesar Chavez and Dorothy Day. He went to marches, fasts, and other farm worker actions. "When I was fifteen we were at an event in Sacramento, and they were showing a film about the United Farm Workers. By chance, I was sitting right next to Cesar Chavez. There you are, fifteen years old, and your hero is sitting next to you. It was one of the things that motivated my work in social justice."

At Tulane University, Mark got a degree in Spanish, then a degree in social work at Louisiana State University. He worked for nuclear disarmament and against the School of the Americas, a U.S. training center in Fort Benning, Georgia, for the Central American military. In 1990 he met an activist nun who was working the poor and the homeless in a section of Shreveport, Louisiana, known as "the bottoms." His work with Sister Margaret helped inspire Mark to study for the priesthood, and in 1996 he was ordained as a priest in the Diocese of Shreveport.

Mark and I met through his mother, a longtime parishioner at Christ the King Parish in Pleasant Hill, a suburb east of San Francisco. Gwen had come into San Francisco to join more than a hundred thousand demonstrators at an antiwar march up Market Street in January 2003. It was one of the biggest protests in the Bay Area since the 1960s.

Gwen, a retired schoolteacher, is proud of her son and his social justice ministry. But don't ask her about her daughter, who favored war with Iraq and sometimes thinks her mother has gone off her rocker. Gwen sighs. "My daughter and I cannot talk about the world situation. She and her husband have their cars and say, 'Where are we going to get our oil? What are you saying, Mother? That we have to ride bicycles, or what?' I tell my daughter that the government is spraying Roundup [a poisonous herbicide] all over Colombia, and she says, 'Mother, I don't know *where* you get your information!' It's hard to believe. We have been practicing Catholics all our lives and have exposed all our children to Catholic faith and morals. What can you do? I began the year 2000 worrying about the world I'm leaving to my grandchildren, and I'm still worried. But at some point the kids and the grandkids have to start taking responsibility for the world."

Gwen Watson's lament got me thinking about the legacy of other families with deep roots in the Catholic left of the Sixties. And when I think "Catholic left" and "Sixties" I think "the Berrigan Brothers."

Stories about these left-wing Catholic priests, Fathers Daniel and Philip Berrigan, were hard to miss during the war in Vietnam and ever harder to find in the 1980s and 1990s. These brother priests were among the Catonsville Nine protesters and served three and a half years in prison for pouring homemade napalm on hundreds of draft cards in May 1968.

Philip Berrigan was ordained as a Josephite priest in 1955. His life as civil rights and antiwar activist began when he was assigned to teach poor and mostly black school children in Louisiana. His first arrest was at a civil rights demonstration in Selma, Alabama, in the early 1960s, and he had lost count of his arrests by 1999, when he was busted for attacking A-10 aircraft with hammers and blood during a protest at the Middle River National Guard base outside Baltimore. His last prison term ended on December 14, 2001.

Less than a year later, on December 6, 2002, Philip Berrigan died of liver and kidney cancer. He was seventy-nine. Among his survivors were his wife, Elizabeth McAlister, a former nun, and three children, Frida, Kate, and Jerry. Father Phil made some of his largest headlines in the spring of 1973, when he and Elizabeth announced that they had been secretly married since the spring of 1969. At his funeral Berrigan was laid to rest in a plain wooden coffin built by his twenty-seven-year-old son.

Reading about his death and that coffin got me thinking about the Berrigan brothers and the next generation, the Berrigan sisters. What had become of Frida and Kate Berrigan? They had grown up in Jonah House, a Catholic war resister commune in a poor, mostly black Baltimore neighborhood. On the Internet I found a story about the Berrigan family published in the *Washington Post* in 1988. Frida was fourteen, Jerry was thirteen, and Kate was six. It was Easter, and the kids had just held their Easter egg hunt on the Pentagon parade grounds, where Mom was protesting. Dad was in prison—again.

> There is Frida, a fourteen-year-old girl whirling around a pole on the Day of Resurrection. Her auburn hair, cropped like a boy's on the sides but long over one eye in a way that maddens her father, saucers about her head, turns all that she sees into fuzz and fleece. Her father has just gone away, perhaps for years, because of an idea. Idea: A weapon that can fly 1,500 miles and murder 100,000 people should not exist.[16]

Where are they now? I tracked Frida down in New York City, where she was working at the World Policy Institute, doing research on the arms trade and military budget issues for that left-leaning think tank. It was now February 2003 and she was twenty-eight. She told me one of her first memories of political life was getting up early in the morning to go Dumpster diving with Dad. She was nine or ten. They'd head out in their truck for Baltimore's busy produce market, where lots of perfectly good food was thrown out every day. "It was fun," she said. "We'd take it back home, spending lots of time cleaning it up, cutting out the rotten bits, peeling potatoes. We'd give most of it away to people in the neighborhood. It felt like we were doing something exciting, and it was beautiful to share it with everybody."

Frida was teased at school. She and her brother were the only white kids in class, and they had some pretty funky clothes. She missed her father when he went away to prison. One time Mom went to jail for twenty-six months, which was harder, even though she wrote letters to the kids every day. But there were always between five and fifteen other people in the Jonah House commune. "We had all these amazing people taking care of us," Frida recalled. "Everyone was so committed to this lifestyle. We had a close relationship with many other adults."

All three of the Berrigan kids are still fighting the good fight. Frida's little sister, Kate, is an undergraduate in peace studies at Oberlin College in Ohio. She'd just been arrested at a demonstration outside the White House against the war in Iraq. Jerry is living at a Catholic Worker commune in Wisconsin and rebuilding log cabins. He's gone to Iraq with a peace delegation and has been arrested at a protest against nuclear arms shipments. "You better hurry up if you want to talk to him," Frida told me. "He's going to jail on Valentine's Day."

Frida is often asked why none of the Berrigan kids rebelled against their parents. Why didn't at least one child join the army or become a stockbroker?

"Our parents didn't say one thing and do another," she said. "When it feels like what your parents are doing is right, and it comes out of deep and legitimate beliefs, there is nothing to rebel against. Their life wasn't easy, but they were happy and fulfilled and respected. We saw that growing up. How can you rebel against something that is right?"

Phil Berrigan and Liz McAlister severed their ties to the Roman Catholic Church but not to the "people of God." They personified the antiauthoritarian spirit of the Sixties and passed it on through the lives of Jerry, Frida, and Kate. Like Thomas Moore, they show how Catholics can leave the institutional church without abandoning the social ethics and spiritual wisdom of the Christian tradition.

That's a tougher assignment for spiritual seekers who turned to new religious movements. Many of them felt so alienated from the Jewish and Christian traditions that they sought out fresh revelation, an entirely new message from God. Divine dictations were not hard to find amid all of the channelers, spirit mediums, and New Age prophets of the sixties, seventies, and eighties. But few of them stood the test of time.

CHAPTER 3

Looking for Miracles in a New Revelation

Just one thing then I'll be okay.
I need a miracle, every day!

"I NEED A MIRACLE"
JOHN BARLOW, THE GRATEFUL DEAD 1978

Once upon a time, a strange voice called out to a Columbia University psychologist named Helen Schucman. It wasn't the first time Helen had heard voices in her head, but this time the message was clear. It told her, "This is *A Course in Miracles*. Go take notes." It was October 21, 1965.

Psychologists are not supposed to hear voices in their heads; their patients are. But Schucman confided in William Thetford, a friend and colleague, who suggested she just obey the voice and write down what it told her. Perhaps it would help her deal with some of the other problems in her life.

It turned out the voice had a lot on its mind. Schucman and Thetford spent the next seven years recording, transcribing, and editing the voice. It would be another four years, in the summer of 1976, before it was finally published in three volumes as a 478-page text, a 622-page workbook, and an 88-page manual for teachers. *A Course in Miracles* was born.

For some spiritual seekers, it's not enough to reform the Catholic church, revive ancient wisdom, or study modern philosophy. They need a new revelation—a religion so new that it's not seen as a religion. But nothing comes out of the blue, and neither did *A Course in Miracles*.

There are 750 biblical references in *A Course in Miracles*, but many of them radically reinterpret such familiar Christian terms as Holy Spirit and Son of Man. Some see the Course as a return to the mystical teachings of Jesus, a New Age Christianity without the guilt, sin, fire, and brimstone. For them, the voice is the voice of Jesus. Others see it as a self-taught experiment in spiritual psychotherapy, a tool for personal transformation, and a practical guide for improving day-to-day relationships with family, friends, and colleagues. Either way, it's a strange book. But if there's a Bible of Sixties' spirituality, it may be a toss-up between *A Course in Miracles* and *Be Here Now*, the counterculture classic by Ram Dass.

Some excerpts from the Course, as it is known:

> *This course was sent*
> *to open the path of light to us,*
> *and teach us, step by step,*
> *how to return to the eternal Self*
> *we thought we lost.*
> *The goal of the curriculum,*
> *Regardless of the teacher you choose,*
> *Is "Know thyself."*

> *Miracles are natural.*
> *When they do not occur,*
> *Something has gone wrong.*
> *Miracles are merely the translation of denial into truth.*

> *Fear is not justified in any form.*
> *"There is nothing to fear."*
> *This simply states a fact.*
> *It is not a fact to those who*
> *believe in illusions,*
> *but illusions are not facts.*
> *In truth there is nothing to fear.*

In 1984, when I first started looking into the story behind *A Course in Miracles*, Helen Schucman was dead, having succumbed to cancer in 1981. But I did track down William Thetford, who was staying in a bayside home in the affluent enclave of Tiburon, just across the Golden Gate Bridge from San Francisco. His journey there began in 1975 when he met a woman named Judy

Skutch, who ran a small research institute called the Foundation for Parasensory Investigation and had put on a conference in New York on parapsychology and psychic phenomena. Thetford and Schucman had completed their manuscript but had no idea what to do with it. Judy Skutch did. She and her husband, Robert, acquired the rights, formed the nonprofit Foundation for Inner Peace, and published it. Before they could put the first edition out, hundreds of photocopies of the original manuscript were circulating coast to coast. On June 22, 1976, the first five thousand copies were released and snapped up. Twenty-five years later, there would be more than a million copies in print and countless study groups around the world poring over these eclectic revelations.

When I first interviewed Thetford and Skutch, they had published one hundred eighty thousand copies of the forty-dollar book. They had tried not to institutionalize the Course. There was no church, no leaders, nothing to join. All the foundation did was publish the book. If people could not afford to buy it, they could write in and get it for free. Small groups of people around the country began getting together in private groups to study *A Course in Miracles*. It soon took on a life of its own. "In the beginning we decided we weren't going to proselytize," Skutch told me. "It wasn't a religion. It wasn't a cult. It was a tool."

It seemed true, and refreshing. It was tough getting Thetford to even agree to an interview. "I have no interest in personal publicity," he said. "I don't go around talking to groups of people. I'm not on the guru circuit."

Thetford was a thin, soft-spoken man. There were deep lines under his eyes and curly tufts of gray hair over a receding hairline. A mystical quality emanated from him as he looked up at me after reading a passage from the blue hardcover book. Light seemed to be coming from the book and illuminating his face. Thetford could make you believe in *A Course in Miracles* because there was *nothing* to believe in. You didn't have to buy the story about the mysterious voice. At first, he told me, he had trouble believing it himself. Schucman was an agnostic Jew, he said, and was suddenly talking about Jesus and the Holy Spirit. To Thetford, the words coming out of Helen Schucman's mouth were coming from somewhere else. "They were not trivial statements, and they were not something Helen could think up," he told me. "This was very alien to her intellectual temperament and predisposition."[17]

I later learned that the story behind the Course was not quite as mysterious as Thetford had suggested. Schucman's mother had dabbled in Theosophy and Christian Science. A Roman Catholic governess and a black Baptist maid also influenced Helen. Schucman visited Lourdes, the Catholic pilgrimage site in

France, when she was twelve. There were times in her life when she went to daily Mass, even though she wasn't Catholic. And shortly before the voice ordered her to take notes, Schucman and Thetford visited the Association for Research and Enlightenment in Virginia Beach, the headquarters for followers of Edgar Cayce, the famous psychic.[18] Thetford's parents had studied Christian Science, and Bill Thetford had been a favorite student of Carl Rogers, a leader in the humanistic psychology movement in the 1950s. Rogers believed humans had a natural impulse for self-actualization and personal growth. This history gives the mélange of mysticism and "know thyself" wisdom in *A Course in Miracles* a very traceable source.

Nevertheless, what struck Thetford, and many later readers, was how the course redefined miracles. They're happening all the time, he says, but we just don't see them. "Our perceptions are ordinarily so clouded and obscured by all our defenses and our mental activity that we seldom see anything with real clarity—as it is," he told me. "The miracle is the undoing of all that complexity—all those levels of the ego that we piled on—so that we remove the barriers of our awareness of love's presence."

Thetford died in 1988. He never tried to turn the Course into a spiritual empire. It was a grassroots, open-ended movement. People were free to take the book and do what they wanted with it. At least that's how it was in the early years. In the late 1990s a legal dispute arose between the Foundation for a Course in Miracles, which had been set up in 1983 by Kenneth Wapnick, and the Circle of Atonement, which taught the Course in Sedona, Arizona, the New Age mecca of the scenic Southwest. Wapnick's foundation had long worked with Schucman, Thetford, and Skutch. In 1999 his foundation acquired publishing rights to *A Course in Miracles* and immediately clamped down on who could make use of the channeled writings. One of the Sedona teachers, Robert Perry, was denied permission to quote from the Course in one of his books. On top of that, the newly empowered foundation sought a cease-and-desist order against the Circle of Atonement's publishing efforts, which include commentaries and study guides on the Course.[19] The dispute raised an interesting question: Who owns the copyright when the real author is a spiritual entity? Some veterans of the Course saw an attempt to enforce orthodoxy on a movement that was supposed to have no orthodoxy. And, of course, it was ironic that a bitter dispute had erupted between proponents of a philosophy whose essential teaching was the call to forgiveness. But by then *A Course in Miracles* was too valuable to maintain spiritual purity. Viking acquired the rights to publish one hundred thousand copies of the Course in 1996 and boosted that effort with a $75,000 advertising campaign, even though the voice had originally told Schucman it didn't like advertising.[20]

One of the first people to popularize *A Course in Miracles* was a Marin County child psychiatrist named Gerald Jampolsky. He knew Skutch and got one of the first photocopies of the manuscript. It changed his life. It inspired him to found the Center for Attitudinal Healing, which helps children and families struggling with life-threatening illnesses. It also inspired a best-selling book titled *Love Is Letting Go of Fear*. Jampolsky hit the lecture circuit, traveling around the world as the apostle Paul for the gospel of modern-day miracles. But the greatest popularizer of *A Course in Miracles* was still to come.

For the past fifteen years, Marianne Williamson has been the *Course in Miracles* superstar on the consciousness-raising circuit. This former cabaret singer is a dynamic speaker, with stage presence and lots of chutzpah. She's been on *Oprah* and *Larry King* and even had a tête-à-tête with Bill and Hillary Clinton. Williamson has packed auditoriums from coast to coast. Her books climbed the best-seller lists and wouldn't come down. They told of her rough journey through the sex-drugs-and-rock-'n'-roll scene in southern California and her ultimate salvation through *A Course in Miracles*. "Like a lot of people at that time—late sixties, early seventies—I was pretty wild," she writes in *A Return to Love*. "Every door marked 'no' by conventional standards seemed to hold the key to some lascivious pleasure I had to have. Whatever seemed outrageous, I wanted to do. And usually, I did."

Marianne was setting herself up as the Everywoman of the Sixties. Single women loved her, and so did gay men. She had partied too hard. She had a brief, failed marriage. She had a nervous breakdown. But it was all grist for the mill, the opening act of an exciting spiritual drama.

Williamson is smart, educated, and good-looking. She dazzled crowds in New York and Hollywood. It was quite a show, and quite a transformation. She was raised in a Jewish home in Houston but had become the West Coast star of a metaphysical text starring Jesus Christ. Film producer Howard Rosenman was just one of many southern Californians who found himself among Marianne's faithful. "Here was this gorgeous Jewish chick who obviously came from a sophisticated, neurotic Texas Jewish background, talking in the argot of my generation, bringing together strands of sociology, politics, anthropology, history, science, and the Bible. The community she's addressing is a group that partied and drugged and sexualized through the sixties and seventies, and here comes this woman who looks like one of us, who you know could have been at Studio 54 or dancing at Fire Island Pines with a tambourine on her hip—and yet she's talking like Jesus Christ."[21]

Marianne Williamson has been called "Hollywood's guru" and the "high priestess of pop religion," but when we spoke, in 2001, Williamson was preaching from behind the pulpit in a Detroit church, the Renaissance Unity Interfaith Spiritual Fellowship, also known as the Church of Today. It was the second largest congregation in the metaphysical Unity School of Christianity.

But Williamson sent her eleven-year-old daughter, Emma, to a traditional Jewish Sunday school rather than to her own church. "She knows she's a Jew, but look at her mother! I'm there giving her a metaphysical perspective on just about every event. She just rolls her eyes, pats me on the head and says, 'Sure, Mom,' like she'll be there to comfort me when they come and take me away."

This space between the spiritual lives of parents and their children is not hard to find among students of A Course in Miracles and other New Age revelations. Religious education for the kids was not a priority in many households of the baby boomer generation. Why expose your children to a religious tradition you have rejected or that has little import in your life?

Cathy Harrington, a single mother of three and a longtime student of A Course in Miracles, puts it like this: "When it comes to your spiritual journey, you need to find it yourself. Kids need to come to their own realization." I spoke with Cathy in early 2003, over breakfast at a restaurant near the university campus in Berkeley.

She was born in Joliet, Illinois, and sent to Christian Science Sunday school by her parents. "I gave it up because I never quite understood it," she said.

Her life took a sudden turn just after her eighteenth birthday, when she gave birth to her oldest child. There would be another marriage and two more children. By 1978 Cathy found herself living as a single mom with three young kids. They wound up in South Carolina, where you either belong to a church or get lots of invitations to join one. "When it came to religious education for the kids, I never found a church where I felt like I fit in. I tried Presbyterian, Methodist, you name it. I wanted to learn, too, and would end up in the Sunday school for adults. I'd be sitting there, and the leader would tell us how to interpret everything. There was no cross talk. It was just, 'This is what we believe.' I just couldn't go there with that."

Cathy's father was an early disciple of A Course in Miracles and had given her a copy of *A Return to Love,* the mega-seller by Marianne Williamson. "My dad had been sending me all this *Course in Miracles* stuff—like little bookmarks with *Course in Miracles* sayings on them. I'd say, 'Oh, that's nice.' Then he sent me *Return to Love,* and I threw it in a drawer."

Harrington was busy working as a hairdresser and raising her kids. One day a client canceled, and Cathy was sitting around her beauty shop, bored to death. "I picked up this magazine, and it had an article about Marianne Williamson and her book. I was just blown away by the article, then remembered that I had that book. I went home that night and read that book. I couldn't put it down. It just spoke to me. It was like that saying, 'When the student is ready, the teacher will appear.' Marianne Williamson brought *A Course in Miracles* down to earth."

Meanwhile, Cathy's marriage was breaking up. She saw seven counselors. Her husband wouldn't go with her to any of them. She found a group that met to talk about *A Course in Miracles* at the Clemson Unitarian Universalist Church in South Carolina.

Her younger son went to a summer Bible camp in South Carolina and came back terrified. "They told him there was a devil, and he thought the devil was in the basement. He didn't understand what they meant by 'down there.' He couldn't sleep, and I started to think that it's dangerous to give your children to people when you don't know *what* is being put in their heads."

Her daughter, the youngest of her three children, had started going to a Baptist church with a friend. "They had a youth group, and it seemed good for her. But when she was twelve she came to the realization that she wasn't a Baptist. The preacher had told her that blacks shouldn't marry whites. She came up to me after that and said, 'Mother, I'm not a Baptist, but I'm going to keep going because I really like my friends.' She went all the way through high school and then stopped when she went to college."

Her son's religious fate was sealed—at least for a time—when he fell in love with a Mormon girl he met in his high school band. She was thirteen. He was fifteen. He saved his lunch money and bought her an engagement ring. Since she was a Mormon, her parents wouldn't let her date, but he spent a lot of time at her house. As soon she graduated from high school he joined the Mormon church and they got married.

They went off together to attend the University of Southern California and soon had a baby. "They were *very* into the Mormon church. He didn't drink. He didn't even drink Coke," Cathy told me. "Then his wife decided she wanted to be free, and she left him. It broke his heart. And then it was hard for him to go back to the Mormon church. He really felt abandoned."

With all three of her children out of the nest, Cathy moved to Alaska to run a bakery. She met a woman who had been ordained into the Unitarian Universalist Association there and led a small congregation. Cathy started helping out, and before she knew it she was at the Starr King School for the Ministry in Berkeley, studying to be a Unitarian Universalist minister herself.

When we met in early 2003, Cathy was working as an intern minister at the 730-member First Unitarian Universalist Church in Austin, Texas. "You know," she told me, "I really regret that I didn't find Unitarian Universalism earlier. They have a great Sunday school program where kids learn about all the world's religions, and then they can make their own choices."

Harrington and Williamson are among a generation of seekers that were reluctant to force religious education on their children. In the sixties and seventies many of us became rightly suspicious of American institutions, including religious institutions. We either formed alternative networks or decided to go it alone.

On the spiritual front, personalized religion was one of the options. In his book *Habits of the Heart*, sociologist Robert Bellah discovered "Sheilaism," a private religion named after one of his interview subjects, a young nurse named Sheila Larson. "I believe in God," Sheila said. "I'm not a religious fanatic. I can't remember the last time I went to church. My faith has carried me a long way. It's Sheilaism. Just my own little voice."[22]

In the 1980s and 1990s many of the same people who left the church to found their own "ism" started looking for new forms of community, and they found it in all kinds of small groups. Men's groups. Bible study groups. Meditation groups. Twelve-step groups. Catholic feminist groups. Baha'i faith groups. Dream groups. Cancer patient support groups. *Course in Miracles* groups.

Some of these small groups got very large. In many cities today it's not hard to find an old mainline church that's mostly empty on Sunday but busy the rest of the week with people seeking self-help or spiritual solace at small group meetings. Many are part of the burgeoning recovery movement. Its twelve-step spirituality is based on a technique devised in 1935 by an Ohio surgeon and a former New York stockbroker, two alcoholics who had a spiritual awakening in the midst of drunkenness and despair. Sometimes called "the secret church," Alcoholics Anonymous helps its members overcome addiction and rekindle a sense of the sacred through the now-famous twelve steps, which include taking "a fearless inventory" of themselves, making amends to those they have harmed, and improving their "conscious contact with God." Many other groups—from Shopaholics Anonymous to Cocaine Anonymous—use this model. Other groups, such as the burgeoning Adult Children of Alcoholics, use a similar format to unearth the psychological and spiritual fallout of abusive families. Then there are the Co-dependents Anonymous meetings, for people who "let another person's behavior affect them and are obsessed with controlling that person's behavior."

John, a successful Marin County businessman who asked that his last name not be used, was the child of two alcoholics, one in recovery and one still drinking. Four years ago he started his own recovery when he attended a meeting of Adult Children of Alcoholics and, later, a Workaholics Anonymous group. "My life had become unmanageable with compulsive work," he said. "When I was in the office pounding out projects, doing deals, I had this feeling of exhilaration, omnipotence, and excitement. It seemed like the essence of what life was about. It was like the two-billion-dollar corporation I was working for couldn't survive without me. I lived to work."[23] John began cutting back on his work hours, and his firm added more employees. He took a leave of absence and started spending more time with his wife and two children. He got involved in community work, and he joined a local Episcopalian church to nurture the spiritual dimension he discovered in twelve-step groups.

Another indication of the recovery boom in the eighties and nineties was the phenomenal success of John Bradshaw, the Texas addictions counselor and pop psychologist who took his message to the public television airwaves. Bradshaw, a former Catholic seminarian and recovering alcoholic, became a self-help superstar and the guru of the recovery movement. His approach combined the raw honesty of an AA meeting and the pop psychology of the Adult Children of Alcoholics movement, delivered with the fiery charisma of a TV preacher. "What the twelve steps say is the only way to heal addiction is to have a spiritual life—to find a spiritual center," Bradshaw told me in an interview at the height of his popularity. "The great thing about the twelve-step program is that it is God as you understand God. That's what has kept it from becoming a religion."[24]

Not everyone applauds this new idea of community in America—one based on recovery. James Hillman, a Jungian psychologist and social critic, sees the explosion as part of the "psychologizing of America," and he views it as a troubling trend. "You used to belong to a real community, go to ward meetings and fight over political issues, over neighborhood issues," Hillman told me in an interview. "Now our emotional loyalties are tied to other fat people or other alcoholics. It's selfish. It's drawn a tremendous energy away from other causes, away from politics and ecology. They have drawn citizens into thinking of themselves as patients, rather than citizens."[25]

These countless recovery meetings and other small group gatherings also pose a collective challenge—and opportunity—for organized religion and the psychological establishment. Americans are taking control of their own spiritual lives and emotional well-being and turning away from both institutions. "Religious leaders are losing touch with the grass roots," said Robert Wuthnow, a sociology professor at Princeton University. "These groups are not interested in theological traditions, denominational distinctions, or church policy statements. They are producing a do-it-yourself religion—a very pragmatic faith. The litmus test is whether the group makes them feel better, whether it helps them get through the day," Wuthnow said. "It is a new kind of family, a new kind of community."[26]

Small groups are a big part of Jerry Jampolsky's Center for Attitudinal Healing, the early organization inspired by *A Course in Miracles*. "Small groups create a wonderful peer support system when people are life-threatened," says a counselor there. "They meet other people who know what they're going through—whether it's chemotherapy, losing your hair, or being a family member of someone who is ill." Like most small groups, those at the Marin County center are a mix of the spiritual and the psychological. "Our work is based on the belief that it's possible to choose peace rather than conflict," she adds, "love rather than fear."

Small groups are also changing American ideas about God. "These groups see God as a deity that can be known fairly easily by following a few simple steps," Wuthnow said. "It's a God of acceptance and love rather than a God of judgment, justice, or mystery."

That kind of God, the one of acceptance and love, is the deity in *A Course in Miracles*, and the God that Marianne Williamson worshiped at her Detroit church.

"What is emerging in the new spirituality is a move away from strict doctrinal identification," Williamson said. "As the *Course in the Miracles* says, teachers of God come from all religions and no religion. Mysticism is not a religion. It's a conversion of the heart. That's what people long for. To be a good Christian is the same as being a good Buddhist or a good Jew—having infinite compassion for all living creatures, to love our neighbors as ourselves."

Over the last two decades many Unity churches have embraced *A Course in Miracles*. Nevertheless, Williamson and Unity did not get along. After five years at her Detroit pulpit, Williamson announced that she was leaving the church. Many congregants were upset when she changed the name of the church and tried to take it out of the denomination. She found that writing books about love and acceptance was easier that running a big church based on those principles.

"When I was just writing books and giving lectures, if people disagreed, they just didn't buy your book or attend your lectures," she told the *Detroit Free Press*. "But if you're leading a congregation, people feel they have the right to tell you what you should or shouldn't talk about. And that hasn't always been easy for me."27

Even when she was preaching in the Unity School of Christianity, Williamson did not consider herself a Christian convert. Her father raised her in the Conservative movement of American Judaism, and she has not renounced that tradition. "You are born a Jew and you die a Jew," she told me. "Converting to Christ's *perspective* is not necessarily a conversion to the Christian *religion.*"

Before she discovered *A Course in Miracles,* Williamson studied Western philosophical traditions in college and dabbled in Eastern traditions. "I would read Hegel and do the I Ching on the same day, then throw in a little Mary Baker Eddy," she recalled. "When I read *A Course in Miracles* I saw Western and Eastern in one book. There's a path for everyone. That's the one that fit me. I had read about forgiveness before, but I never *got it* before—that there is no coming to God without forgiving other people. That was and remains radical information in my life."

Today Williamson is on a new mission. She wants to salvage the damaged reputation of her fellow baby boomers, to revive some of that idealism and social commitment that somehow got lost along the way. "There's a lot of Sixties bashing out there, and a lot of it is true," she said. "Those of us who rebelled against excessive materialism became the most excessive materialists on record. . . . At a certain point spiritual seekers need to face a broader array of issues than the internal self, or it becomes just another chapter in our developing narcissism. . . . But we're not finished yet. We are just starting the third act. We need to go back and reclaim the best of Sixties, but from a more mature and courageous place.

"It's hard for younger people to believe this now, but in the Sixties we actually had a naive belief that we could change the world, and we could change this country, that we could have a society that genuinely worked for a majority of people," she said. "I think the 1960s was the last time in the United States that there was a genuine effort to express philosophical idealism through politics. We were not yet gobbled up as a culture by this prevalent propaganda that economic good is the same as social good."

At the same time, Williamson thinks the generation following Generation X, the one coming of age with the new millennium, could form an alliance with aging boomers resurrecting the old idealism. It's a theory—perhaps more a hope—that I heard three or four times in my interviews with Sixties diehards. "Generations are like keys on a piano," she said. "You have dissonance with the one next to you but harmony with the one after that. I think there is a natural resonance between boomers and many young people today."

On the political front Williamson is trying to promote new forms of community and social change through something called the Global Renaissance Alliance. Small groups of spiritual activists gather in living rooms or church basements for "holistic political conversations." The meetings are a response to the kind of criticism from people like James Hillman—that we were gathering as victims rather than citizens. Williamson's new alliance calls its small groups "Citizen Circles" that are "committed to cultivating the intimate fabric of deep community, and through our individual and joint efforts to create real change in ourselves and the world around us." To promote that vision, she collected essays from a variety of popular spiritual authors and published the results as *Imagine: What America Could Be in the 21st Century*. There's Dean Ornish on health, John Robbins on food, Peter Coyote on the arts, John Bradshaw on the family, John Gray on children, Deepak Chopra on the soul, James Redfield on intuition, Thomas Moore on religion, Neale Donald Walsch on life, and an American prayer from Rabbi Michael Lerner, who first made a name for himself as an antiwar activist in the Vietnam era.

When we spoke, Williamson had come to northern California to be a keynote speaker at the MasterPeace 2001 conference at Stanford University. At first glance, I almost brushed off this meeting as another Bay Area gathering of crystal gazers, tree huggers, and Black Elk wanna-bes. But looking over the program, I saw sessions devoted to politics and economic justice. "We all acknowledge that the present structures, institutions, and systems no longer can address the complexity of life as we are now experiencing it," it states. "We have more data and less knowledge, more experiences and fewer intimate encounters, more things and less sustenance."

What we need, Williamson says, is love. And, as Jesus said, that means loving our enemies. "What I need healed is my left-wing arrogance that I know more than they do," Marianne confessed. "I have to be harmless in my heart toward George Bush. As Martin Luther King said, you have no persuasive power among people who feel your underlying contempt."

Williamson's confession points to one of the pricklier legacies of the Sixties, the feeling that it was us against them. There was a real feeling of "Whose side are you on?" It was culture or counterculture. Establishment or antiestablishment. Black or white. Gay or straight. Sexist or feminist. Young or old. Those divisions remain in many ways, but especially in the realm of race, economics, religion, and politics. Blame the white man. Blame the black man. Blame feminists. Blame men. Blame the rich. Blame the poor. Blame the Arabs. Blame the Jews. Blame the religious right. Blame the secular left.

Can the New Age left get it together, form real political coalitions, and truly change the world? It's a tall order, Williamson says, but now is the time. "This is the baby boomers' last chance. In the sixties, we were stopped by conditions outside ourselves and conditions inside ourselves. Often, we were stoned on one thing or another. But there is a sobriety among us now—at least among enough of us. We want to take one more shot at it."

We can always hope, but it seems like Marianne Williamson took her shot and missed. Her efforts to go beyond personalized spirituality and to inspire social engagement were admirable but ultimately unsuccessful. Williamson was supposed to be one of the big draws at MasterPeace 2001, but the Stanford conference was a financial disaster.

Her collection of essays on a new social vision bombed in the marketplace. And her efforts to get off the lecture circuit and find real community in a religious congregation lasted only a few years.

Spirituality sells, and Marianne Williamson is in the spirituality business. Social justice inspired by religious commitment remains a powerful force in American society, but it cannot be measured by the standards of the marketplace.

Cathy Harrington, the hairdresser and mother who found the *Course in Miracles* in a Williamson book, went on to ground those spiritual insights in the social teachings of an established religious tradition. After her training in Austin as an interim Unitarian minister, Harrington found two vocations—helping the poor in Nicaragua and working with the Faithful Fools, an innovative street ministry for homeless people in San Francisco.

Like many of us, Harrington found her spiritual path and social vocation later in life, after her children had left the fold. Looking back, she wishes she'd found Unitarian Universalism sooner, when there was still time for her and her children to live out a common religious tradition.

This has also been a challenge faced by Sixties parents who sought religious insight in Buddhism, Hinduism, and other imported traditions. We now turn to those families—parents and children living in the wonderland between East and West.

Turning East

As we saw in part 1, the Sixties search for another God could be about cultivating the God within, re-visioning an ancient faith, or embracing a new, improved revelation. But many other seekers in the sixties and seventies turned East, to the great mystical traditions of Buddhism, Hinduism, and Taoism.

Buddhism found fertile ground in the West. Since the 1960s hundreds of Buddhist meditation and retreat centers have been established across the United States. Popular teachers such as the Vietnamese Zen Master Thich Nhat Hanh filled auditoriums with attentive Western converts. Meanwhile, the Fourteenth Dalai Lama became a pop icon, and Nirvana, the apex of Buddhist bliss, morphed into a rock band.

Nevertheless, one of the great challenges facing the new American Buddhism is the "graying of the sangha," the aging demographics of the convert crowd. With its emphasis on meditative practice, Buddhism, American style, has never really been a family affair. But as we'll see in chapter 4, some younger voices are emerging, and a growing number of Buddhist centers have launched programs for children and families. Other clans, most notably the "Jew-Bus," mix and match Buddhism and Judaism, fingering Tibetan prayer beads at their son's bar mitzvah.

Many Buddhist parents took a laissez-faire approach to religious education, not wanting to "lay their trip" on their children. Parents employed exactly the opposite strategy in another East-meets-West movement, the International Society of Krishna Consciousness, with some horrifying results. Chapter 5 tells how children in that Hindu sect, also known as the Hare Krishnas, were sent to austere boarding schools and underwent intensive religious indoctrination. Many kids also suffered sexual, emotional, and physical abuse. Meanwhile, their parents were dispatched around the country with orders to raise money and spread Krishna consciousness.

Perhaps the most fascinating guru to wash onto the American shore was Bhagwan Shree Rajneesh, a former philosophy professor who brewed an enticing blend of Eastern mysticism, Western hedonism, and the kind of avant-garde psychotherapy first popularized at Esalen. Thousands of red-and-orange-clad disciples flocked to the newly incorporated city of Rajneeshpuram, Oregon, where the Bhagwan's penchant for Rolls Royce sedans and free love made him the most infamous guru in the West. Rajneesh saw the traditional family as "the root cause of all our neurosis." But as we'll discover in chapter 6, the alternative community he created had its own form of madness and tore many families to pieces.

Offerings to the White Buddha

Rajneesh

CHAPTER 4

Dharma Kids: Children of the New American Buddhists

My children, my wealth!
So the fool troubles himself.
But how has he children or wealth?
He is not even his own master.[1]

THE BUDDHA, *The Dhammapada*

DharmaCrafts is proud to announce its new DharmaKids Collection, all the stuff Buddhist parents need to send their little ones down the Eightfold Path. On the back of this season's catalog, a curly-haired toddler sits atop a pile of miniature yoga mats. They come in pink, blue, yellow, and Starry Night glow-in-the-dark fabric. They are 100 percent cotton flannel. They are soft and cozy. They are just what this little girl needs as she holds her right hand up to her ear, listening for a still small voice to whisper the Four Noble Truths. "Children learn by imitation," the advertisement advises. "Your child will enjoy practicing meditation or yoga along with Mom or Dad using his or her own child-sized cushion or yoga mat from the DharmaKids Collection." And that's not all. Inside the catalog are miniature *zafus* and *zabatons*, child-sized meditation pillows and cushions just like Mommy and Daddy use. They're stuffed with organic buckwheat hulls and make great little mats for puppies, too. One little pooch, no doubt named Karma or maybe Kerouac, is even pictured in the catalog, attempting a four-legged version of the lotus posture.

There are other tastefully designed products for enlightened moms and dads displayed in the 2002 collection from DharmaCrafts, which offers its Buddhist chic product line out of Lexington, Massachusetts. There are Lotus Pod Table Lanterns from Thailand for $48, Japanese Rin Gongs for $160, and, for the garden, a three-foot-tall statue of the Buddha for $998, available in a rust patina that becomes even more beautiful as it weathers.

And there are ten thousand words of wisdom, on tape and in print, from Buddhist meditation teachers of various sects and incarnations. Among the literary offerings are twelve children's books, including a *Mandala Coloring Book* and *Yoga for Children*. But we get to the heart of the matter with the catalog's most popular kids' book, titled *What Is God?*

"This is a book you will definitely want to have in the house when your child pops the big question," the catalog predicts. "In a simple, joyful way it explores the many ways that people understand God, gives a clear explanation of religion, affirms the child's ability to experience God for himself, and offers a simple technique to do that."

DharmaCrafts is right about at least one thing. God *is* the big question. What *are* Buddhist parents supposed to tell their children about God? We're not talking about Buddhist immigrants from Tibet, Thailand, or Vietnam but mostly Caucasian first-generation converts to the Buddhist path. The Dharma-Crafts demographic are baby boomers who were raised as Catholics or Protestants or Jews, turned away from their Jewish or Christian heritage, then took up Buddhist meditation as a serious, lifelong practice. What do they tell their kids about God when they've embraced a religion that really has no god—at least not one resembling the Jewish or Christian deity they rejected in the Sixties?

To find out, I signed up for Family Practice Day at Spirit Rock Meditation Center, a four-hundred-acre Buddhist retreat on the rural edge of Marin, the California county most entranced by the Middle Way. Nearly a hundred parents and kids from toddler to teen started the day in a large room, with the children sitting up front on the floor and the parents arrayed behind them in a semicircle of padded red chairs. Three workshop leaders shared a raised platform with a large bronze statue of the Buddha. It was not the still, mindful gathering one usually finds at Spirit Rock. On this spring day, the place was buzzing with the collective energy generated by dozens of kids rolling around the floor, jumping up and down, and bouncing off the walls. But that was fine because the theme for this day was "the spirit of play in the dharma."

"What type of play do you like?" workshop leader Betsy Rose asked to an instant chorus of replies: "Marco Polo. Tickle games. Wrestling with my brother."

Rose told the kids and parents that one of the things they teach at Spirit Rock is how to pay attention, how to be present in every moment. "You parents know about attention. Your kids seem to demand it constantly," Betsy said. "And you kids know the adult response. 'I'm too busy now.' One thing you parents can do is notice the places of resistance when you're asked to play with your kids. And also notice the joy when you do play."

Among the many mysteries of Buddhist meditation are constant references to "practice." Buddhists practice and practice and practice. They're constantly practicing, but no one ever seems to ask, "When's the performance?" Betsy told the kids—and the parents—what cellist Pablo Casals once said when someone asked him how often he practices. "I don't practice," he replied. "I just play."[2]

After singing a couple of songs and strumming her guitar, Rose handed the microphone over to Wes Nisker, the Buddhist writer and teacher. Back in the 1970s Wes went by the name Scoop and provided offbeat news commentary on one of San Francisco's alternative FM stations. "Remember," he'd say at the end of every broadcast, "if you don't like the news, go out and make some of your own." Nisker has been practicing meditation for three decades and provides some comic relief in the sanctimonious realms of the consciousness-raising set.

"Listen up, kids," Nisker said. "What important holiday is coming up?" It was late March, and the obvious answers were offered. "Easter," one girl replied. "Passover," another said. "Spring equinox," one parent answered. "Buddha's birthday?" Nisker wasn't impressed with any of the answers. "That's true. Those are coming up. Passover is for Jewish people. Easter is for Christians. Buddha's birthday is for Buddhists. But what's the really important holiday, the holiday that's for everyone?" When there was no reply, Wes pulled out his court jester's hat and shouted, "April Fool's Day! Who wants to be *foooolish?*"

Before long the meditation hall at Spirit Rock looked like the soundstage for *Romper Room.* Mickey Mouse meets the Dalai Lama. After a few minutes of foolishness Nisker told the kids a story about how the Buddha and his disciples were once wandering through a kingdom, and the king was very impressed by how happy all the Buddha's disciples seemed to be. They were so free and graceful; they had minds like gazelles. The king asked the Buddha to tell him the secret of their contentment. "It's simple," the Buddha replied. "They are not thinking about the future and have no regrets about the past. They are just being here now."

Brushing the tip of his jester's hat from his face, Scoop asked the kids, "Have you ever tried to really be here now? Let's try—whoops, it's gone. Let's try again. Ready? Whoops! You missed it again. Don't worry. It always comes around. But you can see how you have to be *really* quick to be here now."

For the rest of the morning the parents and the kids split into three groups and played games modified to embody a Buddhist message. "Duck, Duck, Goose," a game of tag, became "Buddha, Buddha, Bodhisattva," the name for a Buddhist saint who postpones nirvana to help others stuck in the world of pain and suffering. Other games seemed designed to get the parents to drop their defenses, get silly, and roll around the floor with the kids. "We teach the parents the same dharma lesson we're teaching the kids," said Heather Sundberg, the young woman who directs the family and children's program at Spirit Rock.

Later there would be juggling, skits, and yoga for children. This free-spirited catechism was quite a contrast to my memories of Sunday school classes back in a buttoned-down Presbyterian church in Littleton, Colorado, in the 1950s and early 1960s. Those sessions were not fun. It turns out that Sundberg, born in the mid-1970s, was also raised in the Presbyterian church but broadened her spiritual horizons when her mom began a sudden spiritual search. "My mom got into women's circles and meditation," Heather told me. "I've been meditating since I was seventeen."

My mother bowled.

In the afternoon, with the children engaged in other games, the parents went off on their own to the yurt, a canvas tepee meeting space. This is where they would squeeze in a half hour of meditation, listen to a dharma talk by Nisker, and discuss the trials and tribulations of trying to work, raise children, and still find time to meditate. "First of all, forgive yourselves," Nisker advised. "I know how difficult it is to maintain a spiritual practice *without* young children. I doubt that even Buddha could keep his cool."

Nisker suggested that they stop looking at meditation as a serious *practice* with the expectation of some enlightened reward. "Try looking at meditation as a ritual. Try to bring in a sense of *play*. Let go of doing anything or getting anywhere. Be bemused by your own confusion. You are not alone. It is *our* confusion. Meditation is about dropping out of your own psychological story for a while. Just be aware of the body, the breath, the heartbeat."

During the discussion, one father said it's easy to say "be here now" but difficult to find the time when his wife, his kids, and his job are all demanding his attention at the same time. "Meditate? All I want to do is sleep." Amen, said the mother of eleven- and seven-year-olds. "I haven't had a regular meditation practice for eleven years." Another mom pointed out that one of the problems with sitting meditation is that it creates a lap. Kids, like cats, love to crawl into laps. And then there's all that simple wisdom about how Buddhists are supposed to do one thing at a time. Chop wood, carry water. When you are washing dishes, just wash dishes. When you drive, just drive. "Right," one mom quipped. "When you're parenting, you're always multitasking."

Other parents offered some simple tips. One dad said the only way he can find time to meditate is to get up in the morning before anyone else in the house wakes up. Otherwise, the rest of the day and night are shot. Another mom said she found a time to meditate when putting her child to bed. She used to lie in bed with the child but would often fall asleep herself. "Now I sit next to the bed and say, 'Now is the time you need to be quiet, and the time I need to be quiet.' She gets her cuddle and usually falls right asleep, and I get a half hour to meditate."

Spirit Rock is just one of many new centers where Americans who first discovered Buddhism in the 1960s and 1970s have pooled their resources, founding meditation retreats and other institutions to spread the dharma. "Buddhism is coming of age in America," said Jack Kornfield, cofounder of Insight Meditation Society and Spirit Rock. "But at the same time, Buddhism is dying out in much of Asia. Forty-five years ago there were five million monks and nuns in China. Temples in Thailand, Cambodia, and Sri Lanka were full. Now, most of that is gone. In Thailand, people are converting to capitalism."[3]

Many American Buddhist centers have imported Asian culture along with oriental contemplation, either the exotic rituals of Tibetan Buddhism or the stark elegance of Japanese Zen. During the past twenty-five years, however, Kornfield has taught a relatively straightforward form of Buddhism known as Vipassana meditation. At retreats ranging in length from one day to six months, students of this form of Buddhism sit quietly, focus their attention on their breath, and observe the workings of their minds. You don't even have to sit on the floor.

"We emphasize mindfulness, a way to see things clearly, to see how greed, desire, and conflict arise in our lives," said Kornfield, walking down a newly built trail at Spirit Rock. Kornfield trained as a Theravada Buddhist monk in Burma and Thailand in the 1960s but returned to the United States to become a husband, father, psychologist, and Buddhist teacher. Buddhist practice in the United States is much more a movement of ordinary laypeople than in Asia. And unlike the male-dominated, authoritarian temples in Asia, this center is run by a democratically elected council and a collective of twenty meditation teachers, about half of them women. "Eventually, Buddhism in the West will be American in style," said Kornfield. "We've pretty much left behind the Asian style of Buddhism, the bells, the robes, and all that. It has tremendous appeal for people who don't want to put on Zen robes but want some kind of inner spiritual practice."

That conversation with Kornfield took place in 1990. By 2000, Spirit Rock had emerged as one of the nation's major meditation centers. That year the Dalai Lama chose Spirit Rock as the gathering place for a private meeting with Western meditation teachers from various traditions. It was quite a scene. There was the Dalai Lama, surrounded by Tibetan lamas in maroon and yellow robes, Thai monks draped in orange, and an assortment of California Buddhists wearing everything from blue jeans to the traditional Zen vestments of Japan. One of the main questions that emerged at the Marin County gathering was how to separate Buddhism's essential teachings from its cultural trappings. But perhaps the most extraordinary thing about that private gathering of 220 Asian and Western Buddhist leaders was that half of the assembled teachers were women.

According to some estimates, there are between two million and three million practicing Buddhists in the United States, an eclectic mix of Asian immigrants and Western converts. American Buddhism traces its roots to the teachings of Siddhartha Gautama, a wealthy prince who lived in the foothills of the Himalayan mountains six centuries before the birth of Jesus. According to Buddhist lore, the prince left his palace one day and was suddenly awakened to the real world of suffering, sickness, and death. After meditating in a forest retreat, the man who would be Buddha realized that the root of suffering was attachment and desire, an obsessive craving that stifles compassion and inner peace. He began preaching a "middle way" between self-denial and self-indulgence.

San Francisco has long been a magnet for American Buddhists. Chinese laborers who came with the Gold Rush first brought the religion there. In 1893 the World's Parliament of Religions in Chicago introduced Americans to Buddhists teachers from several Asian traditions and opened the door for D. T. Suzuki, a Buddhist scholar who first came to the United States in 1897. Suzuki was still teaching Buddhism at Columbia University in New York in the 1950s and helped inspire such Beat writers as Jack Kerouac, Allen Ginsberg, and Gary Snyder. Perhaps the most influential writer and popularizer of Buddhism in the 1950s and 1960s was Alan Watts, the freethinking Anglican priest who came to New York and eventually set up shop on a houseboat in Sausalito, just across the Golden Gate from San Francisco. Watts saw the true spirit of Zen as a "free-form humanistic spirituality infused with creative potential" that "fit well with the expansive idealism of the early 1960s."[4]

Buddhism blossomed in the 1960s and 1970s, when relaxed immigration laws brought a new wave of Asian immigrants and spiritual teachers from China, India, Tibet, and Japan. Traditional leadership styles—where the teacher is all-powerful—soon led to many scandals involving sex, money, and other abuses of spiritual authority. Many of the pioneer roshis and lamas of the 1960s and 1970s have died, leaving the next generation of Buddhist practitioners to find new, more democratic forms of temple leadership. At the San Francisco Zen Center, founded in 1962 by the late Japanese Zen master Shunryu Suzuki, two rotating co-abbots now serve seven-year terms and share power with an elected board of directors.

Abbess Blanche Hartman, the first woman to lead the Zen center, came to the Marin County meeting with the Dalai Lama in 2000 to talk about the role of women in Buddhism and how to interest young people in Zen meditation. "I'm seventy-four years old now," she told me, "so my main function is to try to pass this on to the next generation."[5]

Largely because of the news media, Hollywood, and other purveyors of pop culture, the protection of Tibetan Buddhism has become a cause célèbre among the spiritual intelligentsia. Books by the Dalai Lama and other Buddhist writers are anchored on the best-seller lists. Films such as *Kundun* and *Seven Years in Tibet* have spread the faith, as have Buddhist movie stars such as Richard Gere and Steven Seagal.

Kornfield sees Hollywood's embrace of Buddhism as a mixed blessing. "It gets people interested, but they may show up and say, 'I want to learn to meditate so I can levitate like I saw the lamas do in the movies.'"

In the spring of 2002 Jack and I sat in a small room off the main meditation hall at Spirit Rock, which combines Asian architecture with a rustic northern

California design. We talked about how far Buddhism has come in the West. His book *After the Ecstasy, the Laundry* looks at the way many longtime meditators have gotten over the romantic notions of Buddhist nirvana. "There was this idea that after five or ten years you'd get enlightened and live happily ever after. You might be more compassionate or wiser or more awake, but you're still the same person. The spiritual life turns out to be less about some spiritual state you've attained and more about the life you live."

Kornfield was born and raised in Boston and Philadelphia in a Jewish family that affiliated with the Reform movement of Judaism, but he has practiced and lived Buddhism for forty years. "Judaism is important to me. I respect where I came from in the tradition, but I haven't gone back to it as a spiritual practice. Being Jewish for me was partly tribal and partly a way to learn social values. There was not much about the inner life and how to touch that," Jack told me. "It's like what Ram Dass said, 'I'm only Jewish on my parents' side.' It's funny, but there's a deeper meaning. We all have our tradition—Irish, Italian, Taiwanese. But the tradition of our spirit or our heart is not just our parents' tradition."

Kornfield is Buddhist. But what about his daughter? Is she Jewish? Her grandparents are Jewish. Jack takes her to Yom Kippur services for the High Holy Days. Is she Buddhist? Well, she certainly grew up around Buddhism. Is she Christian? Her grandmother on her mother's side was Methodist, and she was baptized by the Reverend Cecil Williams, an activist preacher at Glide Memorial United Methodist Church in San Francisco. Is she Hindu? Perhaps. She spent some time in a Hindu temple when Jack was studying there. "One day a friend of hers asked her what her religion was," Jack recalled. "She thought for a second and said, 'Jewish-Buddhist-Hindu-Christian.' All of the above. On the other hand, she's also skeptical—she's eighteen."

Programs for children, teenagers, and families of all sorts have been part of the Spirit Rock program from the beginning. "Raising kids with this kind of consciousness is about the most important thing we can do," said Jim McQuade, who attended Family Practice Day with his wife, Vicki Darrow, and their two daughters, Miriam, eleven, and Amanda, eight. "We're trying to instill a deeper sense that we are all interconnected and teach them that we can't help ourselves without helping others and can't help others without helping ourselves."

Vicki was brought up in Chicago in a devout Catholic family—church every Sunday and many years of parochial school. She and Jim met twenty years ago in medical school at the University of Washington at Seattle. That's when Vicki started meditating. She found it helped her cope with the stress of medical school.

Today the couple lives in Marin County, raising their daughters, working as doctors, and actively participating in Spirit Rock programs. Not everyone who meditates at the center identifies as Buddhist, but Vicki and Jim do and are trying to raise their daughters that way. During a lunch break at Family Practice Day, I asked Vicki what her Roman Catholic parents think about that.

"My mother is still Catholic and is still grappling with what it means to have a Buddhist daughter and Buddhist grandchildren. That's still a work in progress," she said. "What's happened with my mother now that the children are eleven and eight is she's seen that she really likes the way we're raising them. Our kids are kind to other kids. My mom isn't completely sold, but she is more open than she used to be, seeing how the kids have embodied some Buddhist values."

At the same time, Vicki and Jim are not forcing Buddhism on their children. "Raising kids as Buddhists is not telling them to go sit on a cushion, but they've grown up around meditation and are with us when we have meditation groups at our house," Vicki said. "That means meditation groups in our place are not always silent—especially since the girls were born. But we're not pushing it on them or asking them to do anything. We're letting them decide on their own."

There are, however, a few tricks to the Buddhist family trade. "At home, we have a mindfulness bell. When something at home gets too stressful, anyone—including the kids—can go over and ring the bell. We all stop, and we take three breaths. It brings everyone back to their self for a moment. The kids use it more than Jim and I."

Many families pray at mealtime or light candles at home as a religious ritual. Vicki and Jim do the same but with a Buddhist twist. "We believe that part of our practice is for the benefit of all beings and wish deeply for all beings to be free of suffering and pain. So when we light candles the kids say their intentions," Jim said. "One of our daughters was upset because she always got hungry when we went out to the movies. So she lit a candle and said, 'May all beings who get hungry in theaters have food to eat.'"

As we spoke, Amanda and Miriam played with some other kids. They tossed around a beach ball with a Whole Earth design until two boys started fighting over it. Amanda came over to us with a friend. I asked Amanda if she was a Buddhist.

"Yes," she said shyly.

"Do you meditate?"

"Sometimes."

"What does a Buddhist do?" I asked.

There was silence (correct answer!) until her friend jumped into the conversation. "Buddhists do spiritual things," she said.

"Like what?" I asked.

"They like to think about spirits who died and the spirits in nature," she replied.

Then Miriam, the eleven-year-old, informed me that she was *not* a Buddhist.

"What's your religion?" I asked.

She thought for a few seconds. "Kids," she replied.

"What do you like about Family Practice Day?"

"I like that you don't have to just sit here and learn and listen to someone who doesn't talk your language. There's not a lot of boring stuff. There's a lot of kids, so it's fun."

One of the workshop leaders at Spirit Rock was Noah Levine, the son of Stephen Levine, a well-known Buddhist teacher and writer on death and dying. Thirty years ago, when Noah was born, Buddhist parents didn't have Dharma-Crafts or Family Practice Day to show them the way.

Noah's parents, Steve and Patty, lived in a small cabin in Garberville, the northern California town Noah remembers as "hippie central." They divorced when he was just two years old. Four years later Stephen married Ondrea, his third wife and spiritual partner for the next two decades. They met at a "Conscious Living, Conscious Dying" retreat at the Lama Foundation in northern New Mexico. In his memoir Stephen Levine speaks of Ondrea often and lovingly but says little about his marriage to his first wife, just that he and Noah's mother "were not made for each other. We could not agree on how long to cook a three-minute egg."[6]

Growing up in the 1970s and 1980s, Noah Levine went back and forth between his father's place in New Mexico and his mother's home in Santa Cruz. Stephen spent much of the 1970s doing intensive meditation with his first teacher, Sujata, a young Buddhist monk. Later his own work as a meditation teacher with prison inmates led to the publication of a best-selling book, *Gradual Awakening*. In the 1980s Stephen and Ondrea became popular teachers on the once-taboo subject of death and dying.

Meanwhile, Noah didn't see his dad that often. "He was very busy," Noah recalled. "They were doing their book *Who Dies?* and all that and were busy working with patients. I saw that he was committed to service."

This was all ancient history when Noah and I met in the summer of 2001. Several people had mentioned his name when I was looking for young adults with stories to tell about growing up in the midst of the Sixties counterculture. "You should talk to Noah Levine," someone at the San Francisco Zen Center told me. "He's writing *his* memoirs, and he's not even thirty yet."

Noah already had a title in mind, *Dharma Punx,* and he looked the part. His head was shaved, and his arms were covered with tattoos. Actually, the title was more than on his mind; the words *Dharma* and *Punx* were tattooed on the outer edge of his right and left hands, proclaiming the title of his work-in-progress whenever he brought his hands together in prayer.[7]

Like his father before him, Noah got into trouble at an early age—drugs, violence, and petty crime. "At seventeen I got into recovery for my addiction to alcohol, coke, and heroin," he told me. "I got deeply involved in the punk rock movement at an early age. That was a bit of my rebellion against the hippie thing."

His father had been influenced by a mix of Buddhist and Hindu teachings but never forced it on his children. "We would hear stories about Buddha and Krishna, but we didn't have to meditate or offer incense. There were Buddhas around, and my parents would sit and practice. Some of my earliest memories are [of] seeing them sit upright with their eyes closed and asking myself, 'Why are they sleeping in that funny posture?' Looking back, I can see how I was influenced by Buddhist practice. If I hurt myself my father would teach me to soften the pain by sending mindfulness to it rather than pushing it away. But he didn't say, 'Buddha says to do this.'"

By the time Noah came into the world, Stephen had stopped his dangerous dance with addictive drugs. For years his hospice work had given easy access to morphine, but Stephen says in his memoir that he was no longer tempted. Nevertheless, drugs were not hard to find in the post-hippie counterculture in northern California and northern New Mexico where Noah grew up.

"It's not that drugs were acceptable, but they were accessible," Noah recalled. "It was not acceptable for the kids to do it. Our parents were giving us more space because they were so constricted by their parents. They were leaning on the side of letting kids experience life rather than sending them to Sunday school."

Noah left Steve and Ondrea's home in New Mexico at age sixteen and was soon in full punk regalia—Mohawk, leather jacket, studs, boots—and out on the street. They gave him some parting advice: "If you continue to act this way, you're gonna get yourself into a lot of trouble. You're responsible for your own actions."

They were right. At seventeen, after five years of heavy drug use, Noah found himself at Santa Cruz County Juvenile Hall and on the edge of heading to prison. Instead, he got involved with a twelve-step recovery group and started meditating in his cell. "I started looking for happiness in something other than drugs and alcohol." Then his father stepped forward. It was the right place, right time. "It wasn't until I was in all kinds of trouble that my father offered me meditation instruction. It was skillful of him to wait until I was ready for it."

It took that dark night of the soul for Noah to appreciate that his father had something to help him transcend teenage rage. "There are those of us who grew up in the seventies and eighties who thought that the hippie movement didn't work and that they kind of just sold out and became yuppies and didn't really follow through on their intentions. So in response there was this whole punk rock movement, a more aggressive, less peace-and-loving approach. There was a whole generation of punk rockers saying, 'We realize that we're being lied to, that this is all a sham, the American dream, that the Western world is lying to us about what the nature of happiness is.' This attitude was being expressed in violence and fashion and attitudes, even in livelihoods—this feeling we won't participate in the system like our parents' generation did."[8]

As he had with sex, drugs, and music, Noah dived into Buddhist practice. He starting going on meditation retreats, then took a couple of trips to Asia to study. There was a long period of celibacy when he thought about becoming a Buddhist monk. When we spoke, Noah was just finishing up his job leading youth groups at Spirit Rock. He had also taught meditation at the Oakland Juvenile Hall and San Quentin Prison.

While Noah may be "punk" and Stephen "hippie," their lives mirror each other in a number of ways. Stephen Levine was born in New York to Jewish parents of Russian, German, and Polish ancestry. It was not an easy childhood. By the time he was nineteen, Stephen had been arrested four times. He went off to the University of Miami to study and become a jazz musician, but he took his pain and suffering with him. He felt like he was born with a deep dissatisfaction, a condition he'd later describe as "the hungry ghost." These are beings in Buddhist mythology that are just one step from hell. They constantly suffer from hunger and thirst and are sometimes seen as the wandering spirits of departed ancestors whose families failed to make the proper offerings for the next life.9

Stephen met Buddha at a Florida bus station and pulled him down from a rack of paperback books. He read the book, A. E. Burt's *The Compassionate Buddha,* and began meditating in his rented garage. He also discovered the Upanishads. But there were no meditation teachers around, no audiotapes, no weekend workshops. Decades later, he remembered that time this way: "When you are excluded from the family, you have to create your own religion. . . . How could I have been born so far from God?"10

He wound up back in New York, living in the Village, making poems, working as a writer and editor, and just soaking up the scene. "The gods of the beat generation, musically and poetically, were often an odd improvisational mixture of a sometimes nihilistic, somewhat gaudy Buddha and a generous, even inspiring Morpheus."11 His taste for heroin, however, would soon win him a free trip to Rikers Island Penitentiary. He finished his parole in 1964 and headed—where else?—to San Francisco.

In the Haight-Ashbury, Stephen Levine discovered "the family I had left home to find." Despite the war raging in Vietnam and the struggles of the civil rights movement, there was an enlivening optimism in the air. "Working with so many visionary artists and writers propelled my sense of a world community actually capable of peace and service."12

Thirty years later Noah notices something that's obvious to anyone hanging around the meditation and spiritual retreat centers that have sprung up on American soil since the 1960s. Buddhist meditation is a baby boomer pastime. The American sangha, the Buddhist community, is old and getting older. And one reason for that is many Buddhist converts from the 1960s and 1970s were hesitant to indoctrinate their kids into any religion.

"Many of us were edgy about whether or not we should show our kids what we do," said Michael Wenger, the former president of the San Francisco Zen Center and father of a teenage son. "Zen Center still has a lot of members who came of age in the 1960s, when there was uneasiness with traditional religious education. Eventually, there's no choice. Either you cut your children out of your life, or you include them." Wenger took his son with him on a trip to Japan, hoping that might whet his appetite for the Japanese-style Buddhism taught at the San Francisco Zen Center and its Tassajara Monastery in the mountains along the central California coast. "He went to Japan, but left to his own druthers, it would be video games and rap music," Wenger sighed. "But one thing I have noticed about the kids who grew up around a Zen center is they have great social ease. They're not necessarily flamboyant, but they grew up in the middle of a community with lots of different people. But a lot of the kids have gone the way of Americanism, which is no religion."

One of the rituals religion does provide are rites of passage for children moving into adolescence and adulthood. Looking back on his adolescence, and down on his arms, Noah Levine sees his many tattoos as some kind of initiation rite. "Maybe it's just an ego trip, but I feel there's something within me that wants to be expressed in that way. . . . It does set me apart from the mainstream—the mindless, sleeping American culture that I so disdain."

At Spirit Rock, Levine and other staff in the youth program looked at the Jewish bar mitzvah ceremony and the vision quest in Native American culture as they put together a six-week program for teenagers growing up in Buddhist families. As part of that coming-of-age rite, teenagers spend several days alone. "They get the opportunity to practice what the Buddha taught. They're sitting under a tree alone in the forest for two days. They're watching their minds, watching their own nature. They're fasting—no food or water. And as we create this rite of passage we are reminded that there hasn't been an American rite of passage, other than sex and violence and drugs."[13]

That's a bit of an overstatement. Millions of American families in mainstream religious congregations offer their children rites of passage—confirmation for Catholics, bar and bat mitzvahs for Jews, and the born-again experience expected in evangelical Protestant circles. But for millions of secular families and those of mixed faiths, finding meaningful rituals and rites of passage can be difficult.

Some Buddhist practitioners of Jewish heritage, such as Lee Klinger and Marc Lesser, created their own blend of Torah and dharma. Walking past the mezuzah nailed to their doorpost or the menorah in the living room, first-time visitors to the Klinger-Lesser home might assume they have entered a Jewish household. They'd be right. Taking a more careful look around this northern California house, the visitors would notice little altars in the bedrooms, each with tiny Buddha statues and other sacred objects—seashells, favorite rocks, pictures of lost grandparents—laid out on embroidered cloth. They might assume they have entered a Buddhist home. They'd be right. For this Marin County family of four, the recipe called for a teaspoon of Buddhism and a tablespoon of Judaism, stirred together slowly with their own sense of the sacred.

Lee and Marc Klinger-Lesser were both raised in Jewish homes in New York but found a spiritual home at San Francisco Zen Center. "Buddhism has a lot of wisdom, but I was born Jewish and have more connection to that than I realized," Lee said. "But even with Judaism, I feel like I'm growing my own religion. Most of what we are doing now is very much at home, and within the family."

When the Klinger-Lessers held a housewarming party and homegrown ceremony to give their second child her Hebrew name, the proceedings were presided over by two women, a Buddhist priest from the Zen center and a woman studying to be a rabbi. They and about two dozen friends and family ceremoniously circled the new home. They planted three trees—a plum, pear, and apple—in honor of the Klinger-Lesser children and their Jewish ancestors. The mezuzah, a small metal case containing a biblical prayer, was nailed to the doorpost, and everyone helped tap in the nails as they entered the home. Buddhist beads, along with the prayer shawl from Marc Lesser's bar mitzvah, were incorporated into the rites, which included Jewish prayers and Buddhist sutras. The afternoon ended with a potluck feast and inspired Lee to find other ways to bring a blend of Judaism and Buddhism into her home.

After looking into the rituals of the Jewish Sabbath, the family began lighting candles each Friday night and sharing a special meal together. After a year they extended the observance into Saturday, giving up shopping, television, working, and errands. Lee appreciated the spaciousness and simplicity of the Sabbath, how it enabled her family to escape the constant juggling of modern life, how it brought a touch of asceticism into their home. In a way it reminded her of Buddhist meditation and life at the Zen center—and of what she missed growing up on Long Island. "My parents tried to send me to a Hebrew Sunday school in the fourth grade for a year, but it didn't have any meaning for me. They wanted us to be exposed to it, but it wasn't something alive in the house, and I could feel that."

Still, Lee had fond memories of celebrating Passover at her cousin's home—the special smells, the holy foods, the candles and stories. "Those holidays were the most vivid for me. I thought the rituals were wonderful. I didn't know it at the time, but I was hungry for some kind of context beyond my family, some larger place of belonging, some kind of ritual or tradition."

When she was twenty-one Lee was told she had cancer. She sought spiritual relief in Buddhist meditation. "It was frightening, and I was looking for a way of not being so frightened by the suffering and the pain. Buddhist meditation became my way to stop running away from pain." Later, when her mother died and her own children began to grow, Lee began to see the limitations of Zen meditation. "When my mother died, I had Buddhism, but there was no shared practice in my family. Nobody knew how to deal with it. Not having a ritual to share made grieving a lot harder."

Lee's father moved in with the family after his wife died and watched with amazement as his daughter became more and more Jewish. "My father is very cynical," she said, "and has trouble believing I am really doing all these Jewish things—especially knowing that I had a Buddhist wedding and spent so much time at the Zen center."

One Friday night, however, as her son, Jason, was reciting the blessings of the Sabbath, his grandfather surprised everyone by saying he wanted to learn the Hebrew prayers. With the help of his daughter and his grandson, Lee's eighty-four-year-old father learned the blessings and recited them at one of the family's regular Sabbath dinners. "I was so touched—and surprised—by that," she said, her voice trembling. "My father had never said those prayers before in his life."[14]

Lee's story, Noah and Stephen Levine's struggles, and the efforts of Catholic parents at Spirit Rock all point to the difficulties—and the epiphanies—of cultivating a new religious tradition on Judeo-Christian ground. Sixties spirituality is eclectic. It can seem silly at times. It can be condemned as religious syncretism or dismissed as New Age confusion.

In fact, so many Jewish and Catholic seekers have turned to Eastern mysticism that religious authorities in both traditions are sounding alarms. Rabbis have long bemoaned the relatively high percentage of Jews in the *zendo*. And in early 2003 four Vatican agencies issued a joint document citing Zen, yoga, and transcendental meditation as "traditions that flow into the New Age." It warned of a "conscious search for an alternative to Western culture and its Judeo-Christian religious roots." But even Rome acknowledged that "the search which often leads people to the New Age is a genuine yearning for a deeper spirituality, for something which will touch their hearts."[15]

This search for spiritual meaning can be seen as a rejection of our parents' faith. Yet it can also help us rediscover the wisdom of a discarded religious tradition, along with the insights of a new meditative practice. Most of the parents profiled in this chapter used subtle, skillful means to pass along the lessons of Buddhism to their children. They did not impose the zeal of religious conversion onto their offspring. But as we'll see in the next chapter, that was not always the case among Sixties seekers who turned to the East.

CHAPTER 5

Devotion and Abuse in the Hare Krishnas

These ignorant children, bound by duality, think their journey has ended.
Blinded by attachment, they fail to see the Truth.[16]

MUNDAKA UPANISHAD

Dallas is a city famous for its super-sized steaks, but not at Kalachandji Restaurant. On a typical afternoon customers at this vegetarian diner run by the Hare Krishnas relax in a peaceful courtyard, sampling broccoli curry, spicy rice dishes, and freshly baked Indian breads from a sumptuous lunchtime buffet. Texas vegetarians go out of their way to visit this unique eatery, especially since the *Dallas Morning News* praised its "heavenly cuisine," served up in an "oasis of serenity."

That may be true for some, but not for Brigite Rittenour. Her memories of Kalachandji are anything but serene. Brigite was sent here in 1974, when she was just five years old, and one year after her parents joined the Hare Krishnas up in Canada. Back then, this complex of buildings was known not for its trendy vegetarian restaurant but for its *gurukala,* a boarding school run under the strict, ascetic precepts of the International Society for Krishna Consciousness. From across North America, Hare Krishna converts sent their young children to Dallas, freeing themselves to spread Krishna consciousness—and raise money—for this devotional Hindu sect.

Of all the spiritual groups that arose in the United States in the 1960s and 1970s, few left as memorable an impression as the Hare Krishnas. Thousands of hippies, drifters, and druggies converted to Krishna. They shaved off their long hair—saving the trademark topknot—and donned flowing saffron clothes. Embraced by George Harrison, the "spiritual Beatle," the Hare Krishnas seemed to be wherever it was happening—at marches, free concerts, street corners, and airport lobbies—dancing blissfully and forever chanting "Hare Krishna."

In the Sixties Hare Krishna devotees and the new American Buddhists both turned East for spiritual sustenance. Yet their lives as parents are strikingly different. Many Buddhist converts were hesitant to impose their new religion on a new generation. But the intense, devotional, renunciative lifestyle demanded by the Hare Krishna sect seemed to give those parents little choice but to send their children to communal boarding schools for strict religious education. Their guru, Srila Prabhupada, was not known as a big fan of the nuclear family. "Prabhupada believed little hope existed for a child to learn self-control within the nuclear family because of the 'ropes of affection' between parent and child," notes Professor E. Burke Rochford Jr., a religion scholar who has studied the Hare Krishna movement extensively.[17]

Many of the Sixties children profiled in this book felt abandoned by their parents. Like David Price, the boy born at Esalen Institute in the early 1960s, they thought Mom and Dad cared too little about them and too much about saving the world or finding themselves. But many of the kids sent off to Hare Krishna boarding schools in Dallas and West Virginia did not just *feel* abandoned or abused, they *were* abandoned and abused.

Few images seem as Sixties as all those Hare Krishna devotees dancing in the streets. But in many ways this movement was the antithesis of what we are calling Sixties spirituality. The Hare Krishnas certainly weren't antiauthoritarian. In this sect, the guru's words were the golden rules. And this version of the Krishna faith was anything but eclectic. It was the only way. It was totalitarian and totalistic. Krishna converts abandoned their Western clothes and culture in a desperate imitation of Vedic renunciation. Many of them were running away from home, trying to escape life on the streets or an addiction to hard drugs. In retrospect, the horror stories don't seem so surprising.

This story began in 1965 when Prabhupada, an aging Indian devotee of the Hindu god Krishna, came to New York to found the International Society for Krishna Consciousness (ISKCON). By the time Prabhupada died in 1977, the

Hare Krishnas controlled one hundred ashrams, temples, and farm communities around the world.

Two years before his death Prabhupada visited his temple in Berkeley. At the time I was working on my degree in sociology, and these chanting, dancing devotees were a daily sight on the streets of Berkeley and the University of California campus. But few of us knew of the power struggles already under way in the upper echelons of this global religious empire. During one of Prabhupada's visits to the Berkeley temple, just south of the Cal campus, a devotee asked the aging guru a question that was on the mind of many Hare Krishna insiders at the time: "What will happen when you die?"

His answer is enshrined on a plaque inside the ornate temple, between a life-size replica of Prabhupada and flower-bedecked statues of Hindu deities. "I will never die," the India-born guru replied. "I shall live through my books." Two years later Prabhupada was dead. And while his books survive, the Hindu sect he built has been floundering for decades, mired in power struggles and legal troubles. It has also failed to attract a new generation of Western converts, including those *gurukala* kids brought up to be exemplars of this ancient Indian faith.

To understand why, consider the story of Brigite Rittenour. Brigite was born in Toronto in 1969. Her mother was British, born into the Methodist church, and her father was raised in the Catholic church in France. They met in Canada and, until the Lord Krishna came into their lives, were living a typical middle-class life. "They were not hippies at all," Brigite recalled. "They never did drugs or any of that hippie stuff—none at all. My dad worked for a carpet company, and my mother stayed at home with me. They went out dancing once a week—which was as extreme as it got. They stayed home a lot and played dominos."

But looking back, Brigite can now see how her parents wound up joining the Hare Krishnas. "My mother was always searching for something. She wanted to know why things were the way they are and never got satisfactory answers from Christianity. One day she found a copy of the Bhagavad Gita and another Krishna book in a used book store. She read that book and decided that was it. She'd found it. She made contact with the Krishna temple, and the next thing I knew we were going to the temple in Toronto. Our diet changed in one day. She started throwing stuff out and said we weren't eating meat anymore."

On the day after her fifth birthday, Brigite said, her mother flew her down to Dallas from Toronto, handed her daughter over to some Krishna devotees at the airport, and then flew back to Canada. "They told me I would learn about Krishna and get to go on a plane and it would be fun. I'd heard all these stories about Krishna, and it sounded like a fun thing. I didn't comprehend that I was going to stay there."

Brigite was shepherded into a white van and driven to the temple, originally built as a Baptist church in what is now a largely Latino neighborhood in Dallas. Brigite walked into the ashram and down the stairs into the basement, into the first room on the right. She was looking for a bedroom—back home she had a bedroom—but was handed a blanket and told to sleep on the floor with about two dozen other girls.

They went to bed early because the children rose at 3:30 A.M., when they lined up in the hallway to wait for a shower. For some reason they were not allowed to sit on the toilets but had to squat. There was no toilet paper, just a bowl of water shared by all the girls, who learned to use their left hand to clean themselves. There were no toothbrushes or toothpaste, just another bowl of water. They dipped their tiny fingers into the bowl and scrubbed their teeth, remembering to use the right hand for that ritual. Then there were two hours of religious devotions—chanting and dancing and singing—followed by a lecture around the time the sun came up.

There was oatmeal for breakfast, but it was more like a nightmare than a morning meal. "We used to eat in the sanctuary, and the food was infested with giant cockroaches. We called them flying dates. They wouldn't kill the bugs because they can't kill anything. We were supposed to pick them out. We were also supposed to eat ginger root, which burned my mouth. I ended up throwing up and had to lick up the food on the floor. It was really gross. You had to lick your vomit, which, of course, would make you throw up again."

It was quite a lifestyle change for a five-year-old girl.

When we spoke, in the summer of 2002, Brigite was living in Brownwood, Texas, a small town about 150 miles southwest of Dallas. There's a conservative Baptist college in Brownwood and lots of poverty. Brigite, a single mother with six children, had just started a new job selling ads for a local radio station—her latest effort to get off welfare and start a new life.

She was also hoping for some financial relief from the Texas courts. Rittenour was one of the plaintiffs in a huge lawsuit brought against the Hare Krishnas by Dallas lawyer Windle Turley. His $400 million suit was originally filed in federal court but was thrown out by a judge who rejected Turley's effort to go after the religious sect nationwide using the RICO act, a legal device traditionally used against organized crime. That decision forced Turley to go after the Krishnas in various state courts, and he had refiled his lawsuit in Texas and West Virginia on behalf of dozens of children allegedly abused in Krishna boarding schools in the 1970s.

Turley's suit and Rittenour's story paint a nightmarish picture of life in the Texas and West Virginia *gurukalas*. The alleged abuse was emotional, physical, and sexual. Brigite remembers the headmaster of the Dallas *gurukala* as a "sadistic brute."

"He had that crazy look in his eyes. He would get mad and you wouldn't know why. He'd come down and kick us if we moved when we were supposed to sleep. One of his favorite things to do was pick us up by our ears and slam us up against a cinder block wall. He did it to me several times."

Sexual abuse, Rittenour charged, was committed under the guise of medical attention. "It made no sense because when we were really sick we weren't allowed to see a doctor. When I stepped on a rusty nail or had asthma, I was never taken to a doctor. Other times we were taken to the 'medicine room' near the guru's visiting quarters to go to the doctor. Different people would be there and we would lie down and take off our clothes. I didn't know what was happening to me. I didn't like it. But I thought they were doctors. Sometimes it hurt, but I also remember being aroused at that young age. I remember it, and remember feeling ashamed about it."

Rittenour's childhood horrors in the Hare Krishnas were not isolated incidents; neither do they characterize the typical life for a young Krishna devotee in the 1970s. Dallas hosted the first *gurukala* in 1971, but eleven others opened across North America in the mid-1970s. At some of the boarding schools there was relatively little abuse, and it's not hard to find children with positive memories of life in the ashram. It's also worth remembering that Rittenour and Turley were suing the Hare Krishnas and thus putting the worst possible spin on what happened in the temple on Gurley Avenue. That doesn't mean they are lying, but it helps to put Rittenour's story in context. There is often a fine line between child abuse and religious indoctrination in strict, authoritarian sects, be they Christian, Islamic, or Hindu. At the Krishna boarding schools children as young as five years old were forced to live like little monks. But equally horrid stories of sexual abuse have been reported regularly in other religious organizations, including the Roman Catholic Church.

"Child abuse is not limited to new religious movements," said Anuttama Dasa, director of North American communications for the Hare Krishna society. "There was almost an epidemic in the 1970s." Anuttama admits there was a serious abuse problem in the movement but denies the lawsuit's allegations that the Hare Krishnas set up the boarding schools to "permit the parents to be free to solicit and raise money" or that the sect "granted teaching positions to sexual predators so they would have access to children for their sexual gratification."

"These were terrible acts in gross violation of our principles," he said. "We believe that sexuality, for strict devotees, is meant to be performed between a husband and wife for procreation."

At the same time, several factors made the Krishna scene an especially dangerous one for children. In many cases the parents were as much to blame as the leaders of the sect. Some Krishna parents were so swept away by their life-changing conversion that they almost forgot they were parents. This was encouraged by leaders of the sect, who promoted monkish lifestyles over the marriage and family life of ordinary householders. "As a stigmatized and politically marginal group, householders were left powerless to assert their parental authority over the lives of the children. Children were abused in part because they were not valued by the leaders, and even, very often, by their own parents who accepted theological and other justifications offered by the leadership for remaining uninvolved in the lives of their children," writes E. Burke Rochford in his sociological research. "Child abuse stands as a powerful symbol of the failure of ISKCON's traditionalist, communal, hierarchical form of social organization."

Swami Prabhupada was already seventy years old when he arrived in New York in 1965, and he had little patience for the disputes between his married disciples. "I am so disgusted with this troublesome business of marriage, because every day I receive some complaint from husband or wife," he wrote in a 1972 letter. "So henceforth I am not sanctioning any more marriages." Years before, this former businessman and father of five—then known as Abhay Charan De—had walked out on his own family in the pursuit of Krishna consciousness.

At the Dallas ashram children were taught that missing their parents was a form of attachment, something they should transcend. That philosophy also allowed their parents to devote themselves wholeheartedly to the Hare Krishnas. "My parents were in Toronto trying to raise money for the movement," Brigite said. "Dad worked in a factory and made incense. We were told not to have any attachment to our parents—just think about Krishna and Supreme Knowledge. They indoctrinated us with this stuff all day. We were convinced we didn't want to see our parents. We were convinced that was bad—that was to be attached." They were also taught to fear the *karmies,* the unenlightened, materialist people in the outside world. "They would terrorize us with brainwashing. They taught us that people outside the movement were evil, that they ate meat and would eat us."

Today there is no boarding school at the Krishna temple in Dallas. Most of the members are, not Caucasian converts, but Asian Hindus trying to keep connected to their native religion. They are people like Nityananda Dasa, the chief priest of the Hare Krishna temple and the chief apologist in Dallas for the sins of the past.

"Some of our leaders became real fanatics," he told me. "They decided to send all the children here to this school. Sometimes we didn't know where the parents were. They could have just been bums. The children were here and totally unhappy. It's a ripe situation. They walked into a lawsuit. The parents were not being what they were supposed to be, the leaders were not being what they were supposed to be, and the teachers were not qualified. But in a pioneering situation, you can understand how those things can happen. It wasn't as bad as it could have been."

Nityananda is a tall, elegant man. He was wearing Western clothes and had an all-American haircut. No saffron robes. No shaved head with topknot. He doesn't have to dress up in Indian garb to feel like a Hindu. He was born a Hindu and an Indian but has embraced American culture. "I love the Dallas Cowboys," he told me. "I watch every Dallas Cowboys game."

Over lunch in a booth at Kalachandji Restaurant, Nityananda gave his take on what went wrong here back in the 1970s. He blames much of the abuse on zealous American converts imposing a twisted understanding of Indian culture onto the boarding school kids. It's time, he says, for the Hare Krishnas to differentiate between Indian culture and the spiritual teachings of the Bhagavad Gita. "Our approach was too Indianized. Americans are not going to accept an Indianization of American culture. This realization is sinking in among our leadership."

In some ways the Krishna congregation in Dallas is thriving. On Sundays hundreds of worshipers fill an ornate hall of worship. The building used to be the indoor basketball court of the old Baptist church. After the Krishnas bought the property in the early 1970s, they transformed the gym, adorning it with lions carved from rosewood and bright murals of little blue Krishnas cavorting with young consorts.

Nityananda moved to Dallas from Fiji in the early 1990s to help straighten out the troubled temple. His first encounter with the Krishnas was as a lawyer back in Fiji, where he filed a noise abatement complaint when the Krishnas opened a temple next door to his home. "They had these huge speakers that started blaring at 4:30 in the morning." But once he came to understand the religious beliefs of the Krishnas, he decided it was a valid expression of his Indian faith.

Nityananda says about five hundred worshipers come for the main weekly celebration, but the problem is that most of them are recent Indian immigrants, not American converts. That same ethnic shift has occurred at other Hare Krishna temples across the United States. "That was not what we wanted to happen. We really didn't come to the West for the Indians. We came so the Westerners would also get some appreciation for our religion."

And that's no easy task, especially in a place like Dallas. "If we can be relevant in Texas, we can be relevant anywhere else," he says. "To do this in the Bible Belt is a real challenge."

Nityananda's challenge is not unlike the one given to Swami Prabhupada back in 1922, when he was given his mission by his guru, Bhaktisiddhanta Saravati Goswami, the leader of a Hindu revival movement in India. Sri Chaitanya Mahaprabhu, who is believed by his followers to be the reincarnation of the Lord Krishna, founded the sect in the fifteenth century. It is just one of a myriad of religious movements based on the ancient Vedic scripture, the Bhagavad Gita, which recounts a conversation between the warrior Prince Arjuna and his friend and charioteer, Krishna.

Prabhupada's mission was to bring his sect's devotional brand of Hinduism to the English-speaking world. He preached a form of Vaishnavism, a predominantly monotheistic denomination within the broader Hindu culture. It teaches that the human soul is composed of the Lord Krishna's highest energy, but people are deluded by *maya*, the lower energy of their bodily and material desires. Devotees seek a return to Krishna consciousness by chanting, devotion, and living a life free of meat, fish, eggs, gambling, intoxicants, and illicit sex.

This lifestyle of renunciation was strangely attractive to a number of Sixties survivors burned out on sex, drugs, and rock 'n' roll. I remember watching the Hare Krishna parades in the early 1970s in Berkeley and San Francisco. Dozens of devotees would be dancing down the street to great throbbing of drums, clashing of finger cymbals, and amplified organ music, chanting "Hare Krishna" all the way. Presiding over it all on an ornate float would be Prabhupada, sitting serenely on a plush red throne beneath a giant statue of Krishna. There would be a vegetarian feast at the end of the parade. We were urged to join them, promised that the life of renunciation was the road to true freedom. Like George Harrison promised on the radio, "Just chant in the name of the Lord and you'll be free. The Lord is awaiting on you all, just wait and see."[18]

It hadn't been that many years since Prabhupada had installed himself in a grimy East Village storefront in New York City, where he lectured three times a week on the teachings of the Bhagavad Gita. His first write-up was in the October 15, 1966, edition of the *East Village Other*. "In only three months," the alternative paper reported, "Swami A. C. Bhaktivedanta Prabhupada has succeeded in convincing the world's toughest audience—bohemians, acidheads, potheads, and hippies—that he knows the way to God . . . a brand of 'Consciousness Expansion' that's sweeter than acid, cheaper than pot, and non-bustible by the fuzz."

One of the first East Village bohemians to turn to Prabhupada was Keith Ham, the son of a fundamentalist Baptist preacher. Ham had come to New York City to work on a doctorate in religious history at Columbia University. He and some buddies went to 26 Second Avenue to check out the new swami in the Village. After some chanting, and a long silence, Prabhupada spoke. "Krishna is God," he told them. "Not merely an incarnation of God, Krishna is God, the supreme Lord of the universe. He is a person, an eternally youthful, playful child with blue skin. His name means 'reservoir of pleasure.'" According to one account of that encounter, Ham was entranced by this new vision of God. "His father taught fear and punishment; his God was the vengeful, white-bearded Jehovah. The swami preached love; his God was a playful, sensual, blue-skinned boy."[19]

Ham, in the form of Swami Kirtanananda, would become one of Prabhupada's most powerful successors and build the grandest Hare Krishna temple in North America—New Vrindaban. That golden temple in rural West Virginia was also ground zero for some of the worst child abuse and shadiest dealings in the Krishna movement. Kirtanananda wound up serving a nine-year term in a North Carolina prison for racketeering. Expelled from the Hare Krishna movement in 1987, he was one of eighteen individual defendants named in Turley's original lawsuit.

One study of child care—and child abuse—at New Vrindaban uncovered a piece of advice given to expectant Hare Krishna mothers at the temple: "Dump the load and hit the road."[20]

That's pretty much what happened to Tina Hebel, another of the plaintiffs in the Turley lawsuit. "My father brought me there when I was two. I'd stay with different devotees, and he'd come back and forth from India. I never really knew my dad. When I was twenty-two, he gave me a call and told me what happened. He said my mother died. He said he gave Kirtanananda a ton of money to take care of me."

At age five Hebel went to live in the girls' ashram. Every morning, like Brigite Rittenour, she was awakened before dawn for hours of religious devotions. During the rest of the day they would attend classes, cook, clean, or work in the fields. "It was great having the freedom to be out in nature, but there were times when we were not properly clothed or fed," she said. "If you fell asleep in [religious studies] class, you'd get smacked or get cold water thrown on you."

Tina and I met years later in a coffeehouse outside San Jose, California, where she was attending an acupuncture school and trying to put her life back together. A single mother with a seven-year-old daughter, Hebel remembers the West Virginia ashram as a place with "no warmth, no acceptance." She told me, "Most of the adults were rebelling against their Christian upbringing. Pretty much everyone living there were Americans trying to be Indians, to be Hindus. It was very strange."

Tina eventually found a protector and surrogate mother in Susan Hebel, known by the Krishna name Kanka. She helped Tina escape from the ashram in 1987, when Tina was fourteen, adopted her, and brought her into her family.

Back in 1971 Susan's wedding to Steve Hebel, also known as Swarup, was written up in the September 6, 1971, edition of *New York* magazine, making them poster children for all those counterculture seekers who had turned away from American materialism and embraced Eastern spirituality. By the end of the decade, however, Swarup was starting to question the wisdom of child care, Krishna style. Here's one account of his February 1979 visit to the New Vrindaban nursery, where he had gone to visit his four-year-old son:

> *Inside, he heard kids crying. He opened the door. He looked into the kindergarten and froze in his tracks. The room stunk of excrement, vomit, and urine, tinged with eye-stinging ammonia. The floor was littered with soiled diapers. There were fifteen to twenty children crowded in the small room. Some were lying in battered cribs, screaming themselves blue. Others sat in the filth on the floor, playing with a battered doll or a broken toy car or an old diaper. A pregnant woman, holding a shrieking baby under one arm, was dashing around trying to see to everything at once.*[21]

New Vrindaban was also a hotbed for sexual abuse. One woman raised at the West Virginia commune told me a male teacher molested her for two years, between the ages of eight and ten. Then, when she was thirteen, another man at the commune sexually abused her for about seven months. "We had a substitute teacher come in, and she started telling us about child abuse," she said. "I'd never heard of it, but realized I'd been living it my whole life. I remember running out of the classroom crying. Some other girls came out, and we started sharing stories. 'Did it happen to you? Did it happen to you?'"[22]

This woman, who asked that her name not be used, told me that the sect's negative attitude toward women and children and its puritanical doctrines contributed to this physical and sexual abuse. "Women were held to be inferior. They suffered the most," she said. "Young men had to be celibate. That's not natural, so you get perversion and child molestation and abusive relationships. The men were fighting with themselves—fighting with the idea that they don't love Krishna enough if they want to have sex."

Regaining her life, and her sexuality, had been a long and difficult process. "It was really hard. I put on weight, trying to cover myself up. I went inside myself for years," she said. "But you eventually realize that this is your life. I was molested as a child, but I can now choose and claim my own sexuality. To me, that's growth. That's positive. If I want to revert and go back to guilt and anger and shame, I might as well go back and live with them."

For years the Krishna leadership ignored clear signs that there was big trouble in the *gurukalas*. They had done what their guru told them, so it had to be right. But in the years following Prabhupada's death, it was hard to deny the failure of the ashram schools. They were turning out, not saints, but children who seemed more like *karmies*, the nonreligious outsiders. "By the mid-1980s, as the children were growing into teenagers, understandings of the second generation and the *gurukala* began to change," Rochford reports. "To the surprise of many leaders and parents alike, the children raised in the *gurukalas* were less than pure spiritually. Few were committed to a life of renunciation and full-time involvement in ISKCON."[23]

Of course, not everyone who grew up with the Krishnas remembers a life of physical and sexual abuse. But even those young families promoted as second-generation exemplars fail to show anywhere near the total devotion of their convert parents.

Consider the stories of Subal Smith and Tulsi Briones, a second-generation Krishna couple living in a cabin in the Santa Cruz mountains, south of San Jose.

Subal was only six months old when his parents left New York and joined the great hippie migration, heading "straight to the Haight." It was the early 1970s, and the peaceful glow had already faded from San Francisco's counterculture scene, replaced by hard drugs and harder hearts. Smith's parents headed south to Santa Cruz, in search of mellower climes. There they stumbled upon a band of ecstatic, chanting converts—blissfully on the road to cosmic consciousness.

Meanwhile, out in Texas, Tulsi Briones looked out the window of her mother's Austin home. Five Hare Krishna buses were parked outside. It was 1979, Briones was six years old, but she remembers it like it was yesterday. "My mother came to me and said, 'We're joining the Hare Krishnas.' She put me in the car, and I said, 'What about our house? What about our stuff?' She said, 'We don't need material possessions.'"

Briones and Smith both wound up in Hare Krishna schools—one in Dallas and the other in the Sierra foothills in California—and both drifted away from the Hindu sect once they were out on their own. In the mid-1990s they crossed paths at a festival at the Krishna temple in Los Angeles, a kind of reunion for kids who grew up in the movement. "My friends convinced me to go to the festival in L.A. I went with an open heart, to be with Krishna," said Briones, who had recently moved from Texas to southern California. "I met Subal and knew he was my husband."

Briones hadn't been to a Hare Krishna temple since she was eleven years old. But she never really stopped believing. She'd gone to Krishna school to age eleven, then her mother sent her to a Montessori school, then a Catholic school, then a public high school in Texas. "It leaked out that I was a vegetarian and a Hare Krishna, so I was the weirdo. Remember that this is Texas. I'm the only vegetarian in the whole school and the only one who believed in the little blue Smurf God."

Shortly after meeting at the Los Angeles festival, Briones and Smith moved in together. "His parents loved me because I was a Krishna girl," she said. "I loved him because he was a real guy, not some devotee man who was, like, 'you're a wife and that's your only position.'" They were married in a traditional ceremony in the Hare Krishna temple in Berkeley, with Indian garb and a fire ritual. In 1999 their daughter was born, Radha Luna Smith.

Smith has good memories of growing up with the Krishnas. In the mid-1970s his parents wound up at the Hare Krishna temple in Los Angeles, where his mother taught at the ashram school. Later he was sent to a Krishna boarding school in the Sierra foothills. "For me, it was incredible to be living on the land, and being a farmhand. I was ten or eleven and had a great experience. My trip there happened to be very sweet. The person who took care of us was a super-nice soul." But at age thirteen Smith went back to Los Angeles, attended a public high school, and lost interest in the Hare Krishnas.

Today this young family's spiritual leavings can be gleaned from a look around their mountain cabin. There's an altar with Buddha next to the TV and one with Krishna in the hall leading to the kitchen. Yet despite his good times as a Krishna kid, Smith doesn't consider himself a believer. "I'm happy with the way I was raised," he said. "I really am. It gave me a different way to live my life. But I'm not hung up on any sort of philosophy. There's some truth in every religion, but I'm nervous about attaching myself to one thing."[24]

Neither he nor his wife feels they need to visit the Berkeley temple where they were married. Nevertheless, it's a part of their lives. "You don't need to be in the movement to maintain a connection to Krishna or develop a relationship with God," Briones said. "The goal of life is self-realization. We don't have to put Radha into an ashram. We can show her what's available without forcing dogma on her. She hears me chant the Hare Krishna mantra. It gives me safety and comfort. There's no harm in it."

Other children of Krishna, such as Brigite Rittenour, want nothing to do with the exotic deities of their youth.

Brigite's parents took her out of the Dallas *gurukala* when it was shut down in 1976. They moved to Los Angeles for a time, then back to Texas when Brigite was eleven. Her parents were drifting away from the Krishna scene, tired of all the politics and infighting that followed the death of the founding guru. Yet her family's lifestyle remained pretty unstable. "My parents decided that I didn't need an education and could work with my dad, who was already picking out prospective husbands for me. When I was fourteen, my parents set me up in the flea market, selling jewelry."

That's where Brigite met the man who would become her first husband. "My parents invited him over to the house. He'd eat dinner with us. Then my mother told me I was betrothed to the guy." She was fourteen. He was thirty-seven. Brigite had her first child at age fifteen and another baby before they divorced four years later. "I was a kid, and he was thirty-seven, so we didn't really get along. He wanted to sit around, smoke pot, buy old cars, and have spiritual revelations."

Her second marriage lasted thirteen years and produced four more children. Along the way there were a couple of suicide attempts, a rape, a cancer scare, and a conversion to born-again Christianity. "You just become so despondent that you want somebody to shoot you," Brigite confesses. "For a long time, I didn't want to hear anything about God. Everybody says their way is the only way."

When we spoke, however, Brigite was attending services at the Living Word, a nondenominational church in Brownwood. "It has taken me awhile to accept a lot of things with my marriage and my health and to see that there are people who would come to help me. The Krishna people didn't help. The Christian people seemed to care, so I put my trust in God. Now I believe there is a loving God."

Raised with the teachings of another God, Brigite Rittenour returned to her Judeo-Christian heritage, finding protection among the followers of Jesus. Subal Smith came away with the idea that "there's some truth in every religion" but worries about "attaching myself to one thing." Tulsi Briones wouldn't think of sending her daughter to an ashram but still chants "Hare Krishna" while holding her in her arms.

Looking back on her childhood in the seventies, Tina Hebel sees value amid all the insanity at New Vrindaban. "My greatest gift was I was young," she says.

"I always felt like everyone around me was crazy, so I trusted myself. Everything was totally regimented, but you're growing up with a bunch of kids going through the same thing. You develop deep relationships. We are still friends. We are so connected. The culture itself was beautiful—the dance, the cooking, the art. We were raised with a communal ideal. You are not the car you drive. You're not buying into material society or having your kids watch all those pathetic TV shows."

When we spoke, Tina Hebel had an altar in her home. Krishna was not the main deity, but he was one part of her own eclectic faith. There was a picture of a waterfall and a statue of Quan Yin, the goddess of compassion. There was Buddha and a picture of Radha and Krishna, representing love and unity. "I feel like spirituality is the most important thing in my life," she said. "I don't necessarily call Krishna God, but I believe there is one God. You can call him what you want to call him, but there is definitely a higher force, a higher energy."

Tina's story illustrates the multifaceted legacy of new religious movements—that a positive spiritual grounding can be formed in even the most abusive setting. Brigite Rittenour rejected her Krishna upbringing when she was embraced by members of an evangelical church, but the opposite could just as easily have happened. Some of the most dangerous cults today are Christian. A Texan with a troubled life could just as easily wind up in one of those than leave to study Eastern religion. What makes cults abusive are not their beliefs but their practices, the way they treat people.

Peoples Temple was a Christian cult. Jim Jones was an ordained minister in the Disciples of Christ, a mainline Protestant denomination. For most of his time in San Francisco in the 1970s, he was seen as a liberal prophet for social justice, not a crazed cult leader. He had the most racially mixed church in town. He was named chair of the city's Housing Authority and was such a political player that he was invited to the White House during the Carter administration. He also compromised the media and its coverage of his church through intimidation and flattery.

Peoples Temple mixed religious revival, leftist politics, social justice, and the us-verses-them divisiveness of the Sixties counterculture. That's why the horror in Guyana can be seen as a final chapter of the Sixties. It was certainly one of the era's most tragic events. Jones was a charismatic, manipulative man who used politics, sex, religion, and social idealism to control people and gain power. When he was on the verge of being exposed for who he really was, he fled with his flock to South America, but the horror stories kept leaking out. In response, a group of reporters accompanied Congressman Leo Ryan to Jones's jungle compound, and Ryan tried to return with several defectors. The fuse was lit. Among those murdered in the subsequent implosion were Congressman Ryan and Greg Robinson, a friend and colleague of mine who'd gone to Guyana as a photographer for the *San Francisco Examiner.*

There were 260 children among the 914 people who died in the Jonestown murder-suicide. Many of these kids had parents who were convinced Jim Jones was the people's messiah, a left-wing prophet protecting them from an oppressive United States government. Those children had no choice but to go along on that ill-fated ride. The horror of their stories is numbing. Mothers actually squirted poison down their babies' throats. Many of the Jonestown children were young African Americans who were poor, running out of second chances, and with nowhere else to go. Some were sent there by county governments as an alternative to juvenile hall.

Jonestown did not end the cult wars of the 1970s and 1980s. After the carnage in Guyana, there was the implosion of the Branch Davidians in Waco, Texas, and the bizarre end of Heaven's Gate, the UFO cult in Huntington Beach, California. Today, the word *cult* resides in the American psyche alongside images of blinding obedience and mass death.

Am I saying that any of the new religious movements profiled in this book will end as "another Jonestown"? Absolutely not. Twenty-five years after the carnage in Guyana, two words are all it takes to demonize a new religious movement, whether it deserves the label or not: *another Jonestown.* Nevertheless, the next generation must remember what happened in San Francisco and Guyana. One of the great misconceptions about cults is that only wacky people join them. I've found the opposite to be true. Many of the adherents are compassionate, idealistic people with a longing for social justice. This, writes religious studies scholar Mary McCormick Maaga, helps explain the inexplicable demise of Peoples Temple. Passion for social justice blinded them to their own cause. Reducing the complexity of Jonestown to a madman brainwashing his vulnerable flock, Maaga argues, is too simple an explanation. We tend to focus on Jim Jones because it's easier to pinpoint evil in one human being.[25]

Most of those who study cults, sects, and new religious movements are bitterly divided into two camps—factions of experts branding their adversaries as apologists or alarmists. Cult watchdogs are the alarmists. They believe authoritarian and "totalistic" groups—whether they're organized according to religion, politics, or psychotherapy—pose a real danger to their members and to the broader society. They have little to do with the other camp in the cult wars, scholars and current cult members who argue that most religious sects are relatively harmless and that the crusade against them violates constitutional guarantees of religious freedom. They are the apologists. Anticult activists warn of "brainwashing" and "mind control" while their opponents tell tales of violent kidnapping and coercive "deprogramming." In some ways, both factions are right; they're just asking different questions. Many of the scholars studying cults and sects focus on more abstract questions, such as how religions are born and evolve over time. Meanwhile, the watchdogs focus on the harm done to *some* people who join authoritarian sects. They deal with the real anguish of fractured families whose loved ones have been subjected to "mind control" or who have gone through life-changing religious conversions. In the newspaper and in this book, I've tried to talk to both sides, believing the truth is closer to the middle than at either extreme.

Those of us in the news media are usually put in the alarmist camp. Two scholars of new religious movements, Susan Palmer and Charlotte Hardman, sum up the feeling of many academics: "The public's tendency to believe the horror stories of anonymous apostates quoted in poorly researched media reports, and to dismiss the defensive testimonies of current 'cult members' has exacerbated the 'tribal wars' that are currently erupting around child-centered NRMs [new religious movements]." They go on to say that most of the these unfairly maligned groups are only trying to "heal the maladies besetting the modern family—the broken marriages, the generation gap, the unsupervised dating, the absentee fathers."[26]

Of course, the truth is not so simple, and we can see why those in the academic camp are sometimes labeled apologists. Intense religious movements often destroy marriages rather than heal them. They are as likely to inspire fathers to leave their children as they are to bring them together. But Palmer and Hartman are right about one thing: neither the government nor the news media should tell parents how to raise their children. Lines must be drawn when children are sexually abused or denied needed medical care. But looking at alternative childhoods in marginal groups *can* help us expand our ways of thinking about the family and perhaps help us understand our own.

Religious cults are only a small part of this book, but they illustrate larger issues facing my generation and the next. We'll soon recount the story of one of the most infamous new religious movements of that era, which calls itself "The Family." Then we'll look at the followers of the Reverend Sun Myung Moon and his wife. Those devotees call that couple their "True Parents." Note an emerging theme. Everywhere you looked in the 1960s and 1970s, old forms of family were breaking down. Children raised amid that turmoil looked far and wide for another way of living. Some of those experiments were disastrous, others were dead-ends, but some were stepping-stones to a better way of being family.

As for the Hare Krishnas, the *gurukalas* were a horrid failure. Swami Prabhupada was wrong about the proper way to raise American children, but his disciples could not believe their perfect master could be wrong. His boarding schools produced, not little Krishna saints, but hard memories of abuse and a legacy of lawsuits. Blind obedience to one man's vision inspired many Krishna converts to shirk their parental responsibilities, turning their spiritual dreams into a daily nightmare for their sons and daughters.

Five years after Prabhupada left his body, an Indian guru of a very different sort came to America and set up shop in the dry rolling hills of central Oregon. Bhagwan Shree Rajneesh had been attracting American and European devotees to India since the late 1960s. Long before his arrival in the United States, this former philosophy professor had learned much about the longings of the American psyche and the Western soul. Rajneesh was the first guru to truly mix East and West, and his eclectic blend of mysticism, hedonism, sexuality, and spirituality would soon make him the most infamous guru in the West.

CHAPTER 6

Slouching Toward
Rajneeshpuram

> *Bliss is a strange wine—strange, because*
> *on the one hand it makes you fully aware, and on the*
> *other hand it makes you fully intoxicated.*[27]

BHAGWAN SHREE RAJNEESH

We were the last ones to leave a long and lazy party at a friend's house in Berkeley, an old Victorian with that post-hippie feel, known in these parts as shabby chic. We'd settled into the breakfast nook, emptied a few bottles of wine, and were feeling quite fine, enjoying a warm night of Indian summer, those autumn weeks when the summer fog lifts from San Francisco Bay and damp days are finally gone.

It had been another gathering of the tribe, of old friends who came here in the Sixties and never left. They came from Baltimore, New York, Los Angeles, Indiana, and Israel. I'd hooked up with them in the early 1970s, feeling like I'd missed the best years of the party. On this night, the party *was* over. I got up, looked around the house, and realized most of my friends had gone home.

My attention had been diverted early in the evening by a notorious character operating on the edge of our tribe. We'll call him Moose. He'd been in and out of this circle of friends since the early 1960s, when he gave up a promising medical career and headed out to San Francisco to see what all the fuss was about. Moose had experimented with LSD before most of us had even heard of it, back when it was still legal and used by psychiatrists to open up resistant patients. But Moose never really came down from his trip. He'd been back and forth to India, sitting at the feet of Muktananda, Sai Baba, and other spiritual masters. For a while he followed another East Coast refugee, a decidedly minor guru known as Swami Hate. Swami concluded that all that peace and love talk from the Summer of Love was just talk—that we all *really* hated one other. Swami Hate had a message of antienlightenment for anyone who'd walk up to him on the streets of Berkeley. "I hate you," he'd say. "I fucking *hate* you!" According to one report, Swami Hate's movement collapsed when he fell in love with one of his disciples and kicked the rest of his followers out of his apartment.

Moose rolled into town that October evening with a young German woman we'll call Rainbow. Both were dressed in the orange clothes favored by that season's most infamous guru, Bhagwan Shree Rajneesh. Perhaps it was just a coincidence, but on the very day I ran into Moose, the *San Francisco Examiner* began a series of articles I'd written titled "Rajneesh, Inc." They detailed how Rajneesh, an irreverent philosophy professor formerly known as Rajneesh Chandra Mohan, had begun his global empire in the late 1960s with a few devotees gathered in his Bombay apartment. He opened a bustling ashram in nearby Poona in the 1970s, attracting thousands of *sannyasins,* an Indian term for "wandering monk." Rajneesh appropriated the word to describe his followers even though very few of them appeared to be monks. But they did wander from all over the world to be near their spiritual master.

Rajneesh was as good at raising money as he was at raising consciousness. There were always a lot of well-heeled baby boomers in this guru's inner circle, including a persistent gaggle from Hollywood. In the early 1980s they bankrolled the purchase and development of a sixty-four-thousand-acre ranch in the desolate hills of central Oregon. There they built a small city and farming commune, legally incorporating it as the City of Rajneeshpuram. It was the most unusual municipality in America, with its own police department, taxing powers, and court. Over the next six years, tens of thousands of red-and-orange-clad devotees came to town, drawn by the Bhagwan's enticing blend of Eastern mysticism, Western hedonism, and avant-garde psychotherapy. For the permanent residents, it was a work camp, giant encounter group, and a chance to live close to the master. For the paying guests, it was party time, a kind of Club Meditation for mind-body swingers. During summer festivals thousands of *sannyasins* would fly into this mecca of sensuous spirituality, browsing through boutiques, eating at gourmet restaurants, and stopping in the street for long group hugs, a central element of the communal liturgy.

With his fleet of Rolls Royce sedans and philosophy of free love, Rajneesh sat above it all with a wink and sly smile, like he knew the whole thing was a cosmic joke. One day Rajneesh held a rare press conference at the ranch. He sat on a well-padded chair atop a raised platform. He stroked his long salt-and-pepper beard, looking at the reporters with that twinkle in his eye. He always wore a stocking cap, and whenever I saw him he had a serene, or perhaps stoned, countenance, like Santa Claus on Ecstasy. He claimed to be the reincarnation of Buddha, but he was always the iconoclast, sounding more like Lenny Bruce than Siddhartha. Rajneesh was a jumble of contradictions. He'd say he didn't want to start a religion, didn't want to become another "ism," and then publish a book describing the tenets of "Rajneeshism." At the press conference a small group of journalists sat before "Bhagwan," as his disciples called him, the "Blessed One." Behind us were hundreds of *sannyasins* there to watch the show. Rajneesh was holding a press conference before a live audience, and we were his straight men. One of the first questions came from an ill-informed TV reporter who asked the Blessed One to respond to allegations that he had engaged in sexual relations with his devotees. The audience roared with laughter. Rajneesh paused and slowly replied in his deep Indian accent, "Yes," he said, elongating the *s* with a hiss. "I have made love to more women than any man on Earth."

You gotta love the guy! Was he kidding or not? Nobody knew. Rajneesh always played the trickster. He once told his disciples a joke that did not point to great sexual prowess. "When I take a bath," he said, "I have to leave my robes on because I hate to look down on the unemployed."

Why does this strange scene come to mind? Well, back at that party in Berkeley, Moose had an idea. He'd seen the headline on my story that day, "Controversy Follows the 'Sex Guru' West," and asked, "Why don't we do a little role-playing? You be Rajneesh," Moose said, "and I'll be a reporter who is interviewing you." Now, I'd met Moose only a few times before, and not since he'd started wearing orange pajamas and hanging a little picture of Rajneesh around his neck. Moose grilled me with questions like, "Do you believe in free love, Your Holiness?" and I said something like, "It is a mystery, my son, but I certainly do not pay for it."

We soon lost track of time and, after another bottle of wine, realized that the rest of the house was deserted. As we walked out, Moose said he required a piece of apple pie à la mode and suggested we go to an all-night coffee shop on University Avenue. He and Rainbow had an old van that appeared to serve also as their home away from home, if they had a home at all. I climbed in the back and started strumming on a guitar I found lying atop of a pile of orange clothes. Moose was driving, with Rainbow riding shotgun.

When we got to the restaurant Moose turned to his partner and said, "I'm going to go eat my pie and read my book." He was reading a biography of Winston Churchill and was miffed that his young German girlfriend had never heard of the famous British statesman. "You stay here and make love to Rajneesh. He's a free sex guru."

Rainbow smiled and hopped into the back of the van. Moose came back about a half hour later and told us the apple pie was delicious.

Okay, I admit it. I've always had a love-hate thing with Rajneesh and his band of merry pranksters. Rajneesh's writings often were insightful. He had a real knack for explaining Hindu, Taoist, and Buddhist concepts to a Western audience. He had a working knowledge of Freud, Jung, Reich, and later humanistic psychologists, and he borrowed many of their techniques. He was a sharp critic of all forms of religious hypocrisy—except his own. He could be funny and wise, which is a strong hand when you hold the pair. On top of that, most of his devotees never seemed quite as devoted (some would say brainwashed) as those in other personality cults. Most of his followers seemed to know that it was all just a game and they were free to move on whenever they got tired of the power trips, authoritarianism, and exploitation that eventually cripple most new religious movements.

But there *was* a dark side to the Rajneesh movement, a sinister amorality. Within a few years the utopian experiment at Rancho Rajneesh collapsed into a paranoid, downward spiral of intrigue, infighting, and murder plots. The public later learned that there was a vast electronic eavesdropping network at the commune and that leaders of the sect had hatched a bizarre election-day scheme to sicken voters in the county seat by poisoning local salad bars with salmonella. Bhagwan's boys and girls played hardball, especially Ma Anand Sheela, his pistol-packing personal secretary. Under her regime, the Rajneesh security forces carried Gestapo-style rifles while Sheela vowed to fight "with the last drop of blood" against county and state officials blocking their development plans.[28] In the end, Rajneesh pleaded guilty to immigration fraud and was deported. Sheela pleaded guilty to fraud, wiretapping, arson, and attempted murder charges and served two and a half years of a four-and-a-half-year term in federal prison before being deported to Germany. Through it all, many of the Bhagwan's disciples kept the faith, blaming the madness on Sheela or turning the whole thing into a cosmic lesson.

Rajneesh's reputation as the sex guru was never quite as simple or as sensational as the headlines proclaimed. It all started back in India with reports about nudity and no-holds-barred encounter groups at his ashram in Poona. "Bhagwan tells us not to repress things, and one of the most repressed things in this society is sexuality," one workshop leader told me. "In our groups, we were experimenting in not repressing anything. That is controversial—especially in India. In San Francisco, what we were doing wouldn't have been looked at twice."[29]

Rajneesh never claimed to be a monk, nor did he demand sexual purity from his *sannyasins*. Instead of asking them to repress their sexual desire, he urged them to act it out—to use those impulses to forge what he called "a sensual religion." That was an enticing philosophy for spiritual seekers brought up in religious traditions with condemnatory views of human sexuality. "I am not teaching sex to you," he told his disciples. "If I have to talk once in a while about sex that is because of your Christian, Hindu, Mohammedan repressive traditions. I am not responsible for it. They have made man's life so paralyzed, so crippled and their whole strategy has depended upon repressing the energy called sex." One of the secrets of this swami's success was that he enabled his devotees to think of themselves as sensual, sexual, *and* spiritual. "Sex should be more fun than such a serious affair as it has been made in the past," he said. "It should be like a game, a play; two persons playing with each other's bodily energies. If they both are happy, it should be nobody else's concern."[30] Ultimately, Rajneesh taught that his disciples could transcend the need for sex, but never by repressing it.

"Every man has his woman within him and every woman has her man within her," he said. "Only the mediator comes to know his whole being. Suddenly his inner woman and the inner man melt and merge into each other. That creates an orgasmic state in him. Now it is no more a momentary experience that comes and goes; it is something that continues, day in and day out, like the heart beating or breathing."[31]

Rajneesh died on January 19, 1990, back at his ashram in India. He was fifty-eight. Along the way he changed his name to Osho, and the repackaged guru continued to attract a posthumous following at his old spiritual retreat center in Poona. Most of his old *sannyasins* have scattered back around the world. Many of them started their own careers as personal growth coaches, massage therapists, meditation teachers, and other psychospiritual consultants. Some still struggle to make sense of what happened in Rajneeshpuram, living with the lingering effects it had on them and their families.

Take the story of Satya Bharti Franklin, a disciple who deeply felt the agony and the ecstasy of Bhagwan Shree Rajneesh. We first spoke in 1992, when Satya was in San Francisco to promote a tell-all memoir titled *The Promise of Paradise: A Woman's Intimate Story of the Perils of Life with Rajneesh*. Back in the early 1970s, this recently divorced mother left three young children to follow Rajneesh all the way to India and back again to Oregon. Bored and sexually frustrated, she had started her odyssey by visiting a Rajneesh meditation center in New York, and she soon fell for one of Bhagwan's disciples, a teacher at the center. As they looked into each other's eyes, spellbound, for hours at a time, she wrote, "the energy between us was so intense we shook and tremored at the slightest touch. Sex between us was as powerful as an earthquake."[32]

Jill Franklin dyed her clothes orange and took the *sannyasin* name Ma Satya Bharti, which roughly translates into "the divine truth of India." And that's where she headed, leaving her two daughters, ages nine and eleven, and her son, age six, at home with their father. Rajneesh's following was still small enough that he was teaching in his Bombay apartment. Arriving in India, Satya soon got an up-close-and-personal look at her new guru and fell in love again.

> *Being with Bhagwan was like being on another planet. The charismatic power of his presence, like his eclectic meditation techniques, made me as stoned as any drug. Every thought seemed like a revelation, every word or gesture seemed filled with a multitude of meanings.*[33]

Satya was hooked. On Rajneesh's instructions, she flew back to New York to say good-bye to her children, to "close everything up." Her final instructions from Bhagwan had been, "Bring many of the rich people you know to me, too." Satya bent down and touched her head to her new guru's feet.

> *As he placed his hand gently on my head, I stopped worrying about leaving my kids for good, what it would do to them, to me; stopped judging why I was to bring my rich friends to India. Only Bhagwan's hand on the top of my head existed. Whatever he wanted was fine with me.*

Back home, her children put up a brave front when she told them she was returning to India. "I left," she wrote, "ignoring my own pain and refusing to see the hurt and bewilderment in my kids' eyes."

> I made the abandonment of my children into a moral principle, clothing it in spirituality. What could I offer them that was more important than my own Buddhahood? If I wasn't free, how could I hope that they would be? Rationalizing, justifying. The fact was, Bhagwan told me to come back to India for good; his words were my only reality. Addicted to the ecstasy I found with him, being by his side was the only thing in the world I wanted.34

Franklin was with Rajneesh from 1972 to 1985. This poet and former student at Sarah Lawrence College, this one-time speechwriter for Congresswoman Shirley Chisholm and wife of a successful stockbroker, threw it all away to follow her bliss. In the early years of her discipleship, Satya served as a ghostwriter for her guru. She wrote three of her own glowing accounts of life with her spiritual master, books that attracted countless others into the fold.35 That work got her closer to the guru and also soon made her a threat to other insiders.

Rajneesh faded fast in the 1990s, at least to those of us in the news media. There's still a posthumous cult around the teachings of Osho, but, with a few notable exceptions, leaving your body is not a good career move in the spiritual marketplace. At the same time, old gurus never really die. In the fall of 2001, nearly a decade after my conversation with Satya Franklin, I once again stumbled onto the ghost of Bhagwan Shree Rajneesh.

Like Satya Franklin, Mick Pulver moved to Rajneeshpuram and left behind a teenage daughter. Mick and his wife were already divorced, but right before the move to Oregon Mick and his daughter, Tamara, had been spending a lot of time together in Los Angeles, going out to restaurants, comedy clubs, and hanging with Mick's friends. But at the same time, there was a chasm between Mick and Tamara, who accused Daddy of being a hippie. "I guess I was, in a way," Mick said. "I was a spiritual kind of hippie. I was a classy hippie. I didn't like being dirty. I liked living the good life. I wasn't a live-in-the-van hippie." Mick was no Moose, but he loved Bhagwan.

Mick had invited Tamara up to Rancho Rajneesh, but she wasn't interested. "Actually, the things I was learning and understanding about life, I wanted to share with her. But she was opposed to hearing what I wanted to say. There were things I clung to, things I believed—like the conditioning of society, and stuff that Osho taught, like how we are expected to be a certain way, and I was rebelling against that. She was more like my parents. My daughter was always pretty much of a material girl. It was always like, 'What can you do for me now?' Love wasn't enough. She's a great kid, but that was a conflict we had. I'd always been a go-with-the-flow kind of guy, and she wanted certainty all the time. When I went to the ranch, that was it. She felt like Rajneesh took her father away. I had gone off to a cult. She figured I'd lost it."

Mick and I were sitting in a restaurant, eating pasta and sharing a fine bottle of wine. It was the winter of 2001, and Mick was fifty-one years old. His daughter was thirty-two. He was still a teenager when she came into the world. "She was born in 1968, the year I graduated from high school. I had my resentments. I really didn't want to be a father, but my wife really wanted to have a kid. We were still in high school, and I felt like I lost my youth."

Music has always been Pulver's passion. He grew up in Florida, where his parents owned a beachfront hotel. When he was eight or nine years old, his parents would host fish fries out on the picnic tables, and Mick and his friends would put on minstrel shows. Dad was "against any religion," but Mick's grandparents took him to the Baptist church, where Mick sang in the choir. When he was a junior in high school, Mick started playing bass in a band with two of his brothers. They became the house band for a local music hall that put on the "Clearwater Star Spectacular." When he was still in high school, Mick's group was the opening band for acts such as Chuck Berry and Jerry Lee Lewis. After high school, with a wife and baby girl, he joined a local nightclub band, HY Sledge, which opened for such bands as Three Dog Night and the Allman Brothers. They recorded an album and went on the road, with all that entails. "You get into drinking, partying, womanizing, drugs. I did it all." After tiring of that scene, Pulver moved to California in 1976 with his wife, Linda, and eight-year-old Tamara. It was harder to make a living in the music business on the West Coast, and Pulver wound up getting a job at an upscale restaurant in San Francisco. One day in 1979 one of his customers handed him a book by Rajneesh. Mick was bedazzled. He had dabbled in est, done the Lifespring seminar, gone to psychics, and had read some of his wife's books on G. I. Gurdjieff, the mystic philosopher. But nothing hit Pulver like Rajneesh.

Within a year he was divorced, living in Los Angeles, and hanging out at an exclusive Rajneesh retreat center in southern California called Gitan. There was a hot tub, pool, great food, and some of the top therapists and meditation teachers in the Rajneesh network. There was also a beautiful Australian woman. "It all pointed to becoming a *sannyasin,*" and that's what Mick did, taking the name Swami Lalit, Sanskrit for "beautiful." Rajneesh was just settling into his new base in central Oregon, and Pulver was soon on his way up the coast.

What was the attraction? "I fell in love with him," Mick said. "His eloquence, the artistic way he spoke, his sense of humor. Most of what he said really struck a chord in me. It was the most profound stuff I'd ever heard, and I loved the energy around him. There was a celebratory aspect to it all. I always liked to party. Not just drugs and alcohol, but as a musician being onstage. I've been privy to being in some great concerts, and know those magical moments onstage—the experience of being in the eye of the hurricane. In a way, it's kind of a state of grace. Time really does stand still if you are really there and really present."

Up in Oregon, Pulver landed a great gig, one that got him close to his guru and allowed him to stay onstage. Mick played bass in the commune's house band on the ranch, and at Zorba the Buddha Rajneesh Disco, a music club the sect set up in Portland. "I played bass in the Rajneesh Country Band," he recalls with a smile. "We'd fly from the ranch on a DC-9 to Portland every Friday night. It was an hour flight, complete with Rajneesh air hostesses. It was great."

Pulver lived at the ranch for a few years, working as a bus driver when he wasn't playing in the band. But then he felt the vibe changing, especially among the upper echelon of the cult. Mick left in early 1985, when the loving, communal scene was starting to sour. He came back for the summer festival of 1985, when Sheela and other leaders brought out the side arms and semiautomatic rifles, supposedly to protect their embattled guru from federal marshals or suspected assassins. "Things were happening at the ranch that did not feel good to me," he says. "The loving vibe that had been there was changing."

It wasn't just the guns. Pulver believed that there really were local rednecks who would do anything to get rid of the crazy guru and his invading army of orange-clad hippies. "I had mixed feelings," he recalled. "I didn't want Osho to get hurt. I'd experienced people pointing guns at me. I'd gotten run off the road. I drove a bus that said Rajneesh Buddhafield Transport right on the side, so I put up with a lot of shit."

His dissatisfaction deepened when he got a call from his wife. She was having medical problems and needed help taking care of their daughter, who was now eighteen. Under the commune's rules, he couldn't leave without permission. An unauthorized departure meant that he would lose his resident status and couldn't return to the ranch. "I went to the hierarchy and said I needed to check in with my daughter and former wife—that I needed to help them. They said my daughter should come here. I said, 'She won't.' They said, 'Sorry, you have to leave the ranch.'"

Pulver gave up his resident status and left. "It was hard to leave—and to put myself back into a situation with my wife and daughter, that was just as hard. If this had happened in the first year, I wouldn't have gone. But by that time it felt shitty up there. It was hard to be manipulated. The whole time they're giving you the rap that you're being resistant or you're not saying yes to the commune. My way out was to say I had to go take care of my daughter. If things had been going great, I probably wouldn't have gone. So in a way, to leave because of my daughter was to find an excuse."

Later, after Sheela lost out in a power struggle and Rajneesh was gone, Pulver went back to the ranch to help close it up. "I knew I was done with all that. I'd done the cult thing."

Like many Rajneeshees, Pulver doesn't blame Rajneesh for all the corruption and exploitation that turned a utopian commune into a paranoid compound. "Maybe it was all just a lesson about how power and politics corrupt," Mick says. "Maybe Osho just let it all happen. I don't know if he really cared. He always said that life was a mystery, and he lived it. Why does this man of love have this bitch, Sheela, running things?

"With Osho, you could give your power away, or not. People who got the attention and the juice were the ones who didn't say yes to everything. When people wanted to move to the ranch, the first thing they'd say was, 'Do you own any property? Would you like to sign that over to us?' People who did sign it over were kind of swept under the carpet. Osho liked the rebels, even in his own community. He would just play in it. It's your own journey. He was trying to stir us up. My favorite saying of his was, 'Don't bite my finger. Just look where I'm pointing.'"

Pulver's take on what went down in Rajneeshpuram may make sense or may just be one stupendous rationalization. But it does point to the troubling amorality that permeated life on the ranch. Rajneesh was responsible for nothing because his followers created their own reality. He was just a mirror. It was all a cosmic lesson—or a cosmic cop-out. If Rajneesh had a philosophy, it was relativism. You can't have good without bad. Embrace the shadow to find the light. After Sheela took the fall for the crimes committed in the guru's name, a reporter asked Rajneesh if he didn't see that his personal secretary was an oppressive, mean-spirited manipulator.

"I know!" Rajneesh answered. "But it was needed for all those mean politicians all around. I could not put the commune in the hands of some innocent people—the politicians would have destroyed it."

"You play a very risky game," the reporter said.

"Certainly," the guru replied. "I am a risky person. And it is a game—I know the right timings. I am just a referee, nothing more."[36]

Later, Rajneesh told his devotees at the ranch that he had anointed Sheela "to give you a little taste of what fascism means." Now, he said, it's time for you to "live my way. Be responsible. Remember one thing," Rajneesh added. "Freedom is not license. Freedom is responsibility. And if you cannot take your responsibility yourself, then somebody is going to take the responsibility on your behalf. And then you are enslaved."

Of course, the truth is that Rajneesh did not take responsibility for crimes committed in his name. He blamed Sheela, who went to prison for doing what he needed done to build his commune and collect his fleet of Rolls Royce sedans. Soon after his lecture on freedom and responsibility, Rajneesh tried to flee the United States in his Lear jet, only to be captured in North Carolina, charged with immigration fraud, and deported.

Satya Franklin remained a Rajneesh disciple for thirteen years, and her children grew up without her. When she'd settled back in the United States, living in Rajneeshpuram, she invited them to come visit her at the ranch. In a way she was glad they weren't around.

> Ranch kids were notoriously precocious sexually, teenage girls hopping into bed regularly with men old enough to be their fathers, often at their own initiative. Scores of ranch swamis would have been considered child molesters out in the world. Appalling on one level, it was prevalent enough to seem acceptable on another. If their parents didn't object—at least someone was paying attention to the kids they were ignoring—how could I?[37]

Satya's deepest grief and guilt was not over her daughters, but over what happened to her youngest child, Billy, who was only six years old when she left Riverdale, New York, and went to India to be with Rajneesh. Ten years later, when Billy was sixteen, he wrote his mom in Rajneeshpuram. It was the first time he'd ever written to her.

"When you left, part of me refused to grow up, waiting for your return, hoping, praying," Billy wrote. "I hope you're happy, Mom. I'm happy sometimes, sad sometimes. I sometimes feel like there's a light at the end of all this shit, but it's so hard reaching."

Five years later Billy was dead, murdered by a drunken assailant outside a San Francisco nightclub. Billy, then twenty-one and a college student in New York, was on his way to visit his mother in Vancouver, British Columbia. Satya blamed herself for his death, her sorrow "magnified by my guilt and sadness at all the years I'd missed of my children's lives."[38]

At his funeral Satya was surprised that her surviving children, her former husband, other relatives, and Billy's friends had no harsh words for the woman who had left her young son to follow her bliss. She was a stranger at her only son's funeral but felt unconditional love from those she had left behind.

What inspired Satya Franklin and Mick Pulver to chose Bhagwan Shree Rajneesh over their children? Perhaps that decision is related to their guru's philosophy, which allowed him to avoid taking responsibility for his disciples. Like so many other people who came of age in the 1960s, Mick and Satya were addicted to ecstasy—not the drug but the spiritual intensity. They did not want to grow up, at least not in the conventional manner. They left the painful realities of everyday life for a tempting promise of paradise, for a life of bliss that could be tasted but that was much harder to live. They left their imperfect families in search of an ideal family—or at least another kind of family.

In doing so, they were following the advice of their spiritual master. "The real family is not your father, your mother, your brothers, your sisters, your wife, your husband, your children; they are accidental," Rajneesh said.

> *Your real family is the family of a Buddha. If you are fortunate enough to feel joyful in the company of a Buddha, then dissolve into that company—you have found your family. Don't miss the chance, because the chance is very rare. Only once in a while does somebody become enlightened.*
>
> *The most outdated thing is the family. . . . It is no more needed. In fact, now it is the most hindering phenomenon for human progress. The family is the unit of the nations, of the state, of the church—of all that is ugly. . . . The family is the root cause of all our neurosis.[39]*

Rajneesh was right when he said the family is the source of much of our neurosis. Many families *are* ugly. But was the family he created any less insane? In the end, the biological family of Satya Franklin was not, as Rajneesh claimed, her "accidental" family. Her "family of a Buddha" included those who tried to poison her in India and those who put her on the shit list in Rajneeshpuram, targeting her to be spied on, provoked, and humiliated. Her biological family was the one that stood by her in the end, when the ties of blood proved stronger than the mysteries of the Buddhafield.

Bhagwan Shree Rajneesh, the free sex guru, was not the only spiritual teacher to question the reassertion of traditional family values in the 1980s or to propose a new kind sexual ethic against that conservative backlash. This redefinition of family and reappraisal of sexual morality began in the Sixties and continues to dominate the agenda of most mainstream religious denominations in the United States. It's to that story that we now turn.

Sex, Drugs, Rock 'n' Roll, and Religion

Sex was at the center of the social and spiritual revolution of the sixties and seventies. The Pill separated sexuality from procreation, and as we'll see in chapter 7, there was no heading back. Divorce lost its taboo, and the single-parent family—for better or for worse—spread across all levels of society. There was no-fault religion and no-fault divorce, and the children of the Sixties often paid the price. Later in the era the gay rights movement swept from the ballot box to the altar as churches and synagogues struggled to come up with a new sexual ethic. For many, the question was no longer "What does God tell us about sex?" but "What does sex tell us about God?"

Psychedelic drugs fueled the spiritual renaissance of the 1960s and 1970s. Drugs like LSD, peyote, and magic mushrooms sent countless baby boomers on a quick trip to another level of reality, an expanded awareness and a sense of oneness they never forgot. It provoked in some a terrifying glimpse of madness. For others profiled in chapter 8, psychedelics inspired a serious—and less dangerous—practice of meditation or other spiritual disciplines. Today the "just say no" approach to drug education has put many of those same baby boomers in a difficult spot, wondering what to tell their kids about the dangers and delights of the long, strange trip.

Rock 'n' roll was another vehicle for spiritual transcendence, and not just for unrepentant hippies and tie-dyed followers of the Grateful Dead. In the 1950s they called it the devil's music, but chapter 9 shows how it didn't take long for evangelical and Pentecostal churches to see that rock 'n' roll was here to stay— and a great way to attract the unchurched children of the baby boom generation.

Timothy Leary

Woodstock, 1969

Godstock, 1997

CHAPTER 7

God and Sex: Searching for a New Morality

Why should we take advice on sex from the pope?
If he knows anything about it, he shouldn't.

GEORGE BERNARD SHAW

Rabbi Alan Lew stepped up to the podium to deliver a lecture on human sexuality. Unfortunately, no one at the local Jewish community center told him he'd be facing a skeptical crowd of young, single adults. "Our Jewish tradition has one word to say to you: *Don't,*" said Lew, realizing his address reflected Judaism's traditional beliefs but did not address the real lives of those in his audience. The rabbi delivered his prepared talk, but as he spoke he saw that Judaism must rethink its approach to sex and spirituality. Later, sitting in the study at his synagogue, Lew raised his hands in dismay. "Our traditional sexual ethic has nothing to say to these people about one of the most important aspects of their lives—their sexuality—and that has been a disaster. The problem is people are marrying much later in life, and most are sexually active before marriage."

Unable to ignore the sexual revolution, feminism, and the crusade for gay rights, American religious institutions have embarked on an unprecedented reappraisal of sex, marriage, and the family. At a time when couples routinely live together without marrying, when divorce is commonplace, and science questions the assumption that we were born to be heterosexual, monogamous, or chaste, religious leaders are taking another look at homosexuality, premarital sex, and other practices long condemned as an abomination to God.

Today's search for an ethical, sex-positive spirituality is one of the most powerful—and still-unfolding—legacies of the Sixties. It goes far beyond the cloister of American churches, mosques, and synagogues. From talk shows to computer networks to city council chambers across the nation, millions of Americans are searching for a new sexual ethic—a new moral framework that transcends the "thou shall nots" of Christianity, Judaism, and Islam but is nevertheless informed by the ancient wisdom of religious insight. But steering an ethical course that both celebrates sexual liberation and sets limits on this powerful human instinct is no easy task. "We can change our ethics around, but we're never going to be able to tame the necessity of sexuality to be spontaneous," said James Hillman, a noted psychologist and social commentator. "Sexuality is always irrational, demonic, and fascinating. It is never completely smooth and harmonious."[1]

There has been a flurry of work since the sixties by gay, feminist, and sex-positive theologians, all of whom start from a very different place than traditional religion when talking about sexual morality. Rather than ask what God tells us about sex, many of these theologians ask, "What does our sexual experience reveal to us about God?"

Sex-positive theology has not gone over well, even in the most liberal Protestant denominations, when it tries to make its way into the church's official statements. In 1991 a task force of the Presbyterian Church (U.S.A.) proposed a new "Christian ethic of sexuality which honors but does not restrict sexual activity to marriage." It promoted "justice-love," which it defined as sex that was "responsible, the dynamics genuinely mutual and the loving full of joyful caring." It also advised women to experiment with "learned masturbation techniques that may increase the orgasmic experience." Justice-love and masturbation were something both gays and straights could practice as faithful Christians. Within months, the Presbyterian proposal was buried in an avalanche of conservative criticism.

Next up was the Evangelical Lutheran Church in America. Although its task force did not go as far as the Presbyterians, it proposed that the denomination take a more liberal view of homosexuality and consider blessing committed same-sex unions. It called masturbation "a means of self-pleasuring that is generally appropriate and healthy." Once again, conservatives were outraged. Within six months of the statement's release, more than three thousand written responses had arrived at the Lutheran church's Chicago headquarters. Most of them were negative. Robert Benne, a professor of religion at Roanoke College, a Lutheran-affiliated school in Virginia, said he was shocked by this major shift in Christian sexual ethics. "This makes far too much of our sexual identity. It idolizes it. There is a loosening of the strong connection of sex within marriage." In response to such criticism, the Lutherans backed down.

Other critics say the church's most serious sexual dysfunction can be summed up in one word: *hypocrisy*. Why can't the church practice what it preaches? In the Roman Catholic Church, hundreds of millions of dollars have been paid out to victims of sexual abuse by priests. Most Protestant churches, even conservative evangelical ones, are very selective in their enforcement of what the Bible says about sex, marriage, and the family. About the clearest thing Jesus says on the subject is an explicit prohibition against divorce and remarriage ("What God has joined together, let no one separate").[2] Nevertheless, few Protestant or Anglican churches shun their divorced members, and divorced clergy can be found in even the most conservative denominations.

Both the Catholic church and most mainline Protestant and Jewish denominations condemn homosexual behavior but quietly allow discreet homosexuals to remain in the clergy. Critics of the church's intransigence on homosexuality say the problem goes much deeper than Christians being uptight about men sleeping with men or women sleeping with women. "There is a fundamental fear of sex and pleasure in Christianity," said the Reverend Robert Cromey, pastor of Trinity Episcopal Church in San Francisco. Cromey and other observers trace this fear not to any particular Bible passage but to ancient Greek philosophy and its split between the profane body and the holy spirit. "You even see that in Buddhism and some of the Eastern religions," he said. "They also have this idea that you should be up there on some spiritual plane, that sex is too earthbound." Cromey, who remarried after a "vigorous" eleven-year bachelorhood, does not share that philosophy. "Good sex among people who love and care for each other is one of the highest spiritual experiences you can have, but it's something nobody wants to talk about. Our bishops are good, lusty, sexy guys, but as soon as they get in the pulpit, there's all this guarding and guiding and manipulating around sex."[3]

Millions of young Americans—the ones who are actually having most of the sex—could not care less what Episcopal bishops, Conservative rabbis, Lutheran synods, or Presbyterian conferences think about all this. But that does not mean their sexuality isn't connected to their spirituality or their sense of right and wrong.

Take, for example, Diana Chornenkaya, the creator of a virtual temple devoted to sacred sexuality. Her portable shrine is set up each year in the middle of the Black Rock Desert, a dry desolate lake bed in northwestern Nevada. It's called Women's Temple, and it exists only in this shimmering valley a few days each summer. That's because it's part of the Burning Man festival, an annual extravaganza of art, ritual, and celebration that draws thousands of devotees to this vast plain of emptiness and jagged mountain peaks.

Late in the summer of 2002 the seventeenth annual gathering of this hardy tribe drew an estimated twenty-eight thousand celebrants. They built huge art installations in the desert then burned them up or carried them off. There was Thunder Dome, a geodesic frame covered with live nude people painted green. There was the Temple of Joy, a seventy-eight-foot-tall masterpiece of discarded plywood that resembled a Balinese temple, delicate and dynamic. And there was Water Woman, a giant abstract sculpture of the female body that stood upright, spraying showers of water down from between her legs, cooling off a rotating circle of hot, hugging bodies.

Some Sixties survivors compare Burning Man to Woodstock or to the earlier hippie happenings in San Francisco—to the Trips Festival in January 1966, the Summer of Love, and the Human Be-In held in Golden Gate Park the following January. There are obvious similarities. Burning Man and those ancient hippie fests featured free love, young people in outrageous costumes, audience participation, and spirited celebrations fueled by loud music and psychedelic drugs. But Chornenkaya is not into Sixties comparisons. She wasn't born until 1971.

"To me, this is more powerful than just a bunch of hippies being soft and mellow and yin," she says. "Burning Man is much more of a yang experience—building all this stuff. There are rowdy beer-drinking guys, New Age healers, hippies, musicians, artists. All of them come together and learn from each other. Women get into their yang energy. If it gets to be too much for you, Women's Temple is a place to come. As long as you're not hurting anyone else you can express your passion any way you want. It's not like you have to meditate for a half hour a day to be one of us."

Burning Man dates back to 1986 and an annual fire ceremony and party held at a San Francisco beach. It was started by two artists, Larry Harvey and Jerry James, and has since grown into a small industry and vibrant subculture of "randomly gathered free spirits who surf the bleeding edge of culture, space, and time." After a crackdown by park police in 1990, the mushrooming event moved to Black Rock Desert. But it still culminates each year on a Sunday night, when revelers ignite a giant wooden statue of their iconic man.

Today Burning Man sees itself as "an annual experiment in temporary community dedicated to radical self-expression and radical self-reliance."[4] Women's Temple is just one of scores of smaller tents, domes, or other canopies scattered around Black Rock City. They offer shade along with all kinds of goods and services. Everything is free—once you pay the organizers forty dollars to get in. There's a place where you can make necklaces from bowls full of colorful beads. There's a woman running a workshop on new ways to paint your toes and guys offering to tattoo your arm, pierce your ear, or brand your body with the Burning Man logo.

Diana offers workshops on sex. They take place under a bulbous green dome that from a distance looks like the top half of a giant brain flapping in the breeze. It's right next to Passion Dome and Tulip Temple, a gleaming white tent adorned with tulips, hearts, and luscious red lips. Chornenkaya and her partner, Bernie, offer three different workshops at Women's Temple—one of healing touch, two on sexual boundaries, and another on how to move sexual energy throughout your body. Their workshops are popular, and their dome is often surrounded by crowds of curious people and lots of mountain bikes—the main mode of transport in Black Rock City. Diana's audience is in all stages of dress and undress, although most people outside her open-air dome have some kind of headdress—an American flag, a white T-shirt, or a broad-rimmed hat to keep out the sun. Diana wears red and black lingerie. Bernie stands behind her wearing nothing but tight orange briefs.

Sexual boundaries, they explain, are something new to many of the young people at Burning Man. "Unless you can say no, your yes doesn't mean much," Diana says. "We teach people how to communicate when you want to be touched and when you don't want to be touched—how to say no with compassion and how to receive no with compassion, or how to say yes. It's getting in tune with other people's body language and checking with them if you are in doubt."

Diana had been to Burning Man every year since 1998. "I've never been in an environment where sexuality was so accepted and welcomed and safe. Women are able to walk around naked twenty-four hours a day and feel safe and celebrated. That is very unusual," she says. "Getting naked, to me, is not just about clothes. It's about taking your mask off—revealing yourself, being vulnerable, being who you are. Coming from that place and searching for your real needs. What are you looking for? Operating from the mask, it's hard for you to see the next step."

Diana lives in Berkeley, where she is working to establish Women's Temple on a permanent basis. Most of her workshops in the San Francisco Bay Area are for women only, and they sign up for various reasons. There are women who downplayed their sexuality in the 1970s and 1980s to compete in the corporate world and are now trying to reclaim it. Some have suffered from sexual abuse, everything from incest to teenage encounters with older men. Others are struggling with shame instilled from their religious upbringing. But whatever the reason, most are trying to regain the power of feminine sexuality.

Chornenkaya, a nurturing woman with soft dark hair and soulful eyes, was born in Moscow in 1971 and immigrated to the United States with her parents in the early 1990s. Her father was a physicist in Russia and a "passionate atheist," so her only religious traditions are faint echoes of the Russian Orthodox Church. "My mother was a kind of guilty Christian in her heart," she says, speaking with a Russian accent. "You just bury everything."

To Diana, Women's Temple and Burning Man are not just about nudity or sexuality, they're about spirituality as well. I ask her if she sees Burning Man as an emerging religion or religious ritual.

"I do see it as religion, almost," she replies. "There are thousands of people now who are strong believers. When you go there, people say, 'Welcome home.' We feel like we finally have a right to our home. This is our home. Black Rock City is our home. We do our other stuff, and then we come back home. There is a sense of welcoming yourself. You can be yourself here. You can be a kid again. You can play again. You can be stupid. You can be silly. Anything you want to do is okay and celebrated. Even when we're grown-ups we still need to play. At Burning Man, people bring big toys, and they play with big toys. They build the toys. When you go there, it's like Martians having their play day.

"When we allow ourselves to be children again, we grow. Children grow. We experience that growth again. It's kind of like a mystery, but that's what happens. I have so many people say, 'This has changed my life.' It changes their perception of who they are."

It's also about community—twenty people who live together during their days in the desert. Some at her camp were friends or friends of friends. Others were "newly recruited just for this project" but soon became friends. There was a massage therapist, a graphics designer for a Web company, three lawyers, an artist, and a computer analyst from a brokerage house in San Francisco. There were ten men and ten women. Their mission was to learn to live together, to deal with the harsh conditions at Black Rock Desert, and, of course, to have a good time.

"It's an extremely fertile ground for people to open their hearts and learn from each other. We all have our neuroses. We may have gotten used to them, or maybe our partner has, but when you're living with twenty people they will be in your face. In a community, you face it and you change it. In the desert, you have to come together or you will be miserable. We create a strong bond. It feels like your family." There were three couples in the beginning of the week in Diana's camp, and one or two more formed by the end of the festival. "We were able to create a heart space. There wasn't a lot of sex going on. It was a beautiful heart space."

Diana concedes that these experiences are achieved by some with the help of Ecstasy, a powerful drug that produces feelings of empathy and compassion. But she says these emotional changes also happen without drugs, and the feelings and insights the drugs do inspire remain long after the Ecstasy wears off. "We had one guy with a loud voice who was always interrupting people. He kept talking about how men had to be warriors—how so many of them were too soft and were wimps. He transformed right in front of our eyes in the course of one week. Yes, one day he took some Ecstasy, but it had started before that. He'd already broken down into tears two days into it. He said he had never felt safe. He felt like he always had to fight. That was his armor. Later he said he felt like he had only a shell, his armor, and there was nothing inside. Here he is at Burning Man—he is thirty-two and this is the first time he has softened his armor. It was the first time he gave a man a hug and felt the compassion pouring from his heart. He understood compassion."

Back in the Bay Area, most of the students at the regular Women's Temple workshops are baby boomers old enough to be Diana's mother. The workshops have that kind of amorphous spirituality one finds in the New Age movement. There are visualization exercises and techniques to allow women to get in touch with their bodies. "We teach women how to pay attention to what is going on in their bodies," she says, "connecting to places that are numb." Men are not allowed to attend. "Some people might call our workshops homosexual, even though the majority of women who come identify themselves as hetero-sexual," she says. "If you touch a woman's vagina and massage her to give her sexual pleasure, some people would call that a homosexual experience. But we do it with other women so we can learn about each other's bodies. It's not like we're going to run off and get married."

Diana and I had several long conversations about Women's Temple. This interview took place outside amid the high-rise office buildings of downtown San Francisco. She was on her lunch break from the corporate job she hoped to leave so she could devote more time to her Women's Temple. It was a cold, windy day, and Diana was bundled up in a big coat like someone ready for win-ter in Moscow. It was a long way from the shimmering heat of northwestern Nevada.

"My vision in this work is about empowering women through their bodies," she explained. "God is really inside them. I don't actually use the word *God*. It's really their body that will tell them. To me, that's the deeper connection."

Diana opens her legs a bit, holds her hands in front of her, and lowers them down to her lap, bringing them together to form a V between her thighs. "This is where every woman is plugged into the whole process of creation. To me, this is the definition of God."

There was a pause while I looked into Diana's lap, then back into her eyes. What do you say to a beautiful woman when she puts her hands between her legs and proclaims, "This is my definition of God"? What do you say to that— "Hallelujah!" or "Amen"?

"Do you offer workshops for men?" I asked, then realized that was not the subtlest of segues.

"Not exactly," she replied, smiling. Then she explained that she does work with an organization called Body Electric, which offers groups for men, women, and couples.

"That includes performing an erotic massage for a man you just met yester-day. Some people would say it is sex. We call it an erotic massage ritual," she said, laughing at her own New Age lingo. "We're redefining the whole story. It's pretty out there, except we don't do intercourse. We teach that we are sexual beings and sexual interaction is a part of our life. We don't have to necessarily constrain it to our marriage relationship. For some it works, for some it doesn't."

Diana's nontraditional ideas about sex, marriage, and spirituality prompted my next question. "What do you base a sexual ethic on," I ask, "if not on religious tradition? How do you decide what sexual activity is right and what is wrong?"

There's a long pause. "That's a good question," Diana says, pausing again. "What we teach in workshops for men and women is that you have to connect with yourself, with your own emotions and feelings, before you can connect to another person's feelings. I guess that's the guide. Are you hurting the person, or not? Obviously, with molestation or child abuse, the person does not really want to connect with the child. They want to rob the child of what the child has."

Chornenkaya speaks from experience. When she was fifteen years old and still living in Moscow, her parents sent her off on summer holiday with a man they barely knew and his teenage daughter. Not only was she sexually violated on the trip, but her parents wouldn't acknowledge Diana's molestation when they heard about it from her sister. "When my parents found out, they kind of pushed me out of the family for two or three years," she said. "It was another stab in the heart. There is still so much more healing for me, and more for me to know about my sexuality and attitudes and fears. It's so deep, like a background that covered my own existence. But when you break through it, it's like you were wearing colored glasses and not realizing it until someone takes them off and gives you a different picture of the world."

There was really no feminist movement in Russia. One of the first things Diana noticed when she immigrated to the States was the different way men treated women—a kind of respect she credits to the work of American feminists. "In Russia, if you are pretty, you really have to prove that you are not a stupid slut. Men don't even listen to what you say. They are looking at your legs or your breasts. They pay no attention to anything else."

Under the Communist government, women were "liberated" to do roadwork side by side with men or to toil in factories. "Then they go home and cook and do the dishes while the men lie on the couch and watch television," she said. "It's much worse than here. There were so few men in Russia after World

War II. It was like one man for twenty women. If you had a man in your life, you worshiped him."

By one reckoning, the sexual revolution began more that a decade before Diana was born. It began on May 10, 1960, and was only two inches long. Maybe size isn't everything.

It was a two-inch item in the *New York Times* announcing that the FDA had given G. D. Searle and Company permission to market a new pill called Enovid. The Pill was born, and by 1966 six million American women were on it. Around the world, another six million women had seized the chemical reins of reproductive freedom. It was a revolution, and it showed no signs of slowing down.

Rome does not like revolutions, especially sexual ones, and many Catholics were waiting to see how the pope would respond. In the 1960s the Roman Catholic Church was already one of the few Christian communions still holding the line on birth control. In 1930 the Church of England had become the first major church in the West to bless artificial contraception for married couples. Concerns about overpopulation, the welfare of children, and the changing role of women inspired most major Protestant churches to follow suit and embrace real family planning with reliable contraception.

In the Roman church Pope Pius XI responded to the Anglican reforms in 1930 with the encyclical *Casti Connubii,* condemning artificial contraception as a sin against nature. Later popes affirmed that view, but the development and marketing of the Pill in the early 1960s seemed like it might nudge the church into the modern world. After all, Vatican II was under way, and the spirit of reform was in the air. In the summer of 1964 Pope Paul VI revealed that his predecessor, John XXIII, had appointed a special commission to study the Pill. Catholic doctors urged the church to bless the Pill, notable among them an American Catholic physician, Dr. John Rock, who helped develop the anovulant pill and saw no moral problems in its use. But Pope Paul removed the issue of contraception from the agenda of the Second Vatican Council, arguing that it was already under consideration by the special commission.

Love is in the air every spring, but it was especially so in 1966. In April of that year Bill Masters and Gini Johnson published their landmark work,

Human Sexual Response. It was more clinical than erotic, but sex was out of the closet and Masters and Johnson were instant celebrities. Their scientific studies measured the female orgasm, the erect phallus, and the sexual problems and proclivities of the Judeo-Christian citizenry. There hadn't been so much buzz about sex since 1948, when Alfred C. Kinsey paved the way for Masters and Johnson with the publication of *Sexual Behavior in the Human Male.* His book shocked the American public with reports that half of the white male population had committed adultery by age forty and that two-thirds reported having sex with prostitutes. A later book on sexual behavior in women was even more explosive. Kinsey died in 1956, leaving Masters and Johnson the anointed experts on human sexuality. In his personal philosophy, Masters saw little value in civil laws or moral codes that sought to regulate private sexual activity between consenting adults. He believed women should derive more pleasure from sex and scoffed at the stereotype of the frigid woman. "There is no such thing as a totally non-orgasmic woman," he said. "She may be non-orgasmic in her current marriage with her current mate, but this proves absolutely nothing."[5]

Meanwhile, back at the Vatican, the princes of the church were in a quandary over the Pill. In that sexy spring of sixty-six, the pope's birth control commission produced two theological working papers, one liberal and one conservative, and the liberal report was rumored to be the majority report. Those rumors were confirmed when the *National Catholic Reporter,* an independent weekly newspaper, revealed that a clear majority of the papal commission favored changing the church's condemnation of artificial birth control. Like the season, hope springs eternal. Liberal Catholics felt that change, along with love, was in the air.

There was a long wait, then sudden disappointment. On July 29, 1968, Pope Paul VI ignored his own commission and reaffirmed traditional church teachings condemning all forms of contraception except the rhythm method. *Humanae Vitae* proclaimed that "each and every marriage act must remain open to the transmission of life." His encyclical may have been the most important papal pronouncement of the century, but not in the way the church had hoped. *Humanae Vitae* was instantly ignored by millions of American Catholics. By 1974, 83 percent of those surveyed by pollsters said they disagreed with church teachings on birth control.[6] Most American Catholics dismissed the encyclical, and a number of influential theologians dissented.

Two decades and a new pope have done little to change the climate. In 1986 the Reverend Charles Curran, a respected moral theologian at the Catholic University of America and longtime dissenter on birth control, had his teaching credentials revoked by Cardinal Joseph Ratzinger and his powerful Vatican Congregation for the Doctrine of the Faith.

Pope Paul's encyclical inspired a new era of dissent in the church. If one can question birth control and still be considered Catholic, why not ignore the church's condemnation of masturbation, oral sex, premarital sex, extramarital sex, homosexuality, divorce, or abortion? In fact, that's exactly what millions of Americans did, joining the sexual revolution in a multitude of ways.

Sit down with Katie Morrison and John McNeill, listen to their stories, and ponder the paradox of being gay and Christian, then and now.

John was born in 1925 in Buffalo, New York, to devout Irish-Catholic parents. His mother was an immigrant from Ireland; his father worked as a crane operator. John was the youngest of five, and in his family, in those days, that meant he was destined for the priesthood. One son would be sacrificed, would wear the collar. His mother died when he was four years old, sealing his vocation. His aunt moved in with his father. They took a vow to live together as brother and sister and raise the children. John's mother's dying wish was that her youngest son become a priest. She got her wish.

Katie was born in 1972 in Pasadena, California. Her parents were both public school teachers and elders in the Presbyterian church. They sang in the choir. Katie's grandmother was the church secretary. To Katie, Pasadena Presbyterian Church was not just that big building on Colorado Avenue, right along the route of the annual Rose Bowl Parade. Church was home, church was safe, church was fun. Church was like a second family.

John is old enough to be Katie's grandfather, and in a way he is. They're separated by two generations, the continental United States, and centuries of church history, but they're also soul mates. In the Sixties, John fought the early battles in a crusade that would someday envelop both their lives.

John knew he was a homosexual from his earliest years. From the beginning, that realization and his priestly calling were stitched together like a seamless garment, and John wrapped it around himself like a shield against sin. "There was no positive road for me to take in terms of my sexual commitment," he said. "I was brought up to believe it was impossible to be gay and in God's good graces. I took in the church teaching, internalized the homophobia, entered the priesthood, and tried to commit myself to a life of sexual abstinence." He joined the Jesuits, drawn to their emphasis on education, spirituality, and discernment. John was listening for the will of God and struggling with his sexuality. He discovered a French Catholic philosopher named Maurice Blondel, a scholar who had also struggled to reconcile philosophy, theology, and the human will. Blondel challenged the idea that grace was just a supernatural force divorced from politics and social action. McNeill entered the Society of Jesus in 1948, the year before Blondel died, and went off to Europe for his doctoral studies.

In Europe, in the mid-1950s, John could no longer wall himself off from his sexual desire. "I began to act out my sexual needs and feel terrible about it, yet I couldn't control it. I was compulsively acting out, and close to an emotional breakdown," he said. "Then I met someone and formed a good, loving relationship. There was deep peace and joy with that person in that relationship. Then I had to deal with that, with the idea that gay relationships could be a way to a deeper relationship to God."

Flash forward three decades, out to southern California and Katie Morrison, who was feeling her own call to ministry. At the Presbyterian church, she was active in the youth group. "That's where I first began affirming my gift for leadership," she said, slipping into Presbyterian parlance. "I knew I wanted to be a minister in the Presbyterian church before I knew myself to be a lesbian woman." She went to college in Maine and came out during her first year. It wasn't like the 1950s. It was the 1990s and no big deal, or at least that's what Katie thought at the time. She'd always been kind of an odd, nerdy girl—the only woman on the water polo team. Nobody talked about sex in her Presbyterian church, especially lesbian sex. "When I came out I had no idea that God didn't love me. It was only after the fact that I learned where my church was on this issue."

Many people go out and get drunk on their twenty-first birthday, but not Katie. She asked her parents to send her to General Assembly, the annual policy-making convention of the Presbyterian Church (U.S.A.), for her birthday. At the meeting in Milwaukee, Katie met the Reverend Janie Spahr and other lesbian activists fighting for the right to stand at the Presbyterian pulpit. That's also where she had her first encounter with a conservative Presbyterian preacher sticking a Bible in her face and telling her she was going to hell.

Is *that* what it all boils down to—to the Bible, to the everlasting flames of hell? Long before Katie went to her first General Assembly, I'd lost track of how many Protestant church conventions I'd covered where the main story was yet another vote on whether to condemn gay sex, ordain homosexuals, or bless their unions as holy. They've all run together—Presbyterian, Methodist, Episcopalian, Lutheran. There's one step forward for gay rights in the church, then one step back. How do we view "self-avowed, practicing homosexuals"? Can't we merely expect faithfulness in marriage and chastity in singleness? Should there be a local option for bishops and presbyteries that disagree with the denomination's national ban on the ordination of homosexuals? Over the last two decades, I've written dozens of stories about church conventions debating gay rights, and they often inspire a flurry of letters, e-mail, and righteous indignation telling me that I've missed the point. What's the point? The Bible and the everlasting flames of hell! All I need to do is open up my Bible to Genesis and read about the destruction of Sodom; or turn to Leviticus, where male-on-male sex is condemned as an abomination to God, punishable by death; or read Paul's letter to the Romans, where he repeats God's warning, promising divine retribution for the unnatural, degrading, and shameless acts of homosexual men and women.

Sometimes I get the lecture even before I write the story. Let me take you to the Presbyterian Church General Assembly back in the summer of 2000. And let me introduce you to a guy I met there named Rod. That summer the Presbyterians gathered at the Long Beach Convention and Entertainment Center, and there was lots of entertainment—at least outside the hall. On Sunday delegates from around the nation joined thousands of Presbyterians from across southern California for a worship service inside the Long Beach Arena. For much of the year the arena is the home rink of the Long Beach Ice Dogs hockey team, whose mascot is an angry bulldog with a black studded collar. This image, which stared down at the worshipers as they filed into the arena, became my personal icon for that year's General Assembly. For by the time the Presbyterians reached the safety of their stadium-sized sanctuary, they had already run a gauntlet of angry, competing protesters, including some who looked a lot like that bulldog.

One of them was Rod, a street preacher and anti-gay demonstrator holding a giant, all-purpose placard. It listed the types of people who were certain to burn in hell, from "queers" to "Mormons," "child molesters" to "college professors," "witches" to "astrologers." No one was talking to the guy, so I strolled up and asked him why he was there. Rod told me that he'd read in the local paper that the Presbyterians were coming to town to debate whether they should allow homosexual "holy union" ceremonies in their churches. He could not believe Christians would even consider such a thing. "I'm here to let these people know that they are being sucked into the biggest lie in America, and that's the idea that God loves us just the way we are," Rod said. "I'm here to tell them that God will not let unrepentant Sodomites into heaven."

Just as I was about to ask Rod what he had against college professors, a brigade of antigay reinforcements climbing out of a minibus distracted us. They had their own signs, with such messages as "Thank God for AIDS" and "Fags Are an Abomination."

In Long Beach the Reverend Mel White, who leads a group called Soulforce, organized the pro-gay forces. Mel was a speechwriter for the Reverend Jerry Falwell before coming out of the closet. Before leaving the Christian Right, White learned a lot about media manipulation from the Reverend Falwell. Eighty of his Soulforce protesters were about to engage in a well-choreographed act of civil disobedience. And I mean *civil* disobedience. It was the most polite protest I've witnessed, and I've witnessed many. The Reverend White's demonstrators didn't even yell or chant. Their message was quietly conveyed across the front of their matching white T-shirts. "End the Debate," the shirts read. "Include us! Ordain us! Let us serve!"

White, a minister with the predominantly gay Metropolitan Community Church, was tired of the endless dialogue about homosexuality at conventions like this. "Frankly, we don't care what they do inside," he said, watching more than eight thousand Presbyterians pour into the arena. "They are in the business of making us outsiders. Well, we are not outsiders. We are God's children."[7]

Two weeks before, the Orlando police arrested Soulforce demonstrators during a protest rally at the Southern Baptist Convention. Before that, it was at a meeting of Methodists in Cleveland. Their next stop was an encounter with Episcopalians and the Denver police. In Long Beach, the demonstrators held a silent, smiling vigil while the Presbyterian delegates, church leaders, and other worshipers filed into the arena. Then, while everyone except the media was inside the arena worshiping, the protesters lined up in neat groups of ten, blocked a driveway nobody was using anyway, and were driven off in chartered buses by police. They were driven a few miles away to a park, cited for misdemeanors, and released. Included among those arrested was Janie Spahr, who lost a long battle in the 1980s to keep her Presbyterian ministerial credentials and would soon be standing at Katie Morrison's side at her ordination.

Inside the Long Beach convention center, at working sessions convened during the week, hundreds of policy-making delegates sat before automatic voting machines and piles of church documents. The image of whoever spoke was projected onto giant television screens hung over blue curtains at one end of the cavernous hall. There was lots of routine business, followed by a debate on the hot issue that summer—whether the church should specifically ban holy union ceremonies for same-sex couples. "We can't bless a behavior that we call a sin," said Florida delegate Ed Goebel.[8] He and other traditionalists in the 2.5-million-member denomination quote not only the Bible but also the Presbyterian Book of Confessions, which lists "sodomy and all unnatural lusts" as "sins forbidden by the Seventh Commandment."

Reformers in the church accuse traditionalists of selectively citing scripture and Presbyterian doctrine. They point out that the same paragraph in the Book of Confessions that outlaws sodomy also prohibits "wanton looks, impudent or light behavior and immodest apparel," along with "idleness, gluttony, drunkenness, unchaste company, and lascivious songs, books, pictures, dancing and stage plays." And no one was trying to defrock Presbyterian preachers for dancing.

In Long Beach, the headline was "Gay Forces Lose." The General Assembly narrowly passed a new church law that would prohibit ministers from officiating at holy union ceremonies for gay and lesbian couples. The measure, which passed by a vote of 268 to 251, then went before the church's 171 presbyteries for ratification. For much of the next year, regional Presbyterian bodies held their own debates, voted on the measure, and ended up overturning the vote and rejecting the holy union ban. So the new headline reads, "Gay Forces

Win." In reality, not one word of Presbyterian church law was changed. It was a classic example of the "one step forward, one step back" system of denominational politics.

Presbyterians began the new millennium talking about gay sex, and I wouldn't be surprised if they are still mulling it over in the next millennium. Having gone to three of four of these conventions, I feel the pain of longtime church staffers who sit through this little drama every summer. At the Long Beach assembly, one of those church employees turned to me in the midst of an endless debate. "Only Presbyterians can make sex boring," he sighed. Another staffer confessed that this denomination is so maddeningly democratic that he sometimes wished they had a pope.

Perhaps, but he should first consider the story of John McNeill.

Back from Europe and his sexual awakening, Father McNeill turned his attention to the Bible. Even in the Catholic church, McNeill knew scripture was the first step toward changing hearts and minds. On first reading, scripture seems clear about the immorality of homosexuality. But McNeill and a new wave of Bible scholars argue that scripture is not so clear, not so simple.

John Boswell, a professor of history at Yale University, has done exhaustive research on early Christian attitudes toward homosexuality. Pointing to a long history of mistranslation and misleading interpretations of biblical writings, Boswell concludes that the New Testament takes no clear position on homosexuality. "To suggest that Paul's references to excesses of sexual indulgence involving homosexual behavior are indicative of a general position in opposition to same-sex eroticism is as unfounded as arguing that his condemnations of drunkenness implies opposition to the drinking of wine."[9]

Scholars like Boswell and McNeill argue that the same-sex references in the story of Sodom, the Holiness Code of Leviticus, and the letters of Paul do not refer to loving, faithful homosexual relationships, which were open and celebrated in Greek and Roman culture. They were talking about rape of enemy soldiers and the worship of idols. More study and careful translation shows that these references were to temple prostitution and lack of hospitality, not homosexuality as we know it today. Old Testament prophets were more concerned with the fruits of procreation than the sins of oral copulation. "There was a close link to procreation because of the Jewish covenant to go forth and multiply—that from among you will come a savior," McNeill said. "For Christians, the savior had come, so there was no need, spiritually, to procreate to fulfill God's will. That opened up the possibility of other lifestyles, and the church introduced the celibate, monastic lifestyle."

Christian attacks on homosexuality are explained only partly by the later church's fear and denial of the body and its elevation of the spirit. Boswell points out that the Jesus portrayed in the Gospel stories repeatedly condemns greed and hypocrisy, yet no Christian state has gone out of its way to imprison hypocrites or burn the greedy at the stake. "Obviously," he writes, "some factors beyond biblical precedent were at work in late medieval states, which licensed prostitutes but burned gay people."[10]

If the Bible is not the real source of Christianity's long-standing condemnation of homosexuality, then what is? Certainly not ancient Rome, where the government taxed homosexual prostitution and even gave young male prostitutes their own holiday. "Roman society almost unanimously assumed that adult males would be capable of, if not interested in, sexual relations with both sexes," Boswell writes. "It is extremely difficult to convey to modern audiences the absolute indifference of most Latin authors to the question of gender."[11]

Boswell's research into the roots of gay intolerance begins with early Christian efforts to reconcile Greek philosophy, the Jewish faith, and the teachings of the apostle Paul. It starts with Clement of Alexandria (c.150–c.215), a Greek theologian who asserted that "to have sex for any purpose other than to produce children is to violate nature."[12] According to Boswell, the "Alexandrian rule" was an erroneous effort to blend the Platonic and Pauline ideas of natural law. It would all but disappear for centuries, only to eventually triumph in the moral theology of the church.

Christendom's condemnatory attitude toward all sexual pleasure—and its suspicion of women—was embodied in Saint Augustine (354–430), who infamously wrote, "There is nothing which degrades the manly spirit more than the attractiveness of females and contact with their bodies." For centuries the most scandalous thing about male-on-male sexual intercourse was not its inherent immorality but the idea that a man would lower himself to assume the passive and inferior role of a woman. Or, as Saint Augustine puts it, "the body of a man is as superior to that of a woman as the soul is to the body."[13] In those days, Boswell argues, the same-sex taboo was more about misogyny than sexuality.

Attitudes to erotic and romantic love—gay and straight—changed dramatically by the late eleventh and early twelfth centuries, and the surviving literature of courtly love reveals that it flourished betwixt and between genders. But something happened in the thirteenth and fourteenth centuries to fuel a sudden rise in social intolerance toward subcultures that were deemed deviant and dangerous. These included Jews and other "money-lenders," Muslims and other "heretics," homosexuals and other "sodomites." It was the era of the Crusades and the Inquisition, a time when the governmental machinery of church and state sought to impose political and religious conformity. "Between 1250 and 1300," Boswell writes, "homosexual activity passed from being completely legal in most of Europe to incurring the death penalty in all but a few contemporary legal compilations."[14] And it was in this climate that Saint Thomas Aquinas passed judgment on homosexuality in *Summa theologiae,* the basis of Catholic orthodoxy for centuries to come. Boswell argues convincingly that Aquinas and other high medieval theologians were responding to popular antipathy toward homosexuality and not relying on any solid Christian tradition for that position. "Aquinas played to his audience not simply by calling on popular concepts of 'nature,' but also by linking homosexuality to behavior which was certain to evoke reactions of horror and fear," such as bestiality and cannibalism.[15] Homosexuality was no longer a sexual sin like other sexual sins—such as masturbation, fornication, or adultery. It was an extraordinary evil and had to be severely repressed.

So influential was Saint Thomas that church teachings on homosexuality had changed little through the 1950s, when John McNeill was studying for the priesthood and struggling with his emerging sexuality. McNeill was ordained in 1959, just as the Catholic church was preparing for the Second Vatican Council. Centuries of church hypocrisy seemed to be giving way to something new. "Vatican II made me so optimistic," O'Neill recalls. "There was a new understanding about the two aims of sexuality—one was procreation, but the other was mutual love and fulfillment. Vatican II said those two aims were coequal. Theologically, it should have been the time for the church to rethink sexuality."

But the church did not rethink sexuality. Instead, it issued one of the most controversial, unpopular, and widely ignored teachings in modern church history. *Humanae Vitae* did not just reaffirm the church's condemnation of artificial contraception. It indirectly closed the door on a reexamination of church teachings on homosexuality—that gay sex is "evil" and "disordered" even among loving and faithful partners. McNeill sees the key theological issue as the church's refusal to separate sex from procreation—to truly acknowledge that sexual love has moral value beyond its ability to create a new life. "I think the reason the Vatican wouldn't approve birth control is it would mean having to reexamine homosexuality. The resistance was just too strong."

That didn't stop McNeill from reexamining homosexuality. In the summer of 1970 the Jesuit theologian published a series of articles called "The Christian Male Homosexual." Based on his scholarly research and years of work counseling gay Christians, O'Neill argued that it was time for the church to change the way it ministered to homosexuals. Over the next four years he continued his research and expanded his ideas into a book-length manuscript. Moral theologians in the United States and Rome reviewed it for two more years, and in 1976 McNeill received his official *Imprimi Potest,* approval from his Jesuit superiors, to publish *The Church and the Homosexual.*

Once again McNeill was optimistic about the changes inspired by the Second Vatican Council. Vatican II opened the church to modern science, including the slippery science of psychology, which was changing its ideas about the pathology of homosexuality. Gays were being told by the medical community to accept their sexuality, and McNeill thought the church would soon follow suit. He'd shown in his counseling practice that gay and lesbian Christians could live happy, healthy, and holy lives. "Unless God is sadistic, he doesn't want us to destroy ourselves psychologically," McNeill argued. "What is bad psychology has to be bad theology."

In 1975, when Pope Paul VI still occupied the throne of Peter, the Vatican restated church teachings on homosexuality. Some gays and lesbians in the church found a glimmer of hope in a new declaration of sexual ethics by the Congregation for the Doctrine of the Faith. It appeared to distinguish between two types of homosexuals. There were those with a "proclivity born from bad education or damaged sexual maturity or habit or bad example." And there were those homosexuals with "some kind of almost innate impulse" or "vitiated constitution." Could the church be saying that at least some homosexuals were born that way—made that way by God? If so, gays and lesbians were still sentenced to celibacy by the 1975 Vatican declaration, which concluded that "acts of homosexuality are disordered by their very nature, nor can they be approved in any way whatever."

Today McNeill sees how naive he was to think the church was changing in the 1970s. At the time, his book unleashed a wave of media attention about this homosexual priest and his radical ideas. There were newspaper headlines such as "Pioneer Priest Who Is 'Gay.'"[16] On television, *Today* and *The Phil Donahue Show* brought McNeill into the living rooms of millions of American Catholic families. It was all too much for Rome. In 1977, just a year after the Jesuits gave him permission to publish his book, the Congregation for the Doctrine of the Faith removed its *Imprimi Potest* and forbade him from publicly discussing his views on homosexuality. He obeyed for a decade, then changed his mind and began speaking out. In 1987 he was defrocked and kicked out of the Jesuit order for disobedience.

Actually, McNeill had been disobedient through much of the 1960s and 1970s—just not in public. It is not uncommon for Catholic priests—gay and straight—to bend their vows of chastity and obedience. They are just not allowed to break them publicly. Making scandal is a more serious sin than having sex.

My interview with John McNeill took place in February 2002 in the faculty club at the University of California at Berkeley. Toward the end of the interview, I realized that I'd been doing exactly what the Catholic church had been doing for years, ignoring the presence of Charlie Chiarelli, who has been McNeill's partner for more than thirty-five years, including two decades when John was still a Jesuit priest. Charlie had been sitting quietly next to John for the entire interview, glancing at his watch every few minutes like a long-suffering spouse who's heard the same story a hundred times before. Charlie and John were visiting the Bay Area from their home in Florida, and Charlie looked like he would rather be out sightseeing than listening once again to the life story of John J. McNeill.

Realizing how rude I'd been, I turned to Charlie and asked how long he and John had been together. "Thirty-six years," he replied. "We met at a gay bar in Toronto—many years ago. New Year's Eve 1965–66. It makes it easy for him to remember our anniversary." We all laugh, because it's funny and because we realize how we'd left Charlie out of the conversation. Charlie is ten years younger than McNeill. He was raised in the Catholic church by Sicilian parents who emigrated to Canada. Responding to another question, Charlie told me he was never ordained as a priest. "No, but we did meet in the *Saint Charles* Bar."

John jumped back in the conversation, remembering that it wasn't just Vatican II that made him optimistic in the mid-1960s. "My relationship with Charlie gave me the deepest experience of human love I've ever had," he said, turning to his life partner. "God's love became real for me through Charlie."

There was a similar moment in my interview with Katie Morrison. We were sitting in a gourmet hamburger joint in one of Oakland's trendier neighborhoods, talking about her recent ordination as a Presbyterian minister. Katie's lesbian lover wasn't there, but at a certain point I was reminded that her ordination battle was not just about whether she is in compliance with Article G-6.0106b of the constitution of the Presbyterian church. That 1997 amendment to the church constitution requires Presbyterian ministers and elders to practice "fidelity within the covenant of marriage between a man and a woman, or chastity in singleness." We were not just talking about G-6.0106b. We were talking about Katie and her lover. Before that amendment was added to the church constitution, Presbyterians had another way of limiting ministry based on sexual orientation. Since 1974 the church had prohibited ordination to "practicing, self-affirming homosexuals."

"They get all uncomfortable, and they say, 'Are you practicing?'" Morrison laughed, taking a bite out of her veggie burger. "It's like, 'Practicing *what?*' My partner says I don't need to practice anymore. I've made it!"

The Reverend Morrison's partner is the Reverend Curran Reichert, an ordained minister with the United Church of Christ, one of the few mainline Protestant denominations that officially ordain gays and lesbians. What Katie and Curran actually do in bed is not the official business of the United Church of Christ, but it remains a concern of the Presbyterians. On October 21, 2001, Morrison made history as the first openly gay or lesbian seminary graduate to be ordained by the Presbyterian church. Katie had recently completed her theological training at San Francisco Theological Seminary and had begun working with More Light Presbyterians, a gay rights lobbying group, which continued to employ her as an ordained minister.

Earlier that year Morrison and other gay Presbyterians scored an apparent victory in Louisville when the church's General Assembly voted to remove the 1996 requirement that church leaders practice "fidelity in marriage, chastity in singleness." That vote to amend the church constitution still had to be ratified by a majority of the denomination's 173 regional presbyteries. By February 2002, however, a clear majority of the presbyteries voted to overturn the General Assembly and retain the chastity test. There it is again—one step forward, one step back for gay rights in the church.

This time, between the forward and backward step, the liberal Presbytery of the Redwoods in northern California quietly voted to ordain Katie. During a church hearing before her ordination, Morrison was asked if she "intends to comply with G-6.0106b." That's how Presbyterians like to talk about sex. They didn't ask her if she was having sex. They asked about G-6.0106b.

At the hearing, Morrison simply replied, "Yes, I intend to comply with G-6.0106b." Since everyone in the room knew she was a lesbian, Morrison expected a series of tough follow-up questions from one or two conservative members of her ordination panel. Was she a celibate lesbian? Was she chaste? What does chaste mean to a lesbian couple? To Morrison's surprise, there were no follow-up questions.

Sitting there in the burger joint with Katie, I had a few more questions. She had already told me she lived in the neighborhood for three years with the Reverend Reichert, a former actress she met while at the seminary.

"So," I asked, "are you celibate?"

"No," she replied. "It says 'chastity,' not 'celibacy.'"

My *Webster's* dictionary defines *chaste* as "innocent of unlawful sexual intercourse" or "celibate." Morrison does not equate *chaste* with *celibate*. She went on to cite chapter and verse of the Heidelberg Confession, a Protestant statement of faith compiled in 1562 and one of the foundations of Presbyterian theology. "It talks about chastity as living in pure and right relation, whether in holy matrimony or singleness. It's not referring to physical practice," Morrison says. "I am in a committed, faithful relationship. It's a whole relationship. Sexuality is one component of the relationship."

Here's the difference between Katie Morrison and John McNeill—and one of the important spiritual legacies of the Sixties: Katie was raised with the idea that its okay to be gay, but John had to learn it. McNeill fought the early battles, which are often the hardest. You can see the difference in their faces, and it's not just their difference in age. McNeill's sometimes angry face shows the battles, shows the early years of self-hate. Morrison is fresh-faced, beamingly optimistic. Her national church never officially proclaimed it, but Katie was raised by parents and other Presbyterians who believe gay is good. When Morrison first came out as a lesbian, some conservative members of her southern California presbytery argued homosexuality wasn't "biblical." Katie's dad, Steve Morrison, replied to his daughter's critics with a letter that began:

> One of my pastors, and about half the elders in my church, are women. I don't object to that, but if I did, IT WOULD BE BIBLICAL. I have a dear friend who has been divorced, and who has remarried. I don't condemn her for that, but if I did, IT WOULD BE BIBLICAL. In my own marriage, I don't regard my wife as subordinate to my will and authority, but if I did, IT WOULD BE BIBLICAL.
>
> I fervently pray that you will one day meet a gay man or woman and get to know them sufficiently well to discern, through the fog of that woefully inadequate adjective, homosexual, the actual human face of a kind and generous, intelligent and creative, conscientious and devoted brother or sister in Christ.

Morrison makes an important point. What happened in the 1970s was not just gay liberation. When gays and lesbians came out of the closet, straight church members met them, got to know them, and in their own lives were also liberated. The silence was broken, secrecy crumbled, hypocrisy exposed.

Presbyterians have been battling over gay rights at their annual meetings since a man at the 1974 General Assembly stood up holding a sign asking, "Is anyone else out there gay?" Katie Morrison was two years old in 1974. She was twenty-nine when she was ordained, and she argues that her youth is her greatest asset. Presbyterian church membership has been falling for decades, and the denomination is desperately seeking the Katie Morrison demographic. It didn't take long for the leading strategists in the gay rights movement to anoint this bright Gen-Xer as "our Presbyterian poster child."

"Young people see the church as hypocritical," she told me. "God loves you, but not the way you are? Young people tend to feel judged by their parents anyway, so the church becomes this big parent being judgmental. People know more about the judgment than the love. Who's attracted to a place where they feel judged?"

Another spiritual legacy of the Sixties is this postdenominational divide between liberals and conservatives in American Christendom. It hardly matters if you're talking about Presbyterians, Methodists, or Roman Catholics. The two camps in the new holy war transcend denominational boundaries. They are the forces of "tradition" battling the battalions of "tolerance." And they have already cracked open a slow-motion schism that continues to creep across the American religious landscape. It's not just about sex. It's about scripture. It's about authority. It's about how to envision Jesus. But gay sex is the issue that pushes buttons and points to the larger divide. "We are the scapegoats over deep divisions about how we read scripture and whether Jesus is the only way," Morrison says. "A lot of this is about fear. Folks in the conservative churches are fearful of homosexuality. They're afraid to even talk about it."

Morrison and McNeill's churches have been talking about it at least since 1974, when that gay man raised his sign at the General Assembly and the Jesuits gave McNeill his *Imprimi Potest.* Officially and nationally, gay rights crusaders have achieved little progress in the Roman Catholic Church and mainline Protestant denominations. But in the real world, which is the local church, lesbian and gay clergy have made enormous strides. Church doctrine changes at glacial speed, but it moves from the ground up.

Nevertheless, McNeill knows that systemic change in the Catholic church can happen only with a new pope, one who is not afraid to continue the openness of the Sixties and reforms of the Second Vatican Council. "We are in an anti–Vatican II period," he said. "Vatican II has yet to have its full impact. The next papacy has to either lose its authority or begin to act in accord with Vatican II. It takes a long time to change such an ingrained tradition as homophobia, but I think it is happening. My counseling clients—those gay and lesbian people living whole, happy, and devout lives—they are the Holy Spirit speaking through the people of God. Vatican II redefined the church as the people of God. It became the primary task of the hierarchy to listen to what the Holy Spirit is saying through the people of God and then formulate that into church doctrine. Instead, they are still speaking to people from the top down.

"God blessed the Catholic church with fallibility," he adds. "Feminism and the sexual revolution are movements of the Holy Spirit. They have helped us reach the fullness of human life. Since Vatican II, the vast majority of Catholics have followed their own conscience on birth control. Once the church proves itself fallible, everyone has to discern the truth from their own experience."

What is it about the gay and lesbian experience that draws them to ministry and forces Christian churches to deny the fact that there are thousands of "practicing homosexuals" in their clerical ranks? Mainline Protestant seminaries today are overflowing with lesbians. Catholic religious orders like the Jesuits and the Franciscans have always had large numbers of gay men in their ranks. One way to envision the future of American religion is to look at who is studying in its seminaries. Today they are full of gay men, lesbians, and bisexuals.

Back in the old days, in the 1950s, when McNeill was preparing for his ordination, there were fewer options for gays and lesbians. Joining religious orders and taking a vow of celibacy was a way for them to fight their sexual urges. But there is much more to the story today than an escape from sexuality. "There is a very positive attraction in the gay community to spiritual values," McNeill says. "I've given retreats for years with gay clergy from every denomination. It's not just that we're trying to escape from our past."

For those hoping to change Rome's condemnatory approach to homosexuality, the watershed event was the 1986 Vatican document appropriately named *Homosexualitatis problema*. The tone of the letter, issued by Cardinal Joseph Ratzinger, the prefect of the Vatican's Congregation for the Doctrine of the Faith, shocked many in the church. Those who saw the church starting to differentiate between homosexual orientation and homosexual acts were surprised by the document's assertion that "the peculiar propensity of the homosexual person" is "disordered" and their sexual acts are "evil."

Mark Jordan, a professor of religion at Emory University, argues that Ratzinger's treatise twists church teachings about natural law to justify a political attack against the gay rights movement. "What complicates the relation of this judgment to the natural law is that most Catholic theologies have held that all human sexuality is 'objectively disordered' as a result of Original Sin," he writes. "What does it mean to say that that 'peculiar propensity of the homosexual person' is 'objectively disordered'?"

But the real hypocrisy and self-hatred in *Homosexualitatis problema* is seen only when one realizes that a large percentage of Catholic priests and bishops are homosexuals themselves. What proportion of priestly sexuality is gay sexuality is impossible to say with any degree of certainty. "Homosexual clergy are often more zealous in keeping their lives secret from their superiors or colleagues than anyone else," Jordan notes. "Many superiors these days do not want to know about the homosexual lives of their subordinates, for fear they would have to act on the knowledge."[17]

Most people who look into the matter agree that the percentage of gay men in the priesthood is much higher than in the overall population. In his study of homosexuality in modern Catholicism, Jordan writes that the aesthetics of the liturgy rather than the asceticism of a celibate life draw many gay men to priesthood. In a chapter of his book titled "Clerical Camp," Jordan describes the "liturgy divas" and the "liturgy queens" of the Catholic mass. "Liturgy Queens need not be members of the clergy, but they are typically found in the vicinity of the altar—or at least in the choir loft," he writes. "The performers are praised and compared in the ceaseless gossip of the 'coffee hour,' the planning meeting, the clerical dinner, the monastery 'rec' room, the regional workshop, and the summer institute. It is not just a matter of how he preached or changed, but how he moved, held his hands, handled the censer. What choice did he make among the available vestments."[18]

Carl Jung, a pioneer in the marriage of psychology and spirituality, believed that the "feminine streak" and "aesthetic sense" in the homosexual male made it easier for them to connect with divine power. "Often he is endowed with a wealth of religious feelings, which help him to bring the *ecclesia spiritualis* into reality, and a spiritual receptivity which makes him responsive to revelation," Jung wrote.[19]

Debate over whether homosexuality is caused by nature or nurture continues to this day. For theologians this is an important question, since many gay and lesbian Christians insist that "God made me this way." Officially, the Roman Catholic Church still considers homosexuality to be a "disorder." St. Ignatius of Loyola, the founder of the Jesuit order to which McNeill was drawn, devised spiritual exercises as a way of "preparing and disposing our soul to rid itself of all its disordered affections and then, after their removal, of seeking and finding God's will in the ordering of our soul." So, the question of whether gay sex is a "natural" or "unnatural" act, whether homosexuality is "ordered" or "disordered" remains a central question for many church leaders.

For McNeill, however, that is no longer the central concern. In his view, sexuality is a spectrum; there's really no such thing as a homosexual or heterosexual. He refuses to endorse the ideal that heterosexuality is the ideal sexual state, although he acknowledges that it does have evolutionary advantages. "Obviously, there is a lot of gay sex based in self-hatred—acting out very destructive sexual needs without any context of love. But that's also true for straights," he said. "There is nothing 'ideal' about a penis and a vagina. For heterosexuals and homosexuals, love is the ideal."

When I first started covering religion in the early 1980s, the AIDS epidemic was just taking hold. AIDS decimated the gay population in places such as New York and San Francisco. It was easy to turn promiscuous sex back onto the gay community and blame gay people for the plague that was killing their friends, lovers, and neighbors. It was easy to say God was punishing places such as San Francisco for a decade of sin and sodomy in the bath houses and sex parlors south of Market Street. And some religious leaders—like the president of the Southern Baptist Convention, the nation's largest Protestant denomination—did just that. But something else began to happen in the coming together of the gay and Christian groups around the suffering caused by the AIDS virus. Understanding happened. Reconciliation happened. Compassion happened. Christianity happened.

In the darkening shadow of AIDS, a new spirituality arose among the gay folk in San Francisco. Its sacraments were long hugs and slow, sensuous massage. Its altars were votive candles burning wherever people with AIDS gathered. Its great totem was a sprawling quilt imbued with sacred power. Its high priests were people living with AIDS and those accompanying them into death. It was a search for meaning in the face of a devastating plague—a crusade to experience life fully in the face of the unrelenting march of death. It was a spirituality that traded the judgment and tradition of organized religion for a homegrown theology of unconditional love.

At first gay people pretty much had to fend for themselves. Most of the gay spiritual renewal in the 1980s happened outside the religious mainstream. Alienated by institutions that viewed them as sexual deviants, thousands of gays looked elsewhere for spiritual support in the age of AIDS. They found God among themselves, in their own experience, and flocked to gay-oriented churches, synagogues, and upbeat New Age congregations. In the process, they began changing Christian hearts and minds.

Brother Jeremy Hollinger left his high-ranking post as provincial superior of Mother Teresa's Missionary Brothers of Charity to work in the trenches of AIDS ministry. "It's humiliating to traditional religious folks that their teachers in unconditional love today are gay and lesbian people," he told me. "In the beginning days of the epidemic, people were afraid to go near people with AIDS because they weren't sure how it was transmitted. But the gay community was there. It's a paradox that the outcasts have become the teachers—the least among us have become the greatest."

Christian history is replete with movements inspired by self-proclaimed prophets—messianic leaders who claim to be mouthpieces for God. But few of those prophets were as obsessed with sex as David "Moses" Berg. "We have a sexy God and a sexy religion with a very sexy leader with an extremely sexy young following," Berg told his followers. "So if you don't like sex, you better get out while you can."

For most of the 1950s and '60s, Berg and his family traveled the country, preaching at small Pentecostal churches and performing as the struggling Berg Family Singers. Their ministry languished for years but took off in the late 1960s, when Berg let his hair and beard grow wild and embraced California's hippie subculture. Within a few years the Children of God, later known as the Family, would generate headlines around the world with its notorious blend of Christian evangelism, revolutionary spirit, and sexual freedom.

Today there's a whole new generation in the Family. They are the actual children of the Children of God, a new wave of freewheeling Christian revolutionaries.

According to their detractors, they and their parents are heretics, cultists, and polygamists, spawned by a twisted prophet preaching a strange brew of Christian compassion and free love.

But to Sarah Lieberman, the oldest of ten children born to a woman in the sect, the Children of God have been misunderstood and maligned. "People think this is all about sex," Lieberman told me. "But it's greater than sexual relations. It's about how you relate and feel about people. It's about loving God with all your soul."[20]

Earlier in its history female members of the Children of God used their bodies to win new souls. Berg urged the women in his flock to expand the "law of love" beyond the confines of their Christian sect. They called it "flirty fishing," after Jesus of Nazareth's call that his disciples become "fishers of men."

Miriam Williams was only seventeen when she met some of Berg's disciples in Greenwich Village. It was 1971, and she went off with them to a commune in upstate New York. "It was a campground with about three hundred people," she told me in an interview thirty years later. "People were living together, sharing everything. It was a mixture of Christianity and communism. It appealed to me."[21]

Williams tried to explain how she found herself sharing her body with strange men—all in the name of Christ. "At first it was just flirting, but if necessary, you'd have sex with men to get them to join. Most of us weren't that shocked by it. It wasn't that much different than the whole hippie, free-love thing. We were already having sex with people in the group."

Berg's teachings on sex and marriage were unusual but not unprecedented in American religious history. In 1848 John Humphrey Noyes founded the Oneida commune in New York. Its members, known as Perfectionists, believed they could be freed from sin on Earth by communion with God, renouncing personal property, and practicing "complex marriage," in which all of the adults in the community were married to one another. That practice proved so controversial that the marital system was renounced and the commune dissolved around 1880.

Less than four decades later, in 1919, David Berg was born in Oakland, California, the son of evangelist Virginia Brandt Berg. David Berg was nearly fifty years old when he began preaching in a Huntington Beach coffeehouse run by Teen Challenge, a Christian outreach group. Berg's early flock, a band of hippies, political radicals, and Jesus freaks, left Huntington Beach in 1969, when the prophet predicted an enormous earthquake would soon hit California. In the early seventies they formed Christian communes in California and Texas, the first of dozens of small intentional communities that would spring up around the world. Within a few years Moses Berg disappeared from public sight. But he continued promoting his prophecies in a series of missives, called "Mo letters," dispatched to his far-flung flock.[22]

Berg told his female devotees that the idea for "flirty fishing" was communicated to him through divine prophecy, and he even composed a prayer to inspire his band of sacred prostitutes: "Help her, O God, to catch men! Help her to catch men, be bold, unashamed, and brazen to use anything she has, O God, to catch men for thee! Even if it be through the lure, the delicious flesh on a steel hook of thy reality, the steel of thy spirit. Hook them through her flesh!"

Birth control was forbidden, and the children born into the sect from these casual encounters produced "Jesus babies." Sara Welsh was seven years old when she and her mother left the Children of God. "My mom had eight kids and only three are from the same father," said Welsh, a student at the University of California at Santa Cruz.

One of the most detailed examinations of Berg's prophecies and sexual practices is contained in a voluminous 1995 court judgment in a British child custody case. In his conclusion, Lord Justice Alan Ward wrote that, at least until 1986, there was widespread child-to-child sex and sexual abuse of minors by adult members of the Children of God. "I am completely satisfied that he [Berg] was obsessed with sex and that he became a perverted man who recklessly corrupted his flock," Ward wrote. Citing the prophet's explicit writings depicting young children as sexual beings, the judge ruled that Berg "bears responsibility for propagating the doctrine which so grievously misled his flock and injured the children within it."[23]

Another independent observer who has studied the Children of God, Steve Kent, agreed with Ward's conclusion that the Family has now stopped most of its past excesses. But Kent called on the current leaders to address the continuing psychological damage to the children of the Children of God. "What about the long-term effect on the children from that period?" asked Kent, a professor of sociology at the University of Alberta. "These kids got very little schooling and grew up in a highly sexualized environment. Some have been able to pull themselves up, but many of them wound up in the sex trade."

Berg died in 1994, leaving the leadership of the Family to his latest wife, Maria, an early convert previously known as Karen Zerby. Today the Family presents a very different image. They say they have grown up to be an international fellowship of Christian communities with nearly twenty-seven hundred full-time active members operating in more than eighty countries and a mailing list of seventy-nine thousand "friends and supporters."[24] They emphasize their witnessing and humanitarian work: starting farming projects in South Africa or helping street children in Mexico. Leaders of the Family say that they no longer practice "flirty fishing," although their official policy statement on "law of love" still sings the praises of "sexual sharing" among consenting married and single members. "This ensures that everyone's sexual needs are being provided for in a clean, healthy, safe and loving environment," it states. "Members can partake in such sexual sharing to bring greater unity or additional pleasure and variety into their lives."

Sarah Lieberman, who lives in a communal home in Orange County with ten members of the Family, wishes the news media and more mainstream Christian groups would look beyond the sect's sleeping arrangements. Lieberman married when she was twenty-one and has two small children. "We have doctrines that aren't mainstream, but we don't focus on them," she said.

"Most of us find one spouse is a big enough challenge. We are usually so tired we just hit the bed and fall asleep. I can think of only two people who have multiple partners. We've gone through stages like the rest of society. There was a time when things were a bit looser."

Things *were* looser in the 1970s, when Lieberman's parents hooked up. Her parents, who declined to be interviewed, had five boys and five girls but are no longer full-time members of the sect. Sarah Lieberman was born in Argentina and grew up living in Peru, Mexico, Korea, Japan, and the United States. Her younger brother, Michael, now nineteen, says he enjoyed traveling around as a missionary child. His first memories are of Japan and living in homes with three or four other families. "You'd have all kinds of playmates," said Michael, who declined to give his last name.

Michael, who married in 2000 and has one child, said members of the Family decide themselves if they want to be monogamous or have open marriages. "This is not adultery, which is something that hurts people," he said. "If your wife didn't know about it, and you had sex with another woman, that would be sinful. But if all parties are okay with it, that's another story."

Since the early days the Children of God has been a secretive organization. Few members knew where Berg and his inner circle lived. Today members look to Maria and her new husband, Peter Amsterdam, as the movement's prophets. Michael said he has never seen "Mama" (Maria Berg) or Amsterdam. They communicate to their followers through letters. "I see them both as prophets," he said. "They are mouthpieces for God."

Two former members of the Family—Marina Tafuri and her daughter, Daphne Sarran—are among the sect's most outspoken critics. In 1977 Tafuri was sixteen and living in her native Italy when she met some of Berg's devotees on a train from Rome to Naples. "They can really spot people having a hard time in life," she said. "I wasn't attracted by the born-again Christian beliefs, but I liked the commitment to social causes. They were trying to change the world. We came from a generation that wanted something different."

Marina certainly found something different in the Children of God. "It was superfundamentalist, but with this sexual twist. Women would have six kids or ten kids, and would not know who three of the fathers were."

Tafuri joined the organization, and a year later Daphne was born, the first of four children fathered by her common-law husband. Many of her daughter's earliest memories in the Children of God revolve around sex. "A lot of the escape for children was sexual play. Everything was very sexualized," Daphne told me. "By the time I was four, I knew a lot about sex. We were bombarded with it. By the time I was six, I was getting molested. I'd seen it happen to so many other children, it didn't really seem that strange."

Sarran and her mother left the Children of God in 1990, the year Tafuri says she finally realized that men in the group were sexually molesting her child. "A lot of the parents didn't know because a part of them didn't want to know," Daphne said. "The trick with the whole pedophile thing is they make you feel like you have a choice and that it's love."

Kent, the Canadian professor who has studied the sect, said Daphne Sarran's experiences in the sect were not unusual. He said he has talked to three dozen people who grew up in the Children of God. "A lot of the young men and almost all of the women had sexual encounters with adults when they were children in the group," he said.

When I met Sarran and her mother in the fall of 2000, they were living in Santa Cruz and trying to get a new start on life. Both had enrolled at the University of California campus there. We sat on a patio at the coastal school, looking at the Pacific shimmering in the late afternoon sun. It had been nine years since Daphne, who was twenty-two when I met her, had left the Family. "When I got out of the group, one of the strange feelings I had was feeling guilty for not feeling guilty about what I'd done. Our sexual maps were so distorted. It's a lot of work reintegrating into society, to have a social face, and to find out that everything you lived and believed up to that point was a lie. I still feel like I don't know who I am."

Rebecca Ann Parker is an ordained Methodist minister and president of Starr King School of Ministry, a Unitarian-Universalist seminary and member of the Graduate Theological Union consortium on Berkeley's Holy Hill. We're sitting in her office and talking about sex. She is a short woman with an easy smile and gray hair cut in a short and simple style. Parker and I were both born in 1953, smack-dab in the middle of the baby boom years, and we both came of age in the middle of the sexual revolution.

"I was just coming of age in the early 1970s and remember the sexual freedom of the time. There was a sense that old boundaries were oppressive and destroying the life spirit. In a lot of ways that was true. The old boundaries were not healthy, but not having any values was also unhealthy. It wasn't that good for women, it wasn't that good for children, and maybe it wasn't that good for men either.

"In the last thirty years we've been reconstructing an understanding of right relationship, or ethical boundaries," she said. "You had the women's movement deeply divided over pornography or S&M. Okay. Let's say 'sex is good' rather than 'sex is bad.' I'm for that. But that kind of either-or is not an adequate way of parsing the problem. It's more complex than that. Even when you say sexuality is good, you have to ask 'When is it good?' Sex is this wonderful thing, but it's a little like fire. It can warm you, or it can burn you."

My next question to Parker was about sexual ethics—about the widespread disagreement in America today about what kind of sex is "good" and what kind of sex is "bad." What's the connection between our attitudes about monogamy and homosexuality and our religious tradition?

"There is a connection between monotheism and monogamy. Being faithful to the one true God. You have images of idolatry and apostasy being articulated as adultery or sexual licentiousness. Your right relationship to God is monogamous. You have one God like you have no other loves. Then you've got the notion of God creating male and female to be right with God. Those are the orders of creation. So to follow God's orders is to be heterosexual. Actually, the Bible itself has many more complicated human sexual behaviors than that. But for those of us born in the fifties, the ethics of that era were, monogamous heterosexuality was right and sex outside of marriage was wrong. If you were a Catholic you also had the idea that sex for pleasure was wrong. What evolved from the 1950s was the idea that, well, maybe sexuality is good. Then the idea that sexual diversity was good."

Okay, I replied, so far, so good. But on what do you base a sexual ethic if you don't base it on God, the Bible, or religious tradition?

"I, myself, would base it on what's good for children," Parker replied. "I think it's good for children to have adults who are committed to them without question."

Her answer gave me pause. One of the themes running through my interviews with people born into the spiritual counterculture of the Sixties was this feeling that their parents were not there for them. It didn't matter that they were worshiping strange gods, following some messianic prophet, or living promiscuous lives. It wasn't that Mom and Dad were out saving the world or spreading Krishna consciousness, but simply that they were not available to the family.

Rebecca Ann Parker is the daughter of a Methodist minister. When she was five years old and living in a small town in Washington State, she was molested by a neighbor. His name was Frank. He's dead, but Parker is just now coming fully alive, finally able to put that trauma behind her. She now sees that her reaction to her abuse has everything to do with her strong Christian upbringing. Her religious education taught her to model her behavior on how Jesus reacted to his crucifixion and not to question a theology that says God allowed his only son to go through this horrid ordeal. "God required his son to suffer in order to save the world," she told me. "That is an image of God as a child abuser, and Jesus is imaged as the perfect victim. He accepts the abuse and does it silently. He is praised in his religious community for accepting abuse as the highest form of love."

Parker does not want to throw stones at the church. But she has been trying to understand how her own tradition of liberal Protestantism influenced her life and her relationships with men in the decades following her sexual abuse. "Liberal Protestantism throws out that idea of God as a wrathful father who demands the punishment of sinners and instead has this loving father and Jesus as the example of self-sacrificing love. I swallowed this image of Christian love where one thinks only of the welfare of others and disregards the well-being of the self. There is a lot of value in that, but it also replicates the socialization of women as not having a self that matters. It defines love in a way that the person who is loving disappears."

When we spoke, Parker had recently coauthored a book in which stories of her childhood abuse and two unsuccessful marriages emerge as major themes.[25] She tells how—ten years into her first marriage—her husband convinced her to have an abortion then left her for another woman. She went on to a successful career as one of the first women in the country to run a Protestant seminary in the United States. But she never got pregnant again or had children. "I think the place where I most internalized the theology of self-sacrifice was when I had that abortion. That has remained in my life as a really sad experience. In some ways, it was the worst experience of my life. That was where, well—I don't know."

Rebecca was close to tears. "It was a turning point. It cost me too much, but that was when I really started to question all this," she told me. "Writing is a way of passing something on. For me, this book was a kind of birth giving, becoming more of a whole person. This was the vow I made to the unborn child."

As I sat in Parker's office, the irony of the scene dawned on me. Neither Rebecca nor I had ever had children of our own. It was a loss in both of our lives. In a way, her book and this one of mine are about the children neither of us ever had.

Those of us who came of age after the Pill were almost able to separate sex from love, sex from marriage, sex from children. That was revolutionary, and it was liberating. Rebecca and I were both young enough for the sexual revolution to affect us as children and old enough to live through it as adults. My parents' divorce was a product of those times, and I carried that lesson with me. God was dead, and so was holy matrimony. When I became an adult, the Pill did not always separate coitus from conception, but my sexual partners in the seventies were liberated women who'd won the right to abortion on demand. We conceived. They aborted. In the eighties, when the party was winding down, I did marry. Once we decided to have children, my wife and I discovered fertility problems that made it impossible to conceive. That was hard. The marriage ended. Liberation turned to loss. But the wheel keeps on turning. Loss can also lead to liberation.

Women's liberation and the sexual revolution were among the most powerful forces stirred up by the social and spiritual upheaval on the Sixties, and they continue to shape our lives. Rebecca and I both came of age in the center of that cyclone. For better and for worse, we lived through the sexual revolution as children and adults. It brought us liberation as well as confusion, and that mix of emotions inspired both of us to write it down, to figure out what happened back then and wonder about what follows the bliss.

This book is not about me. It is not a memoir. Yet, like the song says, every picture tells a story, and every book tells something of its author. This book is about the spirituality of the Sixties, but it is also very much about a crisis of faith and family. At some point along the way, I began to see my role in this work as a kind of translator between two generations, the master of ceremonies in a reunion of Sixties' veterans and the children they brought into this world.

Sometimes, as with Rebecca and me, it's about children unborn and babies never conceived. It's about children who die too soon or about those of us not born at the right time. For millions, the Pill was a godsend. The revolution in birth control and the liberation of our libidos allowed us to revel in sexual bliss. But it also sent down many ghosts, melancholy apparitions of what could have been.

Then there were those other pills, some that made you larger and some that made you small. Psychedelics made it easier to see God, but they made it harder to get rid of the ghosts.

CHAPTER 8

God and Drugs:
Coming Home from
the Long, Strange Trip

And you've just had some kind of mushroom
And your mind is movin' along.

"WHITE RABBIT"
GRACE SLICK, JEFFERSON AIRPLANE 1967

It had been twenty-five years since I'd sat down in the Life Sciences Building at the University of California in Berkeley, but this gathering felt more like a flashback than a reunion. At the bottom of the steeply terraced lecture hall, a gaggle of undergraduates crowded around a table piled high with free literature. The most popular items were glossy, full-color postcards describing the ups and downs of various drugs—acid, Ecstasy, cocaine, tobacco, mushrooms, heroin. They're published by DanceSafe, a group committed to "promoting health and safety within the rave and nightclub community." On the purple Ecstasy postcard, a monarch butterfly makes a soft landing in the valley of the *y*. It reports on the back that users of this drug, also known as MDMA, will "experience heightened feelings of empathy, emotional warmth and self-acceptance." It warns that the drug "can take on great importance in people's lives," leading to compulsive use. Users may also be "unconsciously trying to self-medicate for depression."

Standing at the table, one young student grabs another postcard and turns to her friend. "I love this," she says. "It's not like they're telling us what to do and not to do."

These kids have never seen anything like it. They grew up with DARE, the "just say no" approach to drug education, and these proceedings do not have the Nancy Reagan stamp of approval. Reaching around the two co-eds, I collect another brochure. This one asks, "What is Cognitive Liberty?" Published by the Alchemind Society, it explains that "cognitive liberty is freedom of thought—the right of each individual to think independently, to use the full spectrum of his or her mind, and to engage in multiple modes of thought and alternative states of consciousness." It warns that the war on drugs "is a real and present encroachment upon these fundamental freedoms."

We're advised to take our seats because the program is about to begin. It's sponsored by Students for a Sensible Drug Policy, and it's titled "Religious Freedoms, Spirituality, and Shamanic Practices." I sit down about halfway up the lecture hall, next to two guys who look like they're fifteen years old but are probably nineteen or twenty. These errors of perception can occur when middle-aged men return to old college classrooms.

"Have you ever tried speed?" one guys asks the other. "It's just like cocaine but can make you psychotic."

Then they notice the large sign with the title of the program and start a conversation about shamanic practices. One of the guys isn't sure what that means.

"Man, that's been a field of studies since the sixties," his friend explains. "It's studying consciousness and shit like that."

"Wow," the other guy says. "That would be cool if you could use it for something."

It's time to start the program. The place is packed with students sitting in the aisles and filling the window wells. It begins with a slim young woman with long brown hair parted down the middle. She's wearing a turquoise, tie-dyed T-shirt over a long-sleeved black turtleneck.

"My name is Ann, and I'm a survivor of DARE," she begins. "We're going to tell you what DARE didn't teach you."

Ann proceeds to read from a wrinkled pile of pages. Her topic is entheogens, substances that allow you to see God. Entheogens "offer a different lens through which to view nature," she says. Ann's favorite entheogens are magic mushrooms, partly because you can grow them yourself from spores and thereby bypass "the alienating culture of capitalism."

Her talk drags on too long. It sounds like some of those revelatory and really bad college papers I wrote back in my days as a Berkeley undergraduate. Tuning out, I look over the program to see who else is speaking. My eye is drawn to a woman named Mariavittoria Mangini. She's the author of a research paper titled "Yes, Mom Took Acid: The Sociohistorical Impact of Historic Psychedelic Drug Use in Adults."

Mangini is a family nurse practitioner with a Ph.D. in community health nursing from the University of California at San Francisco. But it turns out she's lived most of her adult life with the Hog Farm Commune, a fun-loving group of unrepentant hippies led by the infamous Wavy Gravy. He's that clown who appeared on the stage at Woodstock and said something like "What we've got in mind is breakfast in bed for five hundred thousand." Wavy is an institution in northern California. Every year he and his cohorts sponsor the Hog Farm Pignic on their land near Laytonville, which also happens to be surrounded by some of the finest and best-hidden marijuana fields in America. There is music and food and camping and lots of fun at the Pignic. A few years ago there was a grand parade around the fairgrounds with flowing costumes, banners, and colorful characters on giant stilts. Behind it all was Wavy Gravy, dressed like a Roman emperor, carried on a throne, and holding up a sign that read, People of the World . . . Relax!

So it was with great expectation that I awaited the address of Mariavittoria Mangini, the founder of the Black Oak Ranch Free Medical Clinic at the Hog Farm. Taking the podium, she looked more like a middle-aged librarian than an unrepentant hippie, but perhaps that's because she spent six years of the 1990s in libraries reviewing thousands of articles on the therapeutic use of psychedelic drugs. Mangini is particularly interested in the stories of people over forty-five years of age who took psychedelics at least three times. They have great stories to tell, and from them she has discovered twenty-three themes to these narrative histories. The most universal theme reported by psychedelic veterans are memories of a "sense of connectedness" while tripping on drugs. They report feeling a religious or mystical "state of grace" or an "undifferentiated unity."

Mangini read some of these stories and told us what those people are doing now. She then left her audience with an interesting question: Why is there such a discrepancy between those insights and the way many of those people are living their lives today?

It's a great question. Drugs were a gateway for many of us who came of age in the 1960s and 1970s. Sometimes the right drugs taken in the right place opened doors to powerful experiences of unity, connectedness, empathy, awe, and wonder. Those states do seem similar to the feelings that religious mystics and enlightened masters have been reporting for centuries. Over the years I've interviewed many baby boomers who told me that their interest in meditation, martial arts, or other spiritual disciplines were inspired by a dose of LSD or a bag of magic mushrooms back in the sixties and seventies. Others discovered new levels of intimacy and empathy with drugs such as MDA or Ecstasy, forging lifelong friendships and new ways of relating to people. Yet the wrong drugs taken at the wrong time can open a gateway to hell—to paranoia, hopelessness, and psychosis. Psychedelic drugs are double-edged swords. They can cut through illusion or create it. They can feed your head or cut it off. They can jump-start a spiritual life or destroy it. What seems like revelation one day can reveal itself the next as a cruel joke. What seems like life-changing love can vanish overnight, leaving disillusionment, depression, and despair. Aldous Huxley, the novelist and influential author of *The Doors of Perception,* noted long ago that psychedelic drugs can give us a glimpse of heaven or a trip straight to hell. You have to be smart—or at least careful—to take these things. It's not always clear where the chemical stops and the real love starts. Where's the mysticism, and where's the madness? Tough questions, so let's turn to two of the guys who signed us up for this wonderful mess.

Richard Alpert and Huston Smith were both professors in Massachusetts when the long strange trip began. It was, of course, 1960. Smith was in the humanities department at the Massachusetts Institute of Technology, and Alpert was a young assistant professor of psychology at Harvard. In the fall of 1960 Smith helped bring Huxley to the MIT campus as that year's "distinguished humanist." It was not the first time the two men had met. Smith had been blown away by *The Doors of Perception,* published in 1953, and Huxley's book on mysticism, *The Perennial Philosophy*. A book written by a longtime Huxley associate, Gerald Heard, titled *Pain, Sex, and Time,* had also rocked his world. Smith sought out the two authors, who would be his virtual gurus over the next decade. Smith had long been fascinated by the stories of religious mystics. He had tried meditation and—like many of us—found that nothing extraordinary really happened. He found Heard in a hideaway in Trabucco Canyon outside Los Angeles. Heard led him to Huxley, who was with his wife, Maria, at their cabin hideout in the Mojave Desert.

Flash forward to late 1960. Huxley was a visiting lecturer at MIT. Huston asked Aldous to give him some mescaline so he could finally experience the mystical states he'd been reading and writing about for so long. Huxley suggested that he call a guy at Harvard named Timothy Leary. He did, and the two men met in the Harvard faculty club.

Leary was studying the effects of psychedelics on convicts through the Center for Personality Research. He was also dosing himself and a growing number of student devotees. Leary arrived at the faculty club wearing expensive English tweeds, leather elbow patches, and brand-new white sneakers that glowed like luminescent clouds. Sure, he was happy to schedule a mescaline session, so the two scholars started flipping through their calendars. "How about New Year's Day?" Leary asked, smiling like an Irish rascal. They had a date.

"What a way to start the sixties," Smith reminisced, his eyes widening.

We were sitting in the bright light of a late Berkeley morning at Smith's home in North Berkeley, just a few blocks from mine. More than four decades had passed since that New Year's trip. Professor Smith was in his eighties now. He had trouble hearing and was recovering from a recent hip replacement, but his mind and spirits were in fine shape.

If you took Religious Studies 101 as an undergraduate, you may be one of the two million people who've purchased his classic text, *The World's Religions,* since the first edition came out in 1958 under the title *The Religions of Man.* Smith's lifework and passion have been to explain the religion of others amid an ever-worsening epidemic of religious illiteracy. So before we get to that mescaline trip with Timothy Leary, let's chronicle a few earlier chapters in this amazing life.

Huston Smith was born in China to Methodist missionary parents, and he spent the first seventeen years of his life in a village about seventy miles inland from Shanghai. His maternal grandmother first came to the East on a nineteenth-century clipper ship. Smith's mother was born in China, which by one reckoning makes this man of solid Midwestern stock a second-generation Chinese American. "In those days the missionaries were always pushing to go where Christ had not been preached," Smith told me. "My parents spotted some place on the map, went there, and wound up spending the next forty-three years there, until the Communist revolution in 1949. They were almost at retirement age then anyway. In our town in China, I had only one adult male role model—my father. I grew up thinking that missionaries were what missionary sons grew up to be."

At seventeen Smith made his first visit to the United States, for missionary training at a small Bible college chosen by his father. "I was totally unprepared for the dynamism of the West. It was only a little Methodist college in a town of three thousand in Missouri. But compared to Podunk, China, in those days, it was bright lights and the Big Apple!"[26]

Smith had planned to return to rural China as a missionary, plans that lasted two weeks once he landed in the States. The obvious alternative was to stay in the United States as a Methodist minister, but after two years on that track Smith decided that teaching, not preaching, was his true calling. He taught at Washington University in St. Louis, MIT, Syracuse University, and the University of California at Berkeley. It was at MIT that he met Leary, then a little-known Harvard professor.

On New Year's Day, 1961, Professor Smith ingested his first dose of mescaline at Leary's home in Newton, Massachusetts. "The whole world into which I was ushered was strange, weird, uncanny, significant, and terrifying beyond belief," he wrote the next day. "The mescaline acted as a psychological prism. It was as if the infinitely complex and layered psychological ingredients which normally are smelted down into a single band was weak. Nondescript sensation-impressions were now being refracted, spread out as if by a spectroscope, into about five layers."

Smith suddenly saw what one scholar meant when he described the brain as a reducing valve. He experienced what Buddhist and Hindu mystics had been describing for millennia. But there was a problem: "How could these layers upon layers, these worlds within worlds, be put into words? I realized how utterly impossible it would be for me to describe them on the morrow when I had lost this world of perception."

There was awesome significance to everything, but there was also great terror. There was heaven and hell, just like Huxley had warned. "I was aware of my body, laid out as if half-dead on a slab, cool and slightly moist. But I also had the sense that the body could only function if my spirit chose to return to it, infuse it, and animate it. Should it so choose? There seemed no particular reason why it should do so. Moreover, could it do so if it chose? A number of religious traditions have the idea that no man can see God and live—the vision would be too much for the body to stand, like plugging an electric toaster into a major power source without a condenser, the body would simply shatter."[27]

Huston Smith did come back to his body and had six or seven more psychedelic drug trips in the early sixties. Smith prefers the word *entheogen* to *hallucinogen*, based on his belief that the visions and states of consciousness he experienced were not hallucinations but doorways to divinity. Except for a few peyote trips in the early 1990s—sessions held to better understand the rites of the Native American Church—Smith has stayed away from these powerful plants and chemicals. He had seen the "clear light of the void" along with some darker sides of himself. "Oh, yes," he says. "There were some bummers."

Smith thinks Leary "careened off course" in 1963, after his New Year's Day trip master was kicked out of Harvard and became the world's leading evangelist for LSD. Leary's infamous mantra, "Turn on, tune in, drop out," was not what Professor Smith had in mind. Instead, he took the advice of Leary's partner in his Harvard studies, Richard Alpert, who would reincarnate later as Ram Dass. Spiritual seekers would often ask Alpert if they should continue taking psychedelics as a spiritual practice. "Once you get the message," he advised, "hang up the phone."

Ram Dass has been a harbinger for the baby boomers since his Harvard days. Both he and Leary were fired, but their psychedelic explorations continued in the early sixties at a country estate called Millbrook. "We have parties to hold and research to do," Alpert explained at the time. "We teach the science and art of ecstasy." For better or worse, Millbrook set the stage for a decade of druggies who blasted off toward higher consciousness. Sometimes they never came back to Earth.

Alpert shifted gears and went off to India, where he found a guru and a less-toxic method of mind expansion—meditation and religious devotion. He came back transformed into Ram Dass, the "servant of God," wrote *Be Here Now*, and inspired countless other spiritual seekers.

Richard Alpert was born on April 6, 1931, in the north end of Boston. His father, George Alpert, was a lawyer and leader in the Boston Jewish community, helping children displaced from Germany. Dad also became chairman of the board of Brandeis University and later president of the New York, New

Haven, and Hartford Railroad, where he had his own private rail car. Ram Dass once told me a story about his father coming to see him for the first time in his new incarnation as a guru from the East. His son had white robes, a long beard, and devotees sitting at his feet.

"So what do you think, Pop?" Ram Dass asked.

"One question," his father replied. "Does this make me the Virgin Mary?"

During much of the 1980s and 1990s, Ram Dass continued the charitable leanings of his father, lending his name and energies to a series of humanitarian projects. He also became one of the most sought after speakers on the New Age conference, workshop, and lecture circuit, where he was known for his ability to convey mystical ideas with lucidity, humor, and grace. I've interviewed Ram Dass quite a few times over the years, but the most powerful conversation we ever had was in the spring of 1997, three months after his brain and body were shaken by a massive stroke, leaving him without speech and paralyzing his right side. It was his first interview since the stroke, and this once-articulate teacher spoke with great difficulty.

On that day Ram Dass sat in the darkening shadow of a long evening, his wheelchair pushed against an old picnic table behind his Marin County home. There was a long silence.

"The mind . . . ," he said.

Leaves rustled in a soft breeze. Water tumbled over rock in a small creek behind his overgrown garden.

"The mind . . . ," he said again.

Silence.

His eyes closed, and his head tilt heavenward, searching for words.

"Doctors see the brain as the mind," he said in a sudden rush of language. "What I'm observing with is not necessarily in their purview."

The loss of language frustrated Ram Dass. Nevertheless, if you listened to him with patience, the old message still got through. When explaining how he must now be eloquent with silence rather than words, Ram Dass took a minute and actually said, "If you . . . if you . . . like a friend of me, of mine, said . . . you've been so eloquent . . . um . . . aren't you eloquent with words, uh, with silence . . . eloquent with silence?"[28]

And he still had his sense of humor. When he "got stroked," Ram Dass was trying his hand at talk radio, hoping to raise the consciousness of a medium known for its vindictiveness. "Talk radio," he said with a smile, "is down the tubes." He was also writing a book to be called *Conscious Aging*. When the stroke hit, he saw he had some difficult fieldwork ahead of him. His stroke and recovery in a northern California nursing home changed his thoughts on aging. "I started the book with my Harvard professorial perspective but decided to make it a more personal account. I didn't want this book to be, 'Now we'll look at this spiritually.' Here I was in an old folks' home up in northern California where patients were screaming, 'I want to get out,' from midnight to four. It was like an old folks' jail."

Ram Dass had watched the passing of two other men whose lives embodied the magic and the mischief of the Sixties, Allen Ginsberg and Tim Leary. Leary turned his death from cancer into a media event and protracted party at his Beverly Hills home, broadcasting daily updates of his demise on the World Wide Web. "We met as adventurers and wisdom seekers," Ram Dass recalled. "Tim did something no one ever did before. He tried to show that the dying process could be fun. But he didn't really deal with death itself. People who wanted a wisdom thing from Tim misunderstood it. Tim was playing his role, but he was not that role. It was a performance."

Ram Dass said his stroke and the deaths of his friends have helped him understand why many old people seem to live in the past. "Older people see that getting older has nothing to offer them but strokes and the process of death. Before my stroke, I was looking forward to the things I wanted to do."

"Are you still?"

"No," Ram Dass said.

Silence.

"But," he said with a smile, "I'm still committed to be here now."

A few years later, in a film about his life titled *Fierce Grace,* Ram Dass said he felt "like an advance guard calling back to the baby boomers." His speech was still slowed by the lingering effects of the stroke. "Now I am calling back from aging."

What's the message?

"It will be sooner than you think."

The most powerful scene in the film comes toward the end, when a young woman comes to see Ram Dass to talk about the death of her lover, a political activist who'd been murdered in Latin America. They had a deep love and spiritual bond, and suddenly it was gone and he was gone. She tells Ram Dass about a dream she had a month after the murder. She and her lover were embracing. She was kissing his temples. She asked him what she should do if she finds another lover, someone who can continue what they had begun.

"Abbey," he said in the dream, "that was peanuts. When you find that love, I'm part of it."

Her story hit Ram Dass like lightning. He gasped and managed to say, "Oh ... God! ... Yum! Yum! Yum," before collapsing into ecstasy and tears in his wheelchair. Then, "Whew ... boy ... that's ... strong."

After about a minute, Ram Dass told her, "You had that relationship. You know how few have a relationship like that. . . ."

Abbey started crying. Ram Dass rubbed his forehead and said, slowly, "My guru said suffering brought him close to God. That's the kind of work we do on this plane. The death of a lover is a path."

The stroke brought Ram Dass close to his own death. But he had no great vision or epiphanies—no long tunnels, no white lights. "Here I am, 'Mr. Spiritual,' and in my own death I didn't orient toward the spirit," he said. "It shows me that I have some work to do. I flunked the test."

Coming from a guru, that kind of honesty is extraordinarily refreshing. It reminds me of another story I did involving Ram Dass. It was back in 1988 when Ram Dass spoke at a conference called "Promises and Pitfalls of the Spiritual Path." Gathered at the Tropicana El Rancho Hotel in Santa Rosa, California, was the who's who of the New Age—Eastern mystics, Western psychologists, astral travelers, brain researchers, crystal peddlers, and psychic channelers. But it was Ram Dass who summed up this amorphous movement's twenty-five-year search for peace, love, and cosmic consciousness. "We had this expectation that the spiritual path would be healthy psychologically," he said. "I was trained as a psychologist. I was in analysis for many years. I taught Freudian theory. I took drugs for six years intensively. I have meditated regularly since 1970. I have taught yoga. I have studied Sufism and many kinds of Buddhism. In all that time, I have not gotten rid of one neurosis— not one!"

After luxuriating in the sexual revolution, he said, many spiritual seekers turned to celibate lifestyles of renunciation. "A lot of us just became horny celibates."

While he may have as many neuroses as he did in the early sixties, Ram Dass wasn't suggesting that the last two decades had not changed him. "What has changed is I am much less identified with my known neuroses and my own desires. If I don't get what I want, it's as interesting as if I do get it. It's the game of dying into yourself. If you get phony holy, it ends up kicking you in the butt. You've got to stay true to yourself."

Two years later Ram Dass was at the Claremont Hotel in Berkeley with Leary and six hundred other proponents of enlightenment through chemicals. For nearly twelve hours they tried to assess the social and psychological aftereffects of the long strange trip and chart a future path. Sharing the stage with Leary and Ram Dass were leading psychedelic researchers, a Navajo peyote priest, the widow of Aldous Huxley, and a former Justice Department drug policy analyst wearing a tie-dyed T-shirt. Despite the political climate of the 1990s, Leary and Ram Dass still sang the praises of LSD, psilocybin, and Ecstasy. "Psychedelics allowed us to override our habits of thinking," Ram Dass said. "It opened up our link to the East and to an incredibly rich philosophical, psychological, and spiritual heritage." Millions of people used psychedelics as rites of passage in the sixties and seventies, he said, opening up a generation to ways of thinking that go beyond the rational and intellectual, into the "intuitive, transcendental, unitive perspective."

Sure, there were mistakes of excess in the psychedelic revolution. "Tim and I had a chart on the wall about how soon everyone would be enlightened. We talked about how we would retool Detroit when nobody wanted cars anymore. We found out that real change is harder. We downplayed the fact that the psychedelic experience isn't for everyone." Giving LSD to undergraduates, Alpert said, was "my personal error. . . . I did that for many reasons. Sexual was not excluded."

Nevertheless, Ram Dass said the psychedelic Sixties profoundly changed his life and nudged American society in another direction. "Psychedelics have to be honored, and they will continue to be honored. The profundity of the social changes wrought by the Sixties are inculcated into our culture. There is a deep, meditative investment of those values in our society, whether you call it stress reduction or whatever. It is there, and it is growing all the time. "

Later, in a book published following Leary's death in 1996, Ram Dass described the psychedelic legacy in more graphic terms. "It was a mushroom and it did explode, and it was carried through the hippies, through the minstrels, through the rock-and-roll movement; it was carried into the collective consciousness, and it has mainstreamed in collective consciousness, and it has to do with the relative nature of reality.

"The Sixties scared the hell out of the culture," he added, "because they showed another potential exists for people."[29]

Four decades after Timothy Leary and Richard Alpert were kicked out of Harvard, I stumbled across a story strangely reminiscent of their psychedelic adventure.[30] This time the venue was St. John the Evangelist Episcopal Church, and the protagonists were the members of the Divine Rhythm Society, a group of mostly young seekers with roots in the San Francisco rave scene in the late 1980s and early 1990s.

Historians of rave culture (yes, they do exist) see its roots in the early years of hippiedom. In case you missed them, raves are all-night dance parties held in, among other places, abandoned warehouses in New York, London, and San Francisco. They began as underground events fueled by technomusic, videos, computers, and energizing, empathy-producing drugs such as Ecstasy. But they can be traced back to 1964 and the infamous acid tests held by Ken Kesey and his Merry Pranksters. Shortly before his death, Leary attended a few raves and blessed these "high-tech hippies" for "capturing the spirit of the Sixties."

What does this all have to do with an Episcopal church named after Saint John the Evangelist? Well, flash forward to 2003 and (where else?) San Francisco. Founded in 1870, St. John's is a little gem of a church in a tough corner of the Mission District. Today it is a predominantly gay and lesbian congregation that calls itself "a community of faith welcoming all colors, cultures, and sexual orientations." But that did not stop a bitter fight from breaking out early that year between the old pillars of the church and the young folks in the Divine Rhythm Society.

For six years, the society's All-Night Dance Celebrations had packed St. John's with hundreds of young people seeking connection and community. They'd grown so fast that they far outnumbered this congregation of some eighty Episcopalians. Officially an outreach program for the church, the rhythm society grew into a semiautonomous wing of the congregation, with about twenty folks formally joining both the dance group and the Episcopal parish. But up to four hundred people attended the invitation-only All-Night Dance Celebrations.

They peacefully coexisted with the parishioners until the summer of 2002, when a nonfatal drug overdose and alleged cover-up by the church rector sparked a bitter battle for the soul of St. John's. The young rector supported the rhythm society and attended most of the All-Night Dance Celebrations. That prompted some members of the parish to call for his resignation, charging that he cared more about the pagan revelers than his own Christian flock. Others said the drug issue was a red herring used by conservatives trying to get the rector and the rhythm society out of the parish.

After one Sunday service, I sat in the garden courtyard outside the wood-shingled church, talking to the parishioners. It was now January 2003 and the tensions among the congregants were obvious to any visitor. The divided congregation still went through the motions of gathering together for Sunday worship. The rector and other clergy would don green and gold vestments and walk down the aisle, leading prayers and offering communion. But another spirit was at work inside St. John's. One side or the other passed out leaflets. There was gossip, backbiting, and lots of whispering in the pews. Intrigue ruled the coffee hour.

Episcopal bishop William Swing had held a series of peacekeeping meetings to try to bring the parish together. They failed, and after three days of intense negotiations, the rector agreed to resign, along with the entire parish vestry. The rhythm society agreed to leave the parish, and a new vestry was elected. Swing (yes, that's his real name) told me had no objection to people dancing the night away in the churches of the Diocese of California. "People all over the world dance to commune with God," he said. "Some people kneel, some people dance. The Episcopal Church is not against dancing.

"But to have it drug enhanced," he added, "is to risk the terror and agony of drug abuse."

Swing acted after a member of the church vestry sent him a lengthy report on the activities of the Divine Rhythm Society. It charged that a "significant number" of the participants at the all-night events took Ecstasy. The drug is among a family of chemicals known as entacogens, which translates as "touching within." They produce feelings of euphoria, empathy, and increased energy. But unlike LSD and other psychedelics, they rarely cause users to hallucinate or to lose control of themselves, although there can be harmful physical effects.

Like Huston Smith, some members of the rhythm society saw Ecstasy as an entheogen, a chemical door to greater spiritual or psychological awareness. "We use entheogens to reach for God," one member said, "not to get high."

Some of the celebrants of the Divine Rhythm Society were no doubt taking MDMA or something else. But many of these recovering ravers *were* trying to cultivate the spirit of ecstasy without taking the drug. Many were looking for actual community and connection—not one based on e-mail messages and a quarterly dose. They wanted to go beyond the one-night revelations and instant intimacy found in a crowded warehouse. They referred to their entheogens as "training wheels" and "door openers," implying they were just one step along the spiritual path. Many of them had stopped dabbling in drugs and *were* just dancing toward the divine. And in doing so, they were continuing in the tradition of Ram Dass and other early explorers of altered consciousness, looking for less toxic ways to find God and love one another.

At the same time, there was something wrong with the community fostered by the rhythm society. It wasn't a real community, an actual place in time and space where different kinds of people live together. Like the "Hispanic community" or the "gay community," it was more of an interest group than a true community. They locked the church gates and held private parties. Between their quarterly gatherings, members of the rhythm society kept in touch via e-mail. It was a virtual community. I'm sure some of these folks did use MDMA to forge real and lasting bonds at the All-Night Dance Celebrations, relationships that will last much longer than the marathon dance parties. But for many others, I suspect that the empathy and compassion they felt on Ecstasy was just as fleeting, just as virtual, as the community they thought they had found at St. John's. For them, the church and its stained glass and its peaceful courtyard were a venue. The real community was the Episcopal Parish of St. John the Evangelist.

One leader of the Divine Rhythm Society compared their gatherings to those of the Native American Church, which legally uses peyote as a sacrament in its indigenous faith. In fact, there is no comparison other than the fact that both ceremonies use drugs and go on all night. I know, because I had the privilege to participate in a Navajo peyote rite. It was not fun, but it was unforgettable.

It was the summer of 1989, and Emerson Jackson, the president of the Native American Church of North America, had invited me to participate in a Saturday night peyote ritual not far from the Four Corners Monument. Jackson had waived the church's strict ban on outside visitors because the United States Supreme Court was about to hear arguments in a lawsuit involving two members of the Native American Church in Oregon. They had been fired from their jobs at a drug treatment center for participating in an all-night peyote ritual. Jackson wanted to show my readers and me that these gatherings were not wild drug parties but serious religious ceremonies. I could attend only if I agreed to take the peyote and not to take notes.

We met in a coffee shop in Shiprock, and I followed his car as he roared across the winding dirt roads of the vast Navajo reservation. We wound up outside a giant tepee erected earlier that day on a high bluff in the southeast corner of Utah. It was just before sunset, and members of the tribal clan were still arriving in an assortment of old cars and new pickup trucks. The ritual wouldn't start for hours, but the emotional, eleven-hour ceremony was to be a unique, powerful experience, a rare glimpse at the social, spiritual, and psychedelic world of the Native American Church's Half Moon Ceremony.

These gatherings are usually held for a particular purpose—to pray for a sick child or help a church member work through a life crisis. Terrance Tom's family sponsored the Saturday night session to pray for success in a new job that was taking Tom, his wife, and his three young children off the reservation and into the white man's world.

There was only one problem. Emerson had neglected to tell Terrance that he was bringing a reporter along with him. Some of the older Indians were not happy with the peyote priest and definitely not happy to see me. They wanted to know who I was, what I was going to write, and who was going to read it. There was a series of loud meetings, mostly in Navajo, before Jackson finally convinced the family that the upcoming Supreme Court case was important and people off the reservation needed to have a better understanding of the peyote circle. My story, he promised, would do that.

Twenty of us sat on the ground in a circle inside the tepee. We began the ceremony by rolling our own cigarettes in pieces of dried corn husk, smoking the tobacco as a ritual act of purification, the way Catholic priests use incense before mass. Most of the night was spent passing around a drum, gourd rattle, and peyote staff while we drummed and chanted guttural, fast-paced hymns. Periodically, a glass jar of dried peyote was passed around the tepee, and we chased it down with several swallows of the bitter peyote tea.

Jackson sprinkled some water on a handful of powdered cactus and molded the bitter potion into two balls about the size of strawberries. "This is a sacrament," he said, handing the psychedelic mixture to Tom.

Everyone inside the tepee had already ingested two or three tablespoons of dried peyote. Sometime after midnight, the Navajos' peyote fans—kaleidoscopes of bright feathers and intricate beadwork—took on a pulsing luminescence. American Indian chants, the gourd rattles, and the drum carried the congregation off to another reality. Chief Peyote, the psychedelic cactus button that inspires these ancient rites, was working its magic.

Speaking a mixture of Navajo and English, Tom humbly confessed his fears and insecurities about the coming move to Albuquerque. Tears rolled down his checks and welled up in the eyes of friends and family as they responded with encouragement and stream-of-consciousness prayers of support. Tom's wife and three young children were there throughout the night. Even the children, who slept on colorful Navajo rugs through most of the ceremony, took small amounts of peyote. Intense waves of emotion and empathy thundered through the tepee, forging a powerful unity of twenty souls.

Few foods on Earth taste as bad as peyote, which can easily turn the stomach. You don't leave the tepee to vomit. You do it right there where you are sitting, in the dirt, and someone comes around and cleans it up. I managed to keep the bitter mixture down but still wanted get out of the tepee. My mind was racing. I was torn between just letting the peyote sweep me away and holding on to my reporter's mind to remember everything that was going on. Was I here for them or for me? Meanwhile, I was getting hostile looks from some of the old Indian women, the ones who didn't want me there. They would lower their peyote fans and stare into my eyes with terrifying power.

Feeling claustrophobic and a bit paranoid, I got up and left the tepee. You were allowed to leave the sacred enclosure only briefly, to urinate, but once I got out into the night I could not return. It seemed impossible to leave the revelatory scene that awaited me outside. The stars were so brilliant and alive that they seemed to be, not above me, but surrounding me. Looking out from the bluff, I saw five or six other tepees glowing in the night across the vast reservation. There was a kind of magnetic power pulling me into the earth, so I lay down on the ground, flat on my back, and just melted into the dirt, staring up into the magnificent night. I don't know if I lay there for a minute or an hour before the face of one of the younger Indian men suddenly popped into my field of vision. "You must come back," he said, turning toward the tepee. I didn't want to go. I felt so much more at peace outside the teepee and by myself. But this was not for me. I was there to tell someone else's story.

Back inside, I took my place and watched the Fire Man tend a small fire in the middle of the tepee. There was an altar behind the fire—a three-inch-high sand sculpture in the shape of a long crescent. Chief Peyote—the bulbous cactus flower—sat atop the crescent of sand, watching us all. With amazing artistry, the Fire Man sculpted embers and ash into the glowing image of an eagle in flight. In the early morning hours, as the peyote priest blew on a whistle made from the bone of an eagle's wing, the eagle rose from the swept red dirt floor and flew out the top of the teepee. Amazed by that vision, I looked back down into the faces of the Navajo. One of the old women, one of the hostile ones with a dark and wrinkled face, sent me out a small smile, like she'd seen the same thing.

In the end I understood why the family was hesitant about having an outsider in their tepee. This was not just a religious service. It was also a session of family therapy conducted on psychedelic drugs. It was Thanksgiving dinner, a drug party, a religious ritual, and a visit to the family therapist all rolled into one.

Back in San Francisco, I talked about the experience with Ralph Metzner, who teaches at the California Institute for Integral Studies. A veteran researcher of the psychedelic experience, Metzner was at Harvard back in the early sixties with Timothy Leary and Richard Alpert. He nodded knowingly when I told him what happened with the Navajo.

"Native Americans regard the peyote ceremony as religious, medicinal, and psychotherapeutic. It's an integrated, holistic approach, and a genuine religious experience," he said. "The white man goes to church and hears about God. The Indians go to the peyote circle and talk to God."[31]

For many of us who came of age in the Sixties, going to church and hearing about God were not enough. Psychedelics gave us an experience so powerful that Presbyterian prayers or Roman Catholic communion seemed irrelevant and weak. Mainstream religion seemed to filter these experiences of unity, wonder, and bliss. In the fifties and sixties, churches and synagogues seemed to be more about social convention than spiritual connection. We wanted to talk to God. We wanted to see God. We wanted the experience.

Drugs are like fire. They can ignite the spirit, but they can also fry the brain. Most of us eventually turned down the heat. For many, meditation and other spiritual practices kept the spark alive. And then there were those who found their fire in the Holy Spirit and their ecstasy in rock 'n' roll.

CHAPTER 9

God and Rock 'n' Roll: Conservative Evangelicals Go Electric

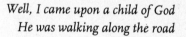

Well, I came upon a child of God
He was walking along the road

"WOODSTOCK"
JONI MITCHELL, 1969

I f you can remember the Sixties, you weren't really there. I can't remember when I first had the following revelation, but I was sitting in some lively Pentecostal church, tapping one foot to the rhythm while the church band and whole congregation rocked and rolled around me. They were swaying in ecstasy, hands and eyes pointed heavenward, while I was sitting there taking notes, trying not to look totally out of place. But what I most remember that morning in church was writing down three words in my reporter's notebook, writing them large and then underlining them so I wouldn't forget:

IT'S THE MUSIC!

There are lots of theories as to why Pentecostal Christianity is one of the fastest growing religious movements on Earth. It is an experiential faith. People have powerful spiritual experiences like speaking in tongues and feeling healed by the power of the Holy Spirit. It is prophetic, giving hope to poor and oppressed people around the world. It is evangelical, spreading its message wherever it goes. They all make a certain amount of sense, but here's my theory:

IT'S THE MUSIC!

Music has the power to take us outside ourselves, just like other vehicles of transcendence, such as meditation or prayer. Christians and Jews have been singing the praises of the psalms since ancient times. Byzantine monks sang *Kyrie eleison* in response to prayers, Roman and Gaelic music fused into the Gregorian chant, and majestic melodies filled the cathedrals of Europe. Martin Luther took music from the priests and gave it to the people, placing the hymnal alongside the Bible in Protestant worship. African Americans took the pain of slavery and the joy of Jesus and brought the world gospel music, soul music, and rhythm and blues. Rock 'n' roll was on its way and here to stay.

Back in the Sixties, you had to go to black churches to find music that swayed the body and the soul. But in recent years I've heard some decent music coming out of white churches. At first it seemed out of place, like the wrong sound track was playing with this movie. Not anymore, not since Christian rock came of age.

Almost four decades ago something that would soon be known as the San Francisco sound blew out the doors of the Red Dog Saloon. Actually, this funky bar is not in San Francisco but in Virginia City, Nevada, an old mining town on the other side of the Sierra. Mark Twain used to write for the local paper in Virginia City, and it's too bad he wasn't around in the summer of 1965. The house band at the Red Dog was the Charlatans, some boys who'd drifted up to town from the Haight-Ashbury district of San Francisco. The boys in the band were not great musicians, but they had a passion for the seminal blues guitar of Robert Johnson. They didn't sound much like Robert Johnson. They didn't sound like much of anything, partly because they were so stoned most of the time. But from these discordant beginnings, the historians of rock 'n' roll trace a musical movement that would soon blossom to include such bands as the Grateful Dead, Jefferson Airplane, and Big Brother and the Holding Company, featuring a young singer who blew in from Texas named Janis Joplin.[32]

Two years later, in the summer of 1967, Joplin gave a scorching performance on the stage of the Monterey International Pop Festival, when the nation's music critics discovered both the San Francisco sound and the new vibe hovering over the region. Monterey set the stage for Woodstock, the event that turned rock music into a billion-dollar business. Scott McKenzie's tribute to the Haight, "San Francisco (Be Sure to Wear Some Flowers in Your Hair)" was on the radio and giving ideas to a whole generation of naive and alienated teenagers—me included. Unfortunately, I never made it to Monterey or San Francisco in 1967. My pilgrimage up Highway 1 came two years later.

Three decades later I *was* on the cutting edge at another rock music festival in Monterey. That weekend crisp guitar riffs and a booming beat thundered through the hills around Laguna Seca Raceway. Peter Furler, leader of the Newsboys, ran toward the edge of the stage and leaned out to a pulsing throng of ecstatic teenagers. "God is not a secret!" screamed the thirty-year-old Australian singer, drummer, and songwriter. "God is not a secret to be kept!"

Thirty years after the Monterey Pop Festival made music history, ten thousand Christian music fans had flocked to the Spirit West Coast festival. It was Woodstock resurrected for a new wave of Jesus freaks. There was pop, rock, grunge, rap, ska, hip-hop, country, and traditional gospel music. What tied it all together was the fact that everyone was singing about Jesus.

Rock 'n' roll—once condemned as the devil's music—has been embraced by American evangelicals. In the 1990s Christian rock was the fastest-growing segment of the mainstream music industry. Gospel rock CDs were going platinum—selling a million copies—and topping the charts as major record companies gobbled up obscure Christian labels. That same month I was in Monterey, in the summer of 1997, Christian pop singer Bob Carlisle's *Butterfly Kisses*, featuring slick, sentimental songs about faith and fatherhood, was number one on Billboard's list of the Top Twenty albums, outselling even the Spice Girls. Just down the list, at number seven, was the twenty-seven-year-old Dallas youth choir leader Kirk Franklin and his gospel/hip-hop album *God's Property*. Other bigtime gospel rock bands such as DC Talk and Jars of Clay (a phrase taken from 2 Corinthians 4:7) had crossed over into mainstream radio, MTV, and such pillars of the rock establishment as *Rolling Stone* magazine.

Backstage at Monterey, I ran into Bob Herdman, who plays rhythm guitar for the Christian rock band Audio Adrenaline. Herdman had started his band seven years earlier at a Kentucky Bible college. "Christian people have accepted this music for a long time," he told me, "but the outside world is noticing it now."

Nevertheless, Herdman said, some Christian concertgoers are not prepared for the rowdy scenes that sometimes break out near the stage when frenzied fans float over the heads of the crowd. "We've had broken bones, but I don't think that's un-Christian," Bob said. "You break bones if you go out and play football, and nobody sees anything wrong with that."[33]

Later in the afternoon one of the teenage fans, Casey Lee, told me the crowds at Laguna Seca were tame compared to ones he's seen at many secular concerts. "There are not as many dirts here," he said, referring to the unwashed fans at some concerts. "Those pits usually stink. And they don't have fights here. Actually, I kinda like to watch the fights."

So much for *Blessed are the peacemakers.* . . .

Casey and three friends sat slumped over a picnic table on the edge of the concert area, seriously bummed out because the security guards had just told them they couldn't ride their skateboards. "They're afraid we'll sue them or something," he moaned. At a nearby tent pavilion, a multitude of Christian businesses and youth organizations had set up displays. There were T-shirts (Satan Is Ugly as Sin), bumper stickers (Warning: In Case of Rapture, This Car Will Be Unmanned), and Christian candy (Testamints—Refreshing Mints with a Message).

Teenager James Samarin was at the Know Him clothing booth, filling out a raffle ticket and hoping to win a surfboard with the Know Him logo. His favorite bands are the Supertones, who were scheduled to play that afternoon, along with Five Iron Frenzy and Slick Shoes. James, a member of Clovis Evangelical Free Church in Fresno, said the major record companies are about two years behind the curve in spotting hot Christian rock. "They realize it's a big market," he said. "But they're not doing it to glorify God. They're just in it for the money."

Christian rock took off in the 1990s, about when America's most influential evangelist, the Reverend Billy Graham, started asking Christian rock bands to warm up the crowds at his youth crusades. Billy Graham, the preacher from North Carolina, had discovered what the late Bill Graham, the rock impresario from San Francisco, found three decades before. Rock 'n' roll is a powerful force, a way to make a lot of money or save a lot of souls. Just a few months after the Spirit West festival in Monterey, Billy Graham drew tens of thousands of Christian rock fans to his San Francisco and Oakland crusades by booking Jars of Clay and DC-Talk, two of the hottest Christian rock bands at the time.

That weekend in the Bay Area, Graham needed all the help he could get. He was already suffering from Parkinson's disease and his prostate cancer had returned with a vengeance, along with several other debilitating ailments. He walked onto the Cow Palace stage in San Francisco with obvious pain and difficulty then gingerly sat down while nearly everyone else in the crowd remained standing for the singing of "Amazing Grace." Wearing a black suit and tie, he preached from a large stage bathed in spotlights of blue and purple, his famous profile projected onto three giant video screens.

In an interview with Graham before he went onstage, I asked America's Preacher about the use of hard rock to save souls:

"Didn't you used to call that the devil's music?"

Graham laughed.

"That's right," he said. "It's not necessarily full-scale rock. It's Christian rock in the sense that the lyrics are Christian, and we try to see that the people get copies of the lyrics so they can follow the music, and the lyrics are really gospel. I think we have to think in terms of generations changing—this is called the Generation X by some. Many people are wondering, 'How can the church appeal to them? How can the church deal with them?' But they have the same problems we had forty years ago. The problems haven't changed in the hearts of young people, it's just the materialism and the sex and the television and the amusements that have changed. Not the individual person. He still suffers from loneliness. He may still suffer from frustration. Most young people today are searching for something. They don't know quite what it is. They want to find something they can hold on to and believe in, something that will take them through the rough times of their lives."[34]

When it comes to attracting alienated youth, conservative evangelicals like Billy Graham always seem to outsmart liberal Protestants. For nearly a century, evangelicals have embraced new technologies (radio, television, direct mail, Internet) and used secular culture (rock music, videos, mystery novels) to get out their message. Today rock music and high-tech entertainment are a major part of the evangelical experience. Even Attorney General John Ashcroft attends Sunday services at an evangelical church with a rock band and a young, ethnically diverse congregation.[35]

Many of the nation's mega-churches are also rock 'n' roll churches. Walk into Jubilee Christian Center, a thriving Pentecostal church in San Jose, California, and you may think you've mistakenly wandered into a rock concert. The church's ten-member band employs three drummers. They and a large, golden-robed choir stand before a giant mural of the Bay Area that depicts the Four Horsemen of the Apocalypse galloping down from the clouds. Like the computer companies of Silicon Valley, this Pentecostal cathedral stands as a towering testament to high-tech religion. Giant video screens and a state-of-the-art sound system beam the preacher's image to all corners of the church while production crews send his fiery sermons out to the world via radio, television, and the World Wide Web.

As rock rhythms rise, one of the giant video monitors flashes "Dance! All Night!" amid a background of exploding video fireworks. Remember, this is church. It's Sunday *morning*, but no one seems to care. It seems like they might be dancing all night. Worshipers clap, shout, and jump up and down, some of them spinning out of control into the aisles. It reminds me more of a Grateful Dead concert than Sunday worship. And as it turns out, Jubilee Pastor Dick Bernal and I may have been to some of the same Dead concerts.

Back in the 1960s, before he was born again, Bernal sought God through doses of LSD at rock concerts at San Francisco's Fillmore Auditorium. Bernal may have found Jesus, but he never forgot the revelatory power of rock 'n' roll. Today he adroitly mixes a rock beat, black gospel music, and Pentecostal power, drawing an unusually diverse congregation of thousands of African Americans, Latinos, whites, and others. His services are studded with celebrities. M. C. Hammer, the born-again rap singer and sports commentator, gives a little talk on sexual addiction. Amid all the glitz on this morning, Bernal seems a little defensive about the celebrity focus at Jubilee. Before his sermon, Bernal tells the congregation, "Now that we've got M. C. Hammer on staff, people are asking, 'Has Jubilee gone Hollywood?'"

"We've been around nineteen years, and no, we're not going Hollywood," he says, answering himself. "But if Hollywood wants to come, we'll have them!"

Some of the finest minds in Christendom are trying to figure out how to sell Jesus Christ to Generation X and the next crowd of young people coming along behind them. They have been called the first post-Christian generation, a slice of the demographic pie raised on MTV and the relativistic philosophy of "whatever." And evangelicals have an even harder time in a city such as San

Francisco. While it's just one hour north of San Jose and Jubilee Christian Center, San Francisco is infamously secular and liberal. But Cornerstone Church, a conservative evangelical congregation in the heart of San Francisco, seems to have found the secret formula:

IT'S THE MUSIC!

Music is a key element every Sunday. Between Sunday services, church leaders and musicians gather in a small room to critique the previous performance, discussing timing and chord changes. "Worship bands have to walk a fine line," said bandleader Phil Piserchio, who plays guitar and writes music. "We practice as hard as anyone else, but you don't want to lose sight of what you're doing and become too performance oriented."

Piserchio grew up in the Roman Catholic Church but fell away from organized religion. He joined Cornerstone in the early 1990s, when the church was just starting to grow. "What attracted me wasn't the music but Pastor Terry and his speaking," he said. "But Terry is a huge music fan. He loves rock 'n' roll."

That would be the Reverend Terry Brisbane, who inherited Cornerstone from his grandfather, the Reverend Albert H. Brisbane, a Pentecostal preacher and onetime city bus driver. Today Cornerstone calls itself an independent, nondenominational church. They've toned down the traditional Pentecostalism—speaking in tongues, faith healing—but kept the conservative evangelical theology. While Cornerstone's creative arts program is innovative, its teachings about sexuality and gender are very traditional. Its women's program stresses motherhood. Like the evangelical movement Promise Keepers, its Men's Inc. groups promote "a more committed and dynamic relationship with Jesus Christ."

Cornerstone goes out of its way to get people in the door, offering Christ with cappuccino. Inside the church, adjacent to its candlelight worship space, is Mission Java, an espresso bar. It even has its own parking garage. Jealous Protestant pastors, envious of Cornerstone's large crowd of demographically correct Christians, have started calling it "the church of the pretty people."

Its congregation is a mix of people with little religious upbringing and Christian refugees from other evangelical movements. Some joined Brisbane's flock after a schism in Vineyard Christian Fellowship, an international association of Pentecostal churches. Others went through the controversial "shepherding movement," a secretive Pentecostal sect that practiced a radical form of Christian discipleship. Leaders in that underground network were accused in the 1980s of infiltrating evangelical churches, exerting excessive control over members' personal lives, and "stealing sheep." Dennis Peacocke, a one-time shepherding movement leader in northern California, has been a guest speaker at Cornerstone.

Peacocke is one of thousands of former radicals and freethinkers who reinvented themselves in the late sixties and early seventies and embraced evangelical Christianity. His "shepherd," evangelist Bob Mumford, first saw Peacocke's potential when the two met at a Bible study group in 1969, just eighteen months after Peacocke had his born-again conversion.

Back in the early 1980s I spent months tracking down the shepherding movement's elusive leadership network. I found Mumford, one of its five international leaders, at the Gulf Coast Covenant Church in Mobile, Alabama. A mustachioed, curly-haired native of Steubenville, Ohio, Mumford had a folksy manner but a strange intensity when he started preaching. He'd spent most of the 1960s as a Pentecostal preacher and Bible teacher, traveling the revivalist circuit, talking about the Holy Spirit. It was back then that he first saw the evangelical potential in Peacocke's generation.

"There is an entire generation out there—the Sixties generation—that has rejected empty religion and is hungry for something real and alive," Mumford said. "They have become burned out on politics, drugs, sex, and now they've blended into the establishment. They are like a sleeping tiger. But with a prophetic word that is real and powerful, they can be awakened."[36]

Peacocke was Mumford's agent for the northern California shepherding flock, where he oversaw eleven churches. And Peacocke has impeccable Sixties credentials. He was a Marxist political science student at Berkeley during the Free Speech and antiwar movements, sought enlightenment with psychedelic drugs, started a flower business in San Francisco on the heels of the Summer of Love, dabbled in Eastern mysticism, and became so disillusioned with the whole thing that he almost blew his brains out with a .357 Magnum. "It was at that point in my life that I had an encounter with Jesus," Peacocke recalled, writing in a shepherding movement magazine called *New Wine*. "Suddenly, I was caught away in a vision in which Jesus was coming toward me across a field. As I looked into his eyes—I'd never seen anything like Him before—He said my name, and I said, 'Master.'"

Peacocke was raised in Seattle by a mother who was a Mormon and a father who was a "pragmatic CPA." As a teenager he was an excellent athlete—an all-city halfback in high school and a star in the decathlon. He came to Berkeley as a recruit for the University of California football team. But he would soon sign with another team, joining the thousands of other former hippies, druggies, and lefties who became Jesus freaks, or the Jesus people.

Vineyard Fellowship was another large church network that grew out of those freakish times. These lively Christian churches have demographics rarely seen among mainline Protestant and Roman Catholic congregations. Scholar Donald Miller attributes their success to upbeat music, young pastors, casual dress, a mild form of Pentecostal worship, and very little hype. "These churches," he says, "are reinventing American Protestantism."[37]

Take, for example, the Vineyard Christian Fellowship in San Francisco. One Sunday morning in the 1990s, Pastor Michael Brodeur stood between his pulpit and a set of drums and told his congregation, "There are some branches of the church that think any music with a backbeat is from the devil." The bearded, thirty-five-year-old preacher quipped, "If it's not Christian Muzak, it's just not right."

Five hundred worshipers were packed into an upstairs meeting room in San Francisco's South of Market area, a church that began only six years ago as a handful of people gathered in Brodeur's living room. Most had Bibles in their laps, but other than that, it looked like the kind of crowd you would find in the latest jazz club or coffeehouse in this trendy neighborhood. Brodeur's church combined a literal reading of the Bible, an ecstatic style of worship, and a decidedly San Francisco ambience. "We are trying to be a church that is indigenous to San Francisco, culturally conducive to baby boom people but consistent with the gospel," Brodeur told me. "We stress genuineness and simplicity. It is real. We're not trying to come up with a lot of hype like at a lot of charismatic or evangelical churches." On this Sunday Brodeur peppers his sermon on the writings of the apostle Paul with jokes about his hippie past and infatuation with Eastern mysticism and New Age spirituality. "I was so spiritual," he tells the flock, "I was more spiritual than God."

This all began in the late 1970s when John Wimber, a pastor in Orange County, California, started the first Vineyard Fellowship. It has grown to three hundred congregations and a hundred thousand members. Because of its emphasis on faith healing and other "gifts of the Holy Spirit," it is often referred to as the "signs and wonder" movement. Brodeur also came out of the shepherding movement and admits there was an authoritarian, cultist style of leadership in some of those congregations. "Some churches have erred on the side of controlling members," he said. "Here, we're trying to have a low amount of control but a high amount of involvement, intimacy, and accountability. People can be involved at whatever level they feel comfortable."

All of these churches are just a small part of a global Pentecostal movement that began nearly a century ago in Los Angeles at a series of revival meetings at a poor church on Azusa Street. Two of the world's largest Pentecostal denominations, the predominantly white Assemblies of God and the mostly black Church of God in Christ, trace their roots to those meetings. While the roots of modern Pentecostalism reach back to evangelical crusades in the nineteenth century, the outside world first learned of the Azusa Street revival in a story published in the *Los Angeles Times* on April 18, 1906, the day of the great San Francisco earthquake. That combination of events helped convince many of Pentecostalism's early leaders that the Second Coming was about to unfold.

Harvey Cox, the author of *Fire from Heaven: The Rise of Pentecostal Spirituality and the Reshaping of Religion in the Twenty-First Century,* sees several reasons for the success of Pentecostalism. Around the world, he said, Pentecostal churches provide community and a new kind of family for people in an increasingly mobile and urban society. It is a brand of religion spread through families and other social networks. Everyone becomes an evangelist. But Cox said the real power is Pentecostalism's emphasis on the "centrality of experience," on powerful, spiritual conversions at emotion-laden, music-filled events. "They major in experience," Cox told me. "People will say, 'I went there and something happened to me.'"

In the market-driven, media-saturated nineties, Pentecostal revivals needed more than a large tent and a fiery preacher. They needed a hook, a theme, a market niche. They needed something to help them take off and establish their own line of books, videos, preaching tapes, conferences, music CDs, and other products. In 1994 it was the Toronto Blessing, a spiritual craze known for wild outbursts of "holy laughter." Then came the Brownsville Revival, a Christian crusade emanating from an Assemblies of God church in Pensacola, Florida. Then it was the "miracle in Smithton," also known as the Cornfield Revival or the "revival in the middle of nowhere," which drew thousands of small-town pastors from across America to rural Missouri.

Music was a big part of the Smithton revival. Working with Integrity Music, a successful Christian record label, the Smithton church put out a CD of high-energy music from its revival. "There's a whole music industry springing up around this," said Don Moen, an executive vice president at Integrity Music. "There's a lot of money being made."38

At first glance the Pentecostal movement, which is largely conservative and evangelical, would seem to have little in common with the New Age movement, which is mostly liberal and eclectic. But some scholars see these seemingly disparate movements as part of a larger religious revival—a new Great Awakening of spiritual fervor. Religion researcher Philip Lucas notes several striking similarities:

- Both seek guidance from spirits and a direct experience of the sacred—whether from the Holy Spirit of charismatic Christians or the more amorphous energy and spirit guides channeled by New Agers.

- Both see the world on the edge of a radical spiritual transformation, whether it is called the New Age or the millennium, the thousand-year period of blessedness that Pentecostals believe will accompany the Second Coming of Christ.

- Both stress spiritual and physical healing through the laying on of hands, prayer, crystals, or other techniques outside medical science, offering a way of healing and empowerment.

- Both arose as movements outside the mainline churches but have grown to the extent they have inspired changes in worship styles in the religious establishment.

"Ultimately, the strategy of many New Agers and charismatics toward mainline churches and institutions seems to be to disappear in their midst and to transform them from within," Lucas reports. His research complements work by American church historians Catherine Albanese and William McLoughlin, who note that both movements came of age in the chaotic period of the 1960s and 1970s, with its "broken families, normlessness, alienation, and focus on self-fulfillment."[39]

There is, however, one important difference between the holy rollers and the crystal gazers. Pentecostal Christians offer lively music with Sunday worship. New Age music, on the other hand, is as insipid as the sounds you hear in elevators. It's supposed to be meditative, but all it really does is put you to sleep. New Agers may have attained higher consciousness, but they desperately need a new sound track. When our religious history is written, the Pentecostals will get at least a chapter. Unless they wake up and hear the backbeat, the New Age movement may warrant only a footnote. They just don't get it:

IT'S THE MUSIC!

PART
FOUR

Paradise Lost

Is this the dawning of the Age of Aquarius, or what?

Harmony and understanding? Sympathy and trust abounding?
Is the moon still in the seventh house? Is Jupiter aligned with
Mars? Isn't peace to guide the planet and love to steer the stars?
If the first few years of the new millennium are the dawning of
the Age of Aquarius, maybe we should just go back to Pisces and
forget the whole thing.

On the other hand, there wasn't all that much peace and love in
the world when *Hair: The American Tribal Love–Rock Musical*
opened on Broadway in 1968. That same year American bombs
and napalm rained down on Vietnam. Richard Nixon was
president. The Reverend Martin Luther King Jr. and Senator
Robert F. Kennedy were assassinated. Riots tore apart inner-city
neighborhoods across America.

Tough times inspire utopian dreams. In the Sixties there were
many versions of the New Age dream. Chapter 10 looks at the
self-centered vision of the Reverend Sun Myung Moon and the
life of a young woman named Donna Collins. Like David Price,
conceived at Esalen in 1963, Donna was born at ground zero of
Sixties spirituality. Her parents were early converts to Moon's

Unification Church. As the first "blessed child" born in the West, Donna was to symbolize the world's races and religions coming together under the messianic leadership of the Reverend Moon. But in her teenage years, Donna saw the dark side of Moon's glorious vision, then spent years getting herself and her parents out of Moon's church.

Chapter 11 profiles other prophets and profiteers of the New Age. Self-help and spiritual solace were for sale like never before in the 1970s, 1980s, and beyond. Its peddlers included Wayne Dyer, the pop psychologist of public TV; spirit medium J. Z. Knight, also known as Ramtha; and New Age sect leader Elizabeth Clare Prophet, whose apocalyptic visions inspired thousands to follow her to a place called Paradise Valley.

Finally, in chapter 12, we visit the Farm, the largest and longest lasting of the hundreds of the hippie communes formed in the 1960s and 1970s. In the beginning, when the group left the streets of San Francisco and headed for the hills of Tennessee, this was the real deal. It was back to the land. Hundreds of hippies turned their backs on capitalism, consumerism, and the nuclear family. They shared everything, including their husbands and wives. Many babies were born. But in the end capitalism triumphed over communalism and the group marriages fell apart, leaving the real children of the Sixties wondering where to go and what to do next.

Rev. Sung Myung Moon

One of the Farm's original buses, 2002

CHAPTER 10

The Reverend Moon, the Messiah, and the Next Generation

Ladies and Gentlemen: The new millennium has just begun. . . .
It is the time when the Parent and the children who have been separated
will meet again. It is an age when the East and West will come
together centering on the Parents of Heaven and Earth.

THE REVEREND SUN MYUNG MOON, JANUARY 2000

Donna Collins opens the door of her new home in the Phoenix suburbs, one of thousands springing up in the subdivisions that ring this blazing desert city. "Sorry," she tells me, "it's a bit hectic in there today." Donna's baby son squirms in her arms. Her slightly older daughter tumbles down the stairs with a friend, riding a piece of cardboard as if it were a sled. The television set blares in the family room, where her husband, Jonathan, talks to a guy from the cable company. It's chaotic and alive, a shrine to the classic American family. It's Ozzie and Harriet. And it's exactly what Donna did not have growing up in Korea, England, and elsewhere as the showcase, second-generation disciple of the Reverend Sun Myung Moon.

"This is exactly what I want—a normal life. We live and have fun and get into arguments, but my daughter knows I'm here for her every day," Collins says a few hours later, toward the end of our conversation. "My daughter's thing at the moment is to ask what I was doing at her age. I don't really go into it. I say, 'I lived in a boarding school,' and she says, 'Didn't you want to live with your mom and dad?' That kind of puts it all in perspective for me."

Collins was conceived in the spring of 1969, shortly after her parents came together in one of the first mass marriages presided over by the Reverend Sun Myung Moon, then a little-known Korean sect leader. As the first "blessed child" born in the West, this cute, curly-haired blond was supposed to embody Moon's vision that the world's religions would soon come together under his messianic leadership. According to church doctrine, children from parents married by the Reverend Moon and his wife are "blessed children." Unlike the rest of us, they are born without original sin.

Many mothers and fathers have high expectations for their children, but few had visions as lofty as the parents of Donna Collins. "When I was born, my dad was surprised I was crying at all," she says. "I was supposed to be perfect—born without sin." From her conception, Collins was to play a key role in the history of the Unification Church. Moon and his wife were the True Parents of a spiritual master race that would spread his message—a mix of Christianity, spiritualism, and right-wing politics—to the four corners of the Earth. Donna was to embody the messiah's message.

Donna and I first crossed paths in the spring of 2000, at a "Cults and the Millennium" conference on the outskirts of Seattle. She was on a panel of speakers at a session titled "After the Moonies," and she had an incredible story to tell.

It begins in 1960, ten years before her birth. Donna's mother, Doris Walder, was living in Oregon, trying to get out of her first marriage. That's when she met Young Oon Kim, the first missionary sent to the West by Moon. Walder was thirty years old and ready for something new. Captivated by Moon's vision of uniting the religions of the world, she signed on as one of the first three U.S. missionaries of the Unification Church, founded by Moon just six years earlier in Korea.

Kim, an early Korean convert to Moon's church, had been a professor of New Testament and comparative religion at Ewha University in Seoul. She arrived on the West Coast on January 4, 1959, and enrolled as a student at the University of Oregon in Eugene. Her real mission, however, was to establish a Moon beachhead in the United States. "I was looking for people who were searching," she said decades later. Kim's strategy was to visit local churches and home meetings of evangelical Christians. That's where she met Donna's mother. "I shared my spiritual experiences, and she told me about hers," Kim recalled. "I also offered her my manuscript because it was awkward to lecture to only one person."[1]

Kim, who died in 1989, moved into a vacant home in Oakhill, a few miles outside Eugene, where she began working with Donna's mother and a half dozen other initiates drawn to Moon's theology, which is described in a treatise called *The Divine Principles*. Moon teaches that Jesus intended to restore the world and cleanse it of sin by marrying but was murdered before he could complete his earthly mission. His followers see Moon as the new messiah, unifying the Christian world and establishing the kingdom of heaven on Earth through his marriage and through blessing the arranged marriages of his devotees.

"My mother had a spiritual conversion, which to her was real," Collins said. "She thought this was the answer. They were going to change the world and save humanity. There was idealism in the organization then that isn't there today. All races are one. All religions are one. These are noble things. It's not like she was joining the KKK."

Doris and other members of the pioneering Oakhill group moved to San Francisco in late 1960, hoping to reach a larger audience with Moon's message. On October 29, 1961, Walder signed the minutes of the first West Coast meeting of the Holy Spirit Association for the Unification of World Christianity. One of Walder's first assignments was to establish the church in San Francisco. She set up an early Unification Church center on Masonic Avenue. It failed, and it would be another decade until the movement found fertile ground among spiritual seekers in northern California. But Kim and Walder laid the legal groundwork for Moon, who would move to the United States ten years later and become the most infamous icon in the cults wars of the 1970s.

Meanwhile, on the East Coast, another key missionary landed in America, a man who would wage Moon's war to garner political power and influence in the United States and spearhead the new messiah's crusade against world Communism. On February 25, 1961, Colonel Bo Hi Pak arrived in Washington, D.C., as a military attaché to the Korean Embassy. Colonel Pak was Moon's point man for a number of church-affiliated political groups, such as the Korean Cultural and Freedom Foundation and Radio of Free Asia. He helped establish two Moon newspapers, the *News World*, later renamed the *New York City Tribune* (1976–91), and the *Washington Times*, a conservative daily that began publishing in 1982.

The Reverend Moon first visited the United States in 1965, starting with a weeklong stay in San Francisco, where he was greeted at the airport by Colonel Pak and Miss Kim. His visit went largely unnoticed except for a breathless article in the Unification Church newsletter, *New Age Frontiers*, titled "Hail to the Brightness." When he stepped off his Japan Airlines flight from Hawaii that February morning, the forty-five-year-old Moon had in his possession fifty-five "holy rocks" from Korea. His purpose on that trip was to prepare America for his movement by burying them across the continental United States, consecrating "holy ground" for his messianic mission. He started at Twin Peaks in San Francisco, on February 15, 1965, then headed south to Griffith Park in Los Angeles, where he planted another. Over the next forty-four days Moon traveled by car to all forty-eight contiguous states, burying rocks in city parks in such places as Paducah, Kentucky; Tampa, Florida; Fargo, North Dakota; Hammond, Indiana; and Central Park in New York City.

Moon was born January 6, 1920, in Cheong-Ju, a village in what is now North Korea, the fifth of eight children. His given name was Yong Myung Moon. When he was ten his parents converted to Christianity and joined the Presbyterian church. According to later church lore, Moon was visited by Jesus when he was sixteen years old, on Easter Sunday morning, when Christ told him that God's mission on Earth was unfulfilled and that it was now up to young Moon to finish the job. Big news, but the teenage Moon did not tell anyone about his startling vision back then, nor did he change his career plans. In 1938 he went to Seoul and then Tokyo to study engineering. During World War II he joined a movement fighting against the Japanese occupation of Korea and spent four months in prison for his activities. He also married (and later divorced) Sun Kil Choi, a devout Christian woman. She gave birth to Moon's first son, Sung Jin Moon, in 1946. That same year Moon started an independent Christian church called Kwang-ya, which practiced a lively charismatic style of the faith. Moon was soon arrested and imprisoned again, this time by Communist authorities trying to quash his new religious movement. After surviving for two and a half years in a North Korean prison camp, Moon and other prisoners were liberated by United Nations forces in the autumn of 1950. Considering the time he spent doing hard labor at Hungnam prison camp, the fierce anti-Communism in Moon's later movement comes as no surprise. Neither does the fervor of Moon's early Korean followers.

Presbyterian and Methodist missionaries established influential churches, schools, and other institutions in Korea in the nineteenth century, and Christianity has been a vital force there since the end of World War II. In more re-cent decades conservative Presbyterian congregations and spirit-filled Pente-costal churches have blossomed in South Korea. They have also flourished in the Korean-American community in the United States, where there are an esti-mated seven hundred Korean-Christian congregations in southern California alone, from buttoned-down Presbyterian congregations to storefront chapels where exorcisms are performed on any Sunday. Today, in an evangelical twist on East meets West, many Korean Americans see themselves as the true mis-sionaries of Christ, destined to bring a spiritually adrift America back to its reli-gious heritage. Moon's movement arose out of that cultural stew, spiced with the kind of messianic zeal that only decades of political oppression can inspire.

Moon founded the Unification Church in Seoul in 1954, calling it the Holy Spirit Association for the Unification of World Christianity. It was soon hit with a wave of accusations that it was as much a sex cult as a church. It's un-clear whether this was a smear campaign, a theological catfight, or a serious charge. But it arose when one of Moon's early disciples wrote a tract titled "The Tragedy of the Six Marys." He charged that Moon practiced sex rituals with six married female disciples. Their mission was to prepare him for a vir-gin he would later marry and bless as the True Mother. Moon denied the allegations but was soon arrested and imprisoned again, this time for draft evasion. He was later cleared of that charge, and more than four decades later the disciple who wrote about the Six Marys recanted the accusations shortly before his death.[2]

These sexual rumors began when a group of students and faculty at Ewha University, a women's school funded by the Methodist Church, found them-selves drawn to Moon's teachings. Among them was Young Oon Kim, the woman who would later convert Donna Collins's mother in Oregon and write *Unification Theology*, an authoritative study of Moon's teachings. In 1955 four-teen students and faculty members were summoned to the dean's office at Ewha and told to leave Moon's church or leave the Methodist school. "The Uni-fication Church is heresy," the dean told them. "They dance around in the nude. You mustn't go there."[3] The students protested, saying the rumors about Moon's sect were ridiculous. "We haven't even danced fully clothed, much less nude," they told the dean, but he wouldn't back down. In the end the women left the university to become disciples of the Reverend Moon.

Naked or clothed, dancing or not, Moon's early followers were playing with heresy—at least from a mainstream Christian point of view. According to *The*

Divine Principles, the New Testament is merely an "interim textbook," and a new and more scientific revelation is needed today. This new Bible turns out to be *The Divine Principles*, which stresses the dualistic nature of creation—masculine-feminine, positive-negative—in a way reminiscent of the yin-yang polarities of traditional Chinese philosophy. Moon rejects the doctrine of the virgin birth, teaching that Zechariah was the father of both John the Baptist and Jesus of Nazareth. *The Divine Principles* argues that Jesus did not complete his mission because he did not have children and predicts—conveniently—that the Lord of the Second Advent will be born in Korea sometime between 1917 and 1930. Moon's much-trumpeted marriage to his current wife, Hak Ja Han, in 1960 set the stage for an era of spiritual eugenics—for the mass marriage ceremonies that would become the new messiah's trademark.

In 1969, after having blessed four hundred thirty couples in Korea, Moon embarked on a world tour, blessing twenty-two couples in Japan, thirteen in the United States, and eight in Germany, including Donna Collins's parents. After her unsuccessful attempt to get the church going in San Francisco in the early 1960s, Doris Walder had been sent to Europe as a missionary for Moon. There she met her future husband, Dennis Orme, while she was giving a talk on Unificationism at Findhorn, the famous spiritual community in northern Scotland. Dennis Orme had been born into the Church of England and had worked as a ship navigator in the merchant navy before joining Moon's ranks.

Dennis and Doris Orme's marriage in Germany was an intimate affair, at least compared to Moon's highly publicized 1982 blessing of 2,075 couples in Madison Square Garden. But the Ormes' service was one of the first ceremonies to include Western converts, and it marked the beginning of a new era in Moon's messianic crusade. Men and women joined together in the Unification Church allow Moon to select their spouse. They also consummate their marriage in a three-day ritual, complete with prescribed sexual positions. Dennis and Doris Orme took Moon's advice to heart, and nine months later Donna Collins was born. Her parents christened her Young Oon, after Moon's pioneering West Coast missionary.

Donna first met Moon at age two. She doesn't remember the encounter, but she has kept a photo of herself sitting on the lap of the messiah, getting a big hug. Donna has a yellow ribbon in her hair, and Moon is beaming like a proud Korean godfather. Donna's first memories of her own life are of living in a group home in England. She didn't live alone with her parents until she was fifteen years old.

During the mid-1970s, leading Korean members of the Unification Church would come visit the first "blessed child" in the Western world. "When I'd walk into the room, they'd all gasp, seeing this little blond, curly-haired child," Collins recalls. "When I was seven or eight, people would actually come and confess things to me about their sex lives. I can laugh about it now, but it was pretty psychotic. I thought I was pretty special, but I was like some kind of china doll. My parents never saw me, and I was always being handed off to other people. They'd take me out of the closet for meetings or for holidays."

Donna's parents declined my requests for an interview, but other longtime Unification Church parents gave knowing nods when I recounted Donna's story. Mose Durst, a longtime Unification Church leader in the United States, confesses that in the early years Moon converts erred in assuming God would provide for the children of devotees. The first kids born into the movement, he concedes, did not always get the parental attention they deserved. "We were trying to build the church up locally. We were hot to build the kingdom," he told me. "There were times in the early years when the hardest thing was building a church while being responsible for your family. You wanted to be part of a spiritual community. People would put their kids in a nursery. When it was not done well, there were all kinds of shortcomings. We made mistakes. We did dumb things."

Durst and I sat in the living room of a spectacular church-owned home in one of Berkeley's finest neighborhoods. The home had an Asian flair, panoramic views of San Francisco Bay, and a portrait of Moon looking down from above the hearth. Durst grew up in an Orthodox Jewish neighborhood in Brooklyn, but his trip to the inner circle of a Korean messiah is not so long, or so strange, as one might think.

In the 1960s he was teaching at a small college in Pennsylvania. "I was the typical radical young professor of the sixties. I was on the side of every cause: for protection of the environment, for civil rights, against the growing war in Vietnam." But his marriage and teaching career soon fell apart. A friend in Oakland, California, invited him to move out to the West Coast, and he got a job at a small urban college. "I began meditating; for the first time in my life I confronted the reality of my inevitable death. I know, now, that I was searching for God."[4]

Durst dabbled in new religions and avant-garde psychology, took an improvisational dance class, and tried to raise his consciousness. Then he met a Korean woman named Onni, who gave him a copy of *The Divine Principles*. His new friend's real name was Yun Soo Lim, who had joined the church in 1960 in Japan, where she was working at the Korean embassy in Tokyo. Onni, her Korean nickname meaning "elder sister," was sent to the States by Moon in 1965 to work in the San Francisco Bay Area as a missionary. Durst says the purity and sincerity of Onni and the small band of Unificationists he met in the Bay Area in 1972 impressed him. "There were, of course, many opportunities for promiscuous sex in California, and everywhere, in the 1960s and 1970s, but I did not take advantage of them. I was repelled by such casual approaches to something as meaningful, and to me sacred, as human sexuality. The purity of Onni and the genuine absence of lust and self-seeking in the few people drawn to this new teaching made the greatest impression on me."5 Durst accompanied Onni to pray atop Twin Peaks in San Francisco, where seven years earlier Moon had planted one of his holy rocks. He went with her to the church's retreat center in Boonville, a former sheep ranch about two hours north of San Francisco.

Durst and Onni became leaders of "the Oakland family," which produced some of Moon's most zealous proselytizers and fund-raisers. Recruits harvested from the streets of San Francisco or the University of California at Berkeley campus were whisked up to the Boonville retreat for days of "love-bombing" and alleged "brainwashing."

"Boonville was always meant to be an environment where our spiritual community could build its foundations through caring relationships," Durst writes in his autobiography. "News media emphasize the 'indoctrination techniques' as opposed to the reality of three one-hour lectures each day followed by discussion. At times, newspapers talk of Unificationists 'love-bombing' those who attend. Such a cynical description."6

Durst has a point. Those of us in the news media do tend to get a bit overheated when writing about religious cults. After a few decades covering new religious movements for secular newspapers, I've learned that the truth is usually somewhere between the glowing accounts of current devotees and the horror stories of defectors and apostates. Leaving a new religious movement is like leaving a marriage. Someone you loved like a saint is suddenly a conniving monster. Chances are that he was neither a monster nor a saint.

My first exposure to Mose Durst was way back in 1977 when he ran a Unification Church–affiliated group called the Creative Community Project. I sat in the living room of a posh Berkeley home and watched him work with a group of worried, skeptical parents who'd been invited to a meeting to learn what was happening to their converted children. "Commitment makes people look crazy," Durst explained. "They smile a lot and work hard."[7] By the end of the night Mose had the skeptical parents smiling.

Twenty-four years later, when Durst and I spoke again in the living room of that even finer Berkeley home, he said it's time to give his church another chance. "People perceive us as a bad religious movement, and they isolate us more," he said. "If you think we're evil, let's sit down and talk. Let's find common ground. Otherwise, you force us into a cul-de-sac, like at Jonestown or Waco."

For years the Unification Church has struggled to make the leap from cult to religion, to win credibility among political and religious leaders in the United States and around the world. Through his newspaper, the *Washington Times,* and through alliances with priests and pastors across the theological spectrum, Moon and company have spent a fortune courting the opinion makers of church and state. During the late 1970s and early 1980s the church reportedly transferred at least $800 million to the United States from its Japanese branch to finance political activities and business operations in the States. These funds came from church-affiliated businesses in Korea and Japan that produce everything from religious icons to machine tools, from weapons manufacture to ginseng soft drinks. Businesses with links to Moon's empire include tuna fleets and fish-processing plants in Alaska and New England, a construction firm in Washington, D.C., and a hotel, bank, and publishing company in Uruguay.[8]

Meanwhile, over in Europe, Donna Collins's father, Dennis Orme, had become the British director of the Unification Church, where the church had an equally sullied reputation. English tabloids were full of exposés about his "sinister sect." Devotees were described by the *Daily Mail* as "robots, glassy-eyed and mindless, programmed as soldiers in this vast fund-raising army with no goals or ideals, except as followers of the half-baked ravings of Moon, who lived in splendor while followers lived in forced penury." On behalf of the church, Orme filed a libel suit against the newspaper. The church lost the case and was ordered to pay court costs, and questions were raised about its tax-free status.

Meanwhile, young Donna was on the blessed fast track. It had long been assumed she was destined to marry one of Moon's sons. At age eleven she was sent off to live in Korea. "Moon said I must learn the language of the fatherland and the spirit world and fulfill my role as the first blessed child," Donna told me that day in Phoenix. She handed me a copy of an account she wrote of her childhood, when she was still trying to understand what happened to her and her family. "I did feel special," Donna wrote.

> The hard part was understanding why. Why my parents left me so often in the care of others, why I was so important, and why I didn't feel safe with anyone. There were other "blessed" children who were also carrying these new genes. But "restoration of the blood lineage" is a heavy concept for a child to understand.

Donna hated Korea. After living in that strange culture for a year, she got seriously ill and was able to reunite with her parents, who were now working for the church in Germany. But at age thirteen she was summoned back to Korea by Moon. "I pleaded with my father not to send me back, but Moon told him something bad would happen to me if I didn't go," Collins said. "They took me back to the airport screaming." Back in Korea, Collins started asking tough questions about what she saw in Moon's inner circle. She was now a teenager. "He and his kids didn't live by the teachings. His sons would come in and swear all the time. They were having steaks flown in from America. I'd been eating rice and kimchi for three years and getting serious dysentery. It was a joke. I started asking myself, 'What is godly about all this?'"

That got Donna a private audience with the messiah. "He got livid that somebody would have the nerve to question him and screamed at me for thirty minutes. I was bawling and shaking uncontrollably. Then he'd hold my hand, and say, 'I am your parent. One day, you will be a great woman for God.' I calmed down and said, 'Thank you. Thank you.' And then I'd write in my diary about how great it was to be with the True Father."

Nevertheless, Collins had gotten a reputation as a rebel, not a good image for the messiah's daughter-in-law. At fifteen she went to live with her parents in New York, where the church had sent them. For the first time in her life she was going to an American high school and living a relatively normal existence. "I started to date and live a double life. I was just being an ordinary person, but I had to make up all these lies when people would ask what my dad did for a living or why I lived in Korea and was named Young Oon."

It was a long process, but by the time she was twenty-two years old Collins finally felt like she had put the Unification Church behind her. After making the break, Collins began working on her parents. "I'd challenge them, asking, 'Why does he own all these villas and châteaus around the world and there are

members of the church who don't have enough to eat and need medical care?'"
Finally, her parents started the long process of separating themselves from
Moon. But after decades of raising money for the church, Collins said, her parents suddenly found themselves living as impoverished senior citizens. "They
were left destitute for a while," she told me. "They were used. A lot of people
joined the church because they met people like my parents. Most members
never meet Moon. But my parents were very charismatic. They laid the foundation for his church."

After staying with her and her husband for a while, Donna's parents pulled
up and moved to Australia. "My dad now believes Moon is the Son of Perdi-
tion—the Antichrist," she said. "My parents still think the nuclear family is
weird. To them, it's insignificant. After living on this roller-coaster for so long,
trying to save the planet every day of their lives, it's not that exciting to just live
and be human."

Collins's story is compelling, but is it typical? What has become of other
children born to "blessed" Western couples in the 1970s? Out of the first
twenty-five "blessed" Westerners, Donna says, around ten have left the church,
ten have remained members, and the rest are somewhere in between. Church
leaders say it's too soon to tell what will become of the next generation because
most of them were born to the 2,075 couples brought together in Moon's infamous mass marriage ceremony in Madison Square Garden in 1982.

And some wedding it was. As a thirty-piece orchestra played Mendelssohn's
"Wedding March," the 4,150 newlyweds filed eight abreast by Moon and his
wife. The brides were dressed in identical white empire-waisted wedding gowns.
The grooms wore dark blue suits. True Mother and True Father wore white
robes and white crowns atop their heads and stood on raised platforms as they
blessed the surreal procession. Meanwhile, the biological parents of the newlyweds sat way up in the stands of the huge arena, struggling to catch a glimpse
of their own children's wedding.

How have those marriages fared? According to a church survey released in
2000, 82 percent of the couples brought together in Madison Square Garden
are still married and still consider themselves members of the Unification
Church. They have had an average of 2.5 children per couple. Because the oldest

kids born from those highly publicized holy unions were still teenagers, the church could not yet say how many would keep the faith. "The real test comes when they are in college and out on their own," one church leader told me.

Among the tested will be Christopher Barker, born in Manhattan in 1983. His father, Garry, who had grown up in the Catholic church and attended parochial school, joined the Unification Church in the 1970s and started a coffeehouse, Aladdin's, on College Avenue in Oakland. Aladdin's had great New York cheesecake and sometimes served it up with a side order of Unification Church theology.

Moon missionaries approached Christopher Barker's mother, Renate, on the street in Munich in 1971, when she was twenty years old. Three days later Renate joined the Unification Church. "My mother was very upset," Renate recalled. "She thought I'd been drugged or something. My parents tried to kidnap me, but I was very dedicated."

What attracted her to Moon? "I was always very religious," she said. "I'd studied the Bible and oriental philosophy, but I looked at people who went to church, and their lives didn't change. It didn't have an impact on their lives." Renate came to the United States in 1973 with seventy other European missionaries. Their mission was simple—to save the world. "The Reverend Moon felt America was so important to the whole world, we thought that if we saved America, we would save the world."

Moon matched Renate and Barker in 1979, but they communicated only through letters for the next three years. They were married in Moon's mass marriage ceremony of 1982 and now live in Hayward, California, with their three children, Christopher, Amalia, and John.

One Sunday morning we were all standing outside the largest Unification Church congregation in northern California, the Bay Area Family Church, housed in a nondescript building in nearby San Leandro, a middle-class bedroom community across the bay from San Francisco. Inside, a band with guitar and drums played upbeat music while about 150 worshipers, a mix of Asians and Caucasians, found seats on rows of red padded pews. There were a lot of children running around the complex, which contains an elementary school, the Principled Academy, for 125 children.

In was late in 2000, and the communal days were over. Most church members lived in their own homes, with their own children, and worked outside jobs. "We still proselytize," said the Reverend Bento Leal, associate minister at the church, "but it's different when you have a house full of kids and a full-time job."

Having heard one side of the story from Donna Collins, I asked seventeen-year-old Christopher Barker what it was like to be a "blessed child."

"My understanding is we were born without original sin, since they were matched by the True Father," he replied. "We are the culmination of all that work, and it's up to us to carry on what they want us to do." Part of that legacy is no sex before marriage and agreeing to a union arranged by the Reverend Moon.

His sister, then fifteen, was saving herself for that day. "You are waiting for that one person, and not wasting your love on other people," Amalia said. "We believe in total fidelity in your marriage, so you're not comparing them with other boyfriends you've had before." Her older brother also has vowed to stay chaste until he marries. "Dating is kind of like practicing for divorce," he said. "When you're done with that person, and when problems come up, you dump them and go on to someone else."

Both teenagers attended the Unification Church's Principled Academy through the eighth grade and then transferred to a Catholic high school in Oakland. "I haven't told anyone there that I'm a Unificationist, or a Moonie," Christopher said. "My friends can see I'm not a normal teenager who has girl-friends and everything."

Renate Barker said she and her husband have learned lessons from the child-rearing mistakes of early Moon parents. "In those days, the thought was that the children would just automatically turn out good, just by God talking to them or something. We thought we didn't really have to take care of them. It was naive."

Garry says only time will tell if the Unification Church is a forgotten cult or a "religious movement with legs."

"All religions start out like this," he said. "The proof is going to be three, four, or five generations from now. When the Reverend Moon dies, nobody knows what will happen. That will be the big test."

Worldwide, the Unification Church claims three million members, with most of them living in Korea and Japan. Some scholars, however, say the ac-tual number of committed adherents may be closer to a quarter million or lower. In fact, nobody knows, but it does seem that church membership has declined rapidly in the United States. After decades of proselytizing in north-ern California, the largest Unification Church in the Bay Area draws only 150 members on a typical Sunday. In the late 1990s Moon indicated that he had all but given up hope of attracting a large membership in the United States, his adopted home since he moved to New York in 1971. In one speech Moon said, "God hates the American atmosphere." In another he called America "the kingdom of extreme individualism, the kingdom of free sex." American women, Moon said in yet another talk, "have inherited the line of prostitutes. . . . American women are even worse because they practice free sex just because they enjoy it."[9]

Yet despite his provocative speeches and declining U.S. membership, Moon still rules over one of the wealthiest religious movements in the world, with extensive business interests and land holdings in Asia, South America, and the United States. Meanwhile, Moon's public addresses have gotten stranger and stranger in recent years.

Sometimes he shocks his audiences by talking about how the husband owns his wife's genitalia and vice versa. "Every man thinks his sexual organ belongs to himself, and each woman thinks her sexual organ is her own," he says in one stump speech. "That is why the world is perishing." Other times, he seems to go out of his way to alienate women. During a visit to Oakland, California, in March 2001, Moon told an audience of two thousand that every woman should bear a child, and if she fails to do so, "you're disqualified as a woman."[10]

In 2002 Moon's church issued an extraordinary document titled *A Cloud of Witness*, which purports to be the minutes of a "seminar in the spirit world" that took place on Christmas Day 2001. Among those present were Jesus, Confucius, Buddha, Muhammad, Karl Marx, Joseph Stalin, and Deng Xiaoping. They all offer personal testimonies proclaiming Moon to be the new world messiah. The report on this historic gathering ends with "a letter from God" in which the Almighty declares Moon to be "the Savior, Messiah and King of Kings of all of humanity."

A Cloud of Witness was the latest in a series of increasingly bizarre conferences, proclamations, and alliances organized to bolster Moon's self-fulfilled messianic prophecies. While the money-losing *Washington Times* has been Moon's main conduit for political power in the United States, he has sought religious credibility by bankrolling a series of ecumenical conferences. Among the more high profile religious leaders to join forces with Moon has been the Roman Catholic archbishop Emmanuel Milingo, a freewheeling African faith healer and exorcist with a long history of confrontations with the Vatican. Milingo even married a Korean acupuncturist in one of Moon's mass wedding ceremonies, but the African archbishop soon renounced his wedding vows after being called onto the Roman carpet by Pope John Paul II. Meanwhile,

Moon has courted the African-American community through his associations with the Reverend George Stallings, who broke with the Roman Catholic Church in 1989 and later married a Japanese woman in one of Moon's mass weddings. Moon has also worked with the Reverend Louis Farrakhan, the controversial leader of the Nation of Islam, cohosting a Million Family March with him in Washington, D.C., in 2000.

Not surprisingly, few of these liaisons have given Moon credibility in the American religious community. Ironically, the chapter in Moon's life that garnered the most mainstream support was his 1982 conviction on charges of tax evasion. Other religious groups felt Moon had been unfairly prosecuted—and that their tax-paying status could also be challenged—so they filed friend-of-the-court briefs on his behalf. Moon was convicted anyway and served thirteen months in federal prison.

But Moon's most serious problems may be with his own family. Among many in the Unification Church, the concerns about the next generation start at the top, with the sons of Sun Myung Moon. In 1998 Moon's former daughter-in-law, Nansook Hong, published a tell-all memoir about her turbulent fourteen-year marriage with the self-proclaimed messiah's eldest son, Hyo Jin Moon. Titled *In the Shadow of the Moons,* she accused the onetime heir to Moon's spiritual and financial empire of alcoholism, cocaine abuse, wife beating, and cavorting with prostitutes. Then in October 1999 one of Moon's other sons, Philip Youngjin Moon, twenty-one, committed suicide by jumping from a seventeenth-story balcony at Harrah's hotel and casino in Reno, Nevada.

Both events are more than personal tragedies. They strike at the heart of Unification Church theology. Remember that Moon teaches that he and his wife are the True Parents of a new spiritual lineage born without original sin. Some Unification Church leaders say problems in Moon's own families have troubled rank-and-file members. "Many members have been disappointed," said national church treasurer Michael Inglis. "It challenges some people's faith."

The Reverend Leal, the associate minister at the Bay Area Unification church, said Moon's children may have been born without original sin, but that doesn't mean they're perfect. "Adam and Eve were born without original sin, but as we know, things can still happen if you make a mistake. The Reverend Moon sacrificed his own children when he was out building the church. We believe there are evil spirits in the world. Those kids are spiritually under siege."

Given the troubles surrounding his eldest son, Moon is grooming his third eldest male child, Hyun Jin Nim, as his successor. In 2000 the Unification Church published a history of its U.S. ministry, *40 Years in America*. It ends with the clear anointing of Hyun Jin Nim. In the book's final chapter Nim admits that many children of Moonie parents "have become disillusioned and have fallen astray." But he promises "to revive the second generation of our movement as well as offer a fresh new vision for the world's youth."

It remains to be seen whether Moon's church will last another forty years in America. As we saw with the Hare Krishna sect, the first big test of a new religious movement is surviving the death of its founder. Moon's passing will most likely divide his Unificationists into competing factions—not the best destiny for a spiritual movement founded to bring the world's religions together. You'd have to be a die-hard devotee to conclude that Moon's vision of the future has come to pass or is likely to anytime soon. With every passing year and every new pronouncement, his prophecies for the coming New Age sound more and more like the desperate fantasies of a failed messiah. But like many other seers from the Sixties, the Reverend Moon was always better at turning a profit than realizing his prophecy.

CHAPTER 11

New Age Prophets and Profiteers

> *The '90s are the '60s*
> *standing on your head.*
>
> WAVY GRAVY

W here have all the flowers gone? What happened to the idealism and spirituality of the Sixties? What became of all those sincere seekers who rejected consumerism, simplified their lives, and embraced the quest for higher consciousness and an ideal society?

Someone put a price tag on it in the 1980s and called it the New Age movement. Spirituality was for sale, and business was brisk for the peddlers of higher consciousness. Convention halls filled with seekers signing up for seminars promising self-help, spiritual peace, and emotional recovery. Meditation and retreat centers sprang up around the country. We spent hundreds of dollars to sit around for a weekend, closing our eyes or keeping them open. We stared at walls. We tried to visualize. We tried not to visualize. We tried to see our dreams. We tried to empty our minds. Enlightenment was promised either way. We wanted to be free, but it wasn't free getting there. It cost money. Back in the 1960s and 1970s, L. Ron Hubbard's Church of Scientology and Werner Erhard's est seminars got us used to the idea of handing over hundreds of dollars for a little piece of the truth or tens of thousands to rise a step or two on the stairway to heaven.

In the 1980s business was booming in the New Age sector, and it was a seller's market. The buyers came to be known as the "cultural creatives." One demographic study put it this way: "People who follow this new path are on the leading edge of several kinds of cultural change. They are interested in new kinds of products and services, and they often respond to advertising and marketing in unexpected ways."

By the 1990s cultural creatives made up 24 percent of the U.S. adult population as compared to 29 percent called traditionalists and 47 percent labeled modernists. For New Age workshop leaders, there was no question which slice of the demographic pie belonged to them. "Cultural creatives are the prototypical consumers of the experience industry, which sells intense, enlightening, enlivening experiences, rather than things. Creatives buy psychotherapy, weekend workshops, spiritual gatherings and personal growth experiences in all forms."[11]

Of course, the great thing about selling experiences instead of things is that the manufacturing and overhead costs are much lower. One of the differences between "spiritual" workshops and "religious" congregations is that purveyors of personal spirituality often charge a fixed fee for their services. While they pass the collection plate in churches, you don't have to pay to get the message, and you decide how much. But this fee-for-service spirituality reflects deeper changes. It's not just another way to pay the bills. Designer religion, the whole search for a personal spirituality, is at its core a very practical approach to faith. So much of the self-help industry is about fixing something, whether it's your sex life, your soul, or your cardiovascular system. It's spun under the mantra of "holistic health," and it can be an obsession with cultural creatives.

Or, as the marketing folks advise,

> Creatives are the core market for psychotherapy, alternative heath care, and natural foods. What ties these together is the belief that the body, mind and spirit should be unified. Creatives may include a high proportion of people whom some physicians describe as the "worried well," those who monitor every twitch and pain and bowel movement, in minutely detailed attention to the body. As a result, they spend more on all forms of health care, even though most are fairly healthy.[12]

Perhaps it should come as no surprise that at the dawn of the new millennium, when the marketplace reigns supreme, Americans are blending consumerism and mysticism. We're an unusually religious—and a stubbornly practical—people. And for growing numbers of us spirituality is more about therapy than theology. It's about feeling good rather than being good. Stress reduction, not salvation.[13]

Where does one advertise to find these seekers? Until the spring of 2002 one venue was *New Age Journal*. In that season the magazine ended a twenty-eight-year tradition and changed its name to *Body and Soul*, dedicated to "balanced living in a busy world." You could see the powerful hand of God in the change. In today's magazine and newspaper business, God takes the form of the overpriced demographics and marketing consultant. He or she issues your company new commandments, the first of them being, "Thou shalt appeal to female readers between the ages of twenty-eight and thirty-five." Exactly why we must do this is something of a mystery, but it has to do with moneychangers in the temple of journalism.

What really seemed to change at *New Age Journal* was the cover of the magazine. Suddenly the smiling faces of healthy and attractive women between the ages of twenty-eight and thirty-five beamed out from the cover. There were beauty tips, but only "natural" beauty tips. There was a weight-loss teaser out front, but it called on the rebel twenty-somethings to "Toss the Diet!" and follow "10 Steps to Healthy Eating." Otherwise, the articles were much like before. There were stories about the environment and headlines informing us that New Age celebrities like Marianne Williamson want us to "choose love over fear." There were interviews with the guru du jour. That season it was Eckhart Tolle, who wrote a book called the *Power of Now*, a kind of *Be Here Now* for the new millennium. There were still full-page ads for *Harmony Sound Wave Energy Healing* CDs and healthy cereal that tastes more like cardboard than breakfast.

New *Age Journal* may have reincarnated as *Body and Soul*, but the San Francisco New Age Expo was still rolling along. I swung by one spring weekend and found a few thousand people milling around the Concourse Exhibition Center on Brannan Street, a thoroughfare named after one of San Francisco's first spiritual pioneers, Sam Brannan. In 1846 Brannan gathered 250 Mormons together in New York, put them aboard a sailing ship, the *Brooklyn*, and headed for San Francisco. They doubled the population of this Spanish outpost, then known as Yerba Buena, when they arrived. Until the Gold Rush brought the rest of the world in 1849, San Francisco was known as a largely Mormon town.

It no longer has that reputation, but it is a great place to heal your inner child, regain your hormonal balance, experience tantric harmonics, and journey to cellular healing. Those were among the offerings at the New Age Expo, along with aura photography, light therapy, and the secrets of the ancient Incans. But my sources told me that the hot ticket that weekend was "Loving What Is" with Byron Katie, so I headed straight over there.

About three hundred people sat on folding white chairs and waited for Byron Katie. I looked in my program to find out more about Byron Katie. "Surviving years of depression, Katie experienced a radical shift in her perception of reality in 1986. She then began to share her way of retaining the gift of clarity, which became known as The Work of Byron Katie." The program said The Work of Byron Katie has transformed thousands of people. "Stress becomes a laughable matter, and peace appears as a fundamental ongoing experience."

Katie appeared in a flowing black dress. She had short gray hair, a nice smile, and *presence*, that centered feeling you get from someone who knows how to work a crowd. She told us about the low point in her life when she found herself on the floor of a halfway house. Bugs crawled over her legs. "In that moment I realized the cause of all my problems," she said. "My thinking."

Those of us in the white folding chairs were given little questionnaires to complete. There were four questions on the yellow card, and we were supposed to fill in the blanks.

1. I'm angry, upset, saddened at _____ because _____.
2. I need _____ to _____.
3. He or she should/shouldn't _____.
4. What three things do you most fear will happen?

When we finished answering the four questions, we were supposed to ask ourselves four questions about our four answers: Are they true? Can we absolutely know they're true? How do we react when we think that thought? Who would we be without the thought? Then we're supposed to turn the thought upside down ask ourselves if that is true or truer.

Katie asked for someone to read from their card. A woman stood up and said, "People should be peaceful."

Katie did not seem to like the answer.

"On what planet?" she shot back. "Who needs God when we have you? It just is what it is until it's not. Argue with that. Who would you be without the thought 'People should be peaceful'? Turn it around. 'I should be peaceful.' What's the opposite? 'People shouldn't be peaceful.'"

Okay. I think I get it. Lesson number one: We shouldn't say "should" or "shouldn't." Oops! There I go again. I said "shouldn't." I must not be transformed. Next lesson: We create our own reality. Our mind is the real problem. Well, my mind certainly can be a problem, but I'm not sure it's the real problem or the only problem. There are little things like hunger, disease, poverty, global terrorism, the new American imperialism. . . .

Byron Katie reminds me of a guy who takes over my television during PBS pledge weeks. His name is Wayne Dyer, and he also likes to tell me that I create my own reality. He's always pacing back and forth before a studio audience telling me how to get my life together. I'm just hoping to watch *Frontline*, but instead I get a self-help show about "How to Get What I Really, Really, Really, Really Want." Sometimes I really, really, really, really want to throw my shoe at my TV set. But I'm enlightened enough to know that when something gets me that upset, it's time to close my eyes, take a deep breath, think peaceful thoughts, and get in touch with my inner therapist.

My inner therapist told me I should confront the source of my anger, so I sat down in a small room and went face-to-face with Wayne Dyer. We didn't start out on a good note. Dyer interrupted one of my first questions when his cell phone rang and he began a long, whispering conversation. Then he ended the call and said, "That was Deepak Chopra. He's a good friend of mine." Chopra is another one of those guys who invades your TV set when you least expect it, telling you how to go about "Creating Affluence" and practice "Quantum Healing." Then there's Suze Orman and "The Laws of Money"? Don't get me started.

Chopra and Dyer are shameless promoters of spiritual syncretism, taking little bits of wisdom out of context from here and there, tossing them together like a bowl of mixed greens. In just a few pages you get a bit of Rumi, a few paragraphs of pseudoscience, a warm and fuzzy Jesus, the thoughts of Carl Jung, and the wise words of St. Francis, everyone's favorite Catholic saint. You never really get anywhere, even though the sales pitch promises enlightenment, affluence, and sexual bliss in three easy steps.

Dyer is unapologetic when I imply that the kind of New Age spirituality he promotes is about as deep as Saran Wrap. "You make an assumption that to go deep into something is better than to take what you can out of it," he replies. "That's like saying the *New York Times* is better than *USA Today*. For me, I don't want to read in depth about everything in the world. I like to skim."

Wrong thing to say to a journalist. It almost seems like Wayne is actually trying to piss me off. He had come to town to promote a new book and a new TV show on KQED, the PBS station in San Francisco. Both are called *There's a Spiritual Solution to Every Problem,* and I guess that includes my problem with Wayne Dyer.

KQED and other PBS stations do not broadcast the Wayne Dyer shows because lots of people watch them. His shows get only about half the ratings as the popular prime-time offerings on public TV. They broadcast Wayne Dyer, Suze Orman, and other self-help gurus during pledge drives because a small number of people get so inspired that they send in money. It's the same reason you can't get Pat Robertson or other televangelists out of your TV set. "Some people really do hate it, and I count myself among them," one KQED manager confessed to me. "But our audience knows it's a necessary evil. The other option is more corporate underwriting, and people don't like that either."

Dyer has been riding the long wave of pop psychology and New Age spirituality since the 1970s, when he came out with his first mega-selling self-help book, *Your Erroneous Zones.* There have been a string of books since then with titles such as *Wisdom of the Ages: 60 Days to Enlightenment* and *Manifest Your Destiny: The Nine Spiritual Principles for Getting Everything You Want.*

His books are a variation on one of the most popular themes in New Age spirituality, that idea that we create our own reality. Dyer's new book is a repetitive meditation upon a circular, self-fulfilling argument. Since all our problems are illusions, they all have a "spiritual" solution. It's the gospel of positive thinking, as American as Chevrolet, Dale Carnegie, and Norman Vincent Peale. Dyer is a great salesman, repackaging Peale with New Age slogans about energy fields.

Having a wrong state of mind causes poverty while illnesses are just symptoms of our "low vibrational fields." This mantra goes from simplistic to scandalous when taken to its logical extreme among those who preach that people with cancer are responsible for their own disease.

In Wayne's world, spirituality and religion have nothing to do with helping others or creating real community. "I'm not a community person," he confesses in our interview. "Maybe my books reflect that." His brand of religion is also a convenient way for the rich and comfortable to be "spiritual" without worrying about those less fortunate.

Isn't that right, Wayne?

"I don't think anybody is out there starving because somebody else gets something good for themselves," he replies. "I don't think there is poverty in the world because there are people who know how to attract abundance into their life."[14]

What about solidarity with the poor and all that good stuff?

"If you meet somebody in a state of poverty and come into that energy field with the same state of consciousness, you will lower the energy field," he explains. "I always had money in my pocket. It wasn't because I was lucky. I always had a burning desire to have abundance."

Dyer says *Your Erroneous Zones* has sold more than ten million copies in the United States. Worldwide, he says, it has sold more than forty million copies and has been translated into forty-eight languages.

So how much money have you made off your books, Wayne?

"Maybe twenty to twenty-five million," he replies.

Abundance, indeed!

Speaking of New Age abundance, whatever happened to Ramtha? Back in the early 1980s, in the glory days of the New Age movement, Shirley MacLaine wrote a book titled *Out on a Limb*. It sold eight million copies, put the New Age movement on the mainstream media map, and propelled an obscure channeler named J. Z. Knight to fortune and fame.

J. Z. brought us Ramtha, the thirty-five-thousand-year-old warrior from the lost continent of Lemuria, and came to represent all that was wacky and weird about New Age spirituality on the Left Coast. Knight, a Seattle businesswoman and cable TV entrepreneur, says Ramtha first appeared in her Tacoma kitchen on a Sunday afternoon in 1977. By the end of 1978 Knight says she learned to channel the spirit of the seven-foot-tall warrior. His timeless wisdom was soon embraced by MacLaine and *Dynasty* diva Linda Evans, rapturing Ramtha into celebrity heaven and making Knight one of the best-known and wealthiest spirit mediums of the 1980s.

Ramtha's basic message was a kind of neo-Gnosticism: the idea that the physical world is an illusion and that enlightenment is achieved through various esoteric teachings and spiritual practices. That's right—we create our own reality.

Those of us in the mainstream media didn't hear much from J. Z. in the 1990s. But in the new millennium, Ramtha decided to attempt a comeback, and where Ramtha goes, J. Z. follows. I caught up with them both on a gorgeous August 2001 weekend at Fess Parker's posh Doubletree Resort in Santa Barbara, California. Ramtha had rented a large meeting room, hoping for a big crowd, and was not pleased to see only about a hundred people. We didn't know that the world would change in a few weeks, on September 11, and neither did Ramtha, the wise seer of future calamities.

But Ramtha does likes to drink, especially when he's in a bad mood. "Do you feel embarrassed that there are not ten thousand people here? Don't worry," he said, filling a golden goblet with red wine. "This is about to take off again—like a firestorm."[15]

J. Z. chose this palatial beachfront resort to roll out Ramtha Redux, the obscenity-spewing prophet who went into hibernation for most of the 1990s at his School of Enlightenment in Yelm, Washington. His three-hour monologue, frequently punctuated with loud breaks of classic Sixties rock 'n' roll, blended the irreverent wisdom of Lenny Bruce with the you-go-girl cheerleading of the *Oprah Winfrey Show*. Plastic glasses of red wine were offered to the members of the audience, who were instructed not to slowly sip but to gulp it down. This gave the workshop a well-lubricated feel—more party than prayer. Two glasses of burgundy were included in the $395 weekend workshop. Not included were meals and housing at the resort, where a roof over your head costs $365 a night.

When channeling Ramtha, J. Z. affects a bad English accent, and it only gets worse as she drinks more red wine from the golden goblet. "Jesus said, 'Remember me when you drink this wine.' He was really saying, 'I love it.' Do you think he drank orange juice, apple juice, or Evian water? Do you think he strained celery and drank it and said, 'Behold. Remember me as celery'? That's not nearly as dashing and as wonderful as what he was saying," Ramtha said. "Wine is a magic elixir that drops the veil of hypocrisy by ceasing time in the mind. When time stops, truth emerges. No wonder Jesus loved it."

Ramtha likes to wear baseball caps and torn blue jeans. At the Doubletree gig, the buttons of his black coat were straining around some extra pounds put onto the physical body of his longtime channeler. But J. Z.'s added girth doesn't bother Ramtha, who encourages women to throw off the shackles of oppressive patriarchy. "What do all world religions have in common? The suppression of women," he/she told the Santa Barbara crowd, where women outnumbered men five to one. "No woman who had an abortion has sinned against God. Fuck all those assholes who tell you that."

Ramtha was getting nasty, and he was rattling on, so I stepped outside the ballroom to talk to Greg Simmons, the marketing director for Ramtha. He's been with Ramtha since March 1982. Simmons has also worked with Anthony Robbins, the guy who walks on hot coal and does lots of cable TV ads and will absolutely positively help you get it all together, guaranteed or your money back. Simmons has quite a story to tell, and he loves to talk, so let's listen:

"For one and a half years I was Tony Robbins's business partner and had an interest in his corporation. He was a big talent without much marketing support. I told him I could help him out. For eighteen months we built that organization. He became better known and published his first book. That was '84–'85. But I wanted to move back to Washington State and study with Ramtha. I could have stayed on with Robbins if my intention was to just make money, which he did. But I had a stronger pull to continue my studies in Washington.

"I first met Ramtha when a friend of mine was driving from San Francisco to Del Mar, where I lived. Just before she was leaving at around midnight, some guy runs into her house, puts a piece of paper on her dresser, and runs out of her house. It was about a seminar with Ramtha the next day, and she was going to just make it in time. She attended it and brought back an audiotape, which they sold right on the spot. She said she'd heard something outrageous and thought I might like to hear it. That was it. I called the organization. I flew up to Seattle in March 1982 and went to my first seminar. Just after we flew over Mount St. Helens, it blew up. I said to my partner, 'This is going to be a very interesting weekend.' It was, and it has been twenty years.

"At the time, I had my own business school and company called Super-Camp—super-learning technologies to get people to learn things quickly. I was always into human potential but not as 'spiritual' as I thought that to be then. I was into meditation ten years before that, but my draw was human potential and what the spiritual people could do.

"In the Sixties I was just a great hippie. I lived in San Francisco and played in a rock 'n' roll band. I was there in '67 and stayed on for two years. I went to Haight-Ashbury because I'd heard about it, but it was not really the love-love scene I'd heard about. It had a hard edge and rough drugs. In '71–'72 I was in New York, taking Sufi dancing lessons. I was back in San Francisco in 1975 and did the est training.

"What we're doing now really incorporates the Sixties. Ramtha felt like that was the only revolution we've had in a long, long time. Nothing since the Sixties has come along to create a spiritual revolution of that magnitude. I was in the middle of it. I was a conscientious objector and marched in Selma, Alabama, with Martin Luther King. Those were my roots."

Ramtha's organization had just released a new rock video about Ramtha, designed to capture the attention of a younger generation. It was full of Sixties song and Sixties images of protest and flower children, spiced with outtakes of Ramtha outrageousness. At this gathering it didn't seem to be working. Most people in the crowd were baby boomers. But Simmons thought it would catch on.

"The younger generation *is* interested. It's the only real true refreshing message people put out right now. With all the decadence today—all the music, the television, the movies are pretty awful. We've just collapsed as a society value-wise. The rock video is to appeal to the younger kids. They need to hear this message in a contemporary venue. Where do they want their life to go? The way of society, or is there another path? Look at rap music, which Ramtha hates. There couldn't be a more unhopeful message there. Ramtha said long ago, he said you'll know you're in the last days of a declining civilization when children kill children without remorse.

"Look at me. I was captivated by the Sixties, and I'm a normal person. I can't imagine why a young person now wouldn't be captivated by the ability to be free. There was truth spoken in the music. They were against issues I'm still against, like war and violence and bias against blacks.

"Ramtha has completely changed the way I live my life. Before I came to his school, I was building a little empire around myself with the proper clothes, the proper address, and the proper investments—not because I wanted to be financially free but because I thought that defined who I was. Now I'm looking for an expanded mind—for adventures I never had before."

Now Simmons was rattling on, so I went back inside to listen to some more Ramtha. Actually, I was trying to find Linda Evans but wasn't sure what she looked like. Perhaps I am the only American of my era who never saw one episode of *Dynasty*. I was told Evans would be in the front row, but there were a lot of beautiful women in that row, and I wasn't sure which one was her. I learned later that even if I been a *Dynasty* devotee, I would not have recognized the star.

Evans was now in her midfifties. She first hit the big time back in 1965 on the TV series *Big Valley*. Back in the sixties and early seventies, Evans was married to John Derek, who dumped her for a younger woman named Bo. Her big comeback was starring in *Dynasty*, the wildly popular eighties TV show. After another failed marriage to Hollywood playboy and real estate magnate Stan Herman, Linda Evans discovered Ramtha. But in a strange foreshadowing of her future life with the New Age warrior, her character on *Dynasty* was named Krystle.

After *Dynasty* Evans gave up on Hollywood and moved to Washington to be close to Ramtha. She has been going to the School of Enlightenment for sixteen years, and when we finally met she told me it had changed her life. Just like it had changed Greg Simmons's life.

"How has it changed your life?" I asked her.

"Me," she replied. "In my mind. In my brain. Me. It's like a totally different person in there."

We were sitting on a little patio outside the Doubletree Hotel. It was Saturday morning, and another teacher, Joe Dispenza, was inside giving the students a lecture on brain chemistry, titled "Molecules of Emotion." Ramtha was long gone. He was supposed to appear again on Saturday night but changed his mind and didn't show up. It had been a pretty small turnout for the once-famous warrior from Lemuria.

Ramtha calls Evans "Star Lady." During his rant the night before, he spent half an hour ridiculing the *Dynasty* star for all the plastic surgery she had back in the eighties. Evans is hardly recognizable from her *Dynasty* days. She's wearing no makeup, and, like Ramtha, she is wearing blue jeans and a baseball cap. But the former TV star does look happy and doesn't mind being the focus of Ramtha's wrath.

"When I left during the break last night, I felt really light," Evans told me the next day. "It was all out on the table. When he says things like, 'Let's talk about you and your face job, Star Lady—do people think you really look like that?' he's trying to get at our secrets. After that, I didn't have to protect anything."

Why get upset, asks Evans, when you know you are God? "All my life I looked outside of me to be loved and accepted," she said. "Then I finally heard that I was God. He is within me."

We all know about the power of celebrity endorsements. It works for sports cars, hair spray, lawn mowers, and fat burners for those chunky thighs. It also works for religion. Hubbard, the founder of Scientology, sought celebrity devotees for his movement back in the 1950s and today counts Tom Cruise and John Travolta in his ranks. Ramtha was launched with Shirley MacLaine, and when he tried his recent comeback it was Linda Evans who was trotted out to speak to the press. Of course, most people who join the Church of Scientology and Ramtha's School of Enlightenment are not celebrities. They are often people with a lot of problems in their lives, struggling through life's difficult transitions.

My first look at Ramtha's world was back in the 1980s, when I spent a lot of time up in the Pacific Northwest talking to middle-aged women who had gone there to follow three female gurus—J. Z. Knight, Elizabeth Clare Prophet, and a channeler named Mafu. They came from places such as Oklahoma and southern California, refugees from a world that seems spinning out of control. They were selling their homes and leaving their families. It was more than a decade before 2000, but there was a real apocalyptic feel to that middle-class migration. What they found was a strange mix of New Age mysticism, radical environmentalism, survivalist fervor, and old-fashioned Christian doomsaying.

Nothing new here, or so it seemed. The United States, founded by people coming from distant lands to practice new religions, has always provided fertile ground for doomsayers, date setters, and religious prophets. But there was something different about this wave, a new kind of apocalyptic fervor.

"It's the ideology of the nineteen-sixties' counterculture, updated and transformed by the political events of the eighties," said Carl Raschke, a professor of religious studies at the University of Denver. "In many ways the sixties were a secular apocalypse. Everything was now, now, now—total transformation. Apocalypse now."

Hundreds of members of Prophet's New Age religious sect, the Church

Universal and Triumphant, had moved to the church's thirty-three-thousand-acre Royal Teton Ranch in the mountains north of Yellowstone National Park. Members were frantically building bomb shelters, stockpiling dried food, and buying weapons to survive what Prophet saw as a dark transition between the old Age of Pisces and the dawning new Age of Aquarius.

Christians who are premillennialists see a final apocalyptic battle between the forces of good and evil—Armageddon—as inevitable. Those predicting the New Age Apocalypse, however, put more power in the hands of humans to alter the course of history through chanting, meditation, positive thinking, political action, or a change in personal lifestyle.

Prophet, Ramtha, and Mafu all borrow heavily from prophets, spiritualists, astrologers, and occult leaders going back two millennia. This cast of cosmic characters begins with the anonymous Jewish-Christian author of the book of Revelation, the last chapter of the New Testament and a classic apocalyptic work. Probably written around A.D. 95, the book of Revelation was designed to comfort Christians being persecuted by the Roman Empire, although its author's dreams, visions, and bizarre imagery about the end of the world hardly seem comforting, especially for the unsaved.

Elizabeth Clare Prophet's spiritual lineage shows that there's nothing new about the so-called New Age. She looks to Saint-Germain, an alchemist, oracle, and almost legendary wonderman who dazzled the royal courts of eighteenth-century France before his ascension as a heavenly prophet of God. Generations of occult leaders, including Prophet's late husband, Mark Prophet, have claimed to receive divine dictations from "le Comte de Saint Germain."

Both Prophet and J. Z. Knight draw heavily from Helena Petrovna Blavatsky, the infamous occultist who was born in Russia in 1831 and founded the Theosophy movement. Reacting to the stifling conformity of the Victorian Age and the materialism of the Industrial Revolution, Blavatsky created a magical universe of disembodied spirits of white light, Hindu mantras, Buddhist saints, and a Great White Brotherhood of heavenly masters. Prophet received divine dictations from ascended masters immortalized a century ago by Blavatsky while Ramtha came from Lemuria, the mythical lost continent described in Blavatsky's 1888 opus, The Secret Doctrine.

Knight and Prophet also follow in the footsteps of Annie Besant. This Englishwoman succeeded Blavatsky as head of the Esoteric Section of the Theosophy society and anointed a young Indian boy, Krishnamurti, as the new messiah to lead the world into the age of cosmic consciousness. Krishnamurti later renounced his role as New Age savior and spent decades urging people to think for themselves.

Two other precursors of Mark and Elizabeth Prophet were Guy and Edna Ballard. These Midwestern migrants to California founded the Mighty I AM movement, a Theosophy offshoot that struck a resounding chord during the Great Depression. At its peak in 1938, some one million followers were drawn to this mix of the occult, positive thinking, cataclysmic predictions, patriotic fervor, and strident anti-Communism. Prophet's church uses a meditation chart nearly identical to that of the Mighty I AM movement. Knight's church was incorporated in Washington State as the Church I Am.

Elizabeth Clare does not like being reminded of the similarities between her church and the I Am movement of the Ballards. She made that perfectly clear during an interview we had at the height of the apocalyptic fever up at her spread in Montana.

Prophet arrived an hour late and seemed tired as she sat down at a dining room table in the century-old farmhouse used as the headquarters building at Royal Teton Ranch. The place was meticulously restored, decorated with lace curtains and simple furniture to project a feeling of frontier homeyness. As she leaned against the oak table, sipping tea from a rainbow mug, something did not quite add up about her demeanor. It was as if her body was exhausted but her mind was racing. Her eyes did not say "sleepy." They said "get on with it." They were clear and open wide, intense and impatient, waiting for the first question. Prophet had agreed to set aside a couple of hours that day to discuss the religious beliefs of her Church Universal and Triumphant—to explain how her New Age theology justified spending countless hours and millions of dollars to build a huge underground sanctuary and bomb shelters to survive the New Age apocalypse.

She had been born Elizabeth Clare Wulf in the New Jersey shore community of Red Bank on April 8, 1939. At an early age, according to church lore, this only child of a Swiss mother and strict German father began to search beyond her parents' Lutheran faith. Those Sunday sermons were only words. Young Elizabeth wanted to experience God face-to-face. At the age of five she began remembering past lives. She had out-of-body experiences while waterskiing on a New Jersey river headed toward the sea.

Prophet studied political science and economics at Antioch College in Ohio and Boston University, where she joined the headquarters staff at the Church of Christ, Scientist, in Boston and worked briefly at the *Christian Science Monitor*. At school she met a young Norwegian law student, Dag Ytreberg, who became the first of four husbands. It would not be long, however, until Elizabeth met her true soul mate, her "twin flame."

They met when she attended one of Mark Prophet's lectures in Boston. "When I sat down, I found myself sitting opposite the messenger, Mark Prophet. I looked into his eyes. I had been looking for that pair of eyes all my life. I'd describe them as a pair of eyes that had met the eyes of God. I had found the one who could open the door of consciousness. I found my teacher."[16]

Marcus L. Prophet was born on Christmas Eve, 1918, in Chippewa Falls, Wisconsin. *Prophet* was both his actual family name and a spiritual status Mark would ultimately claim. His father died when Mark was nine years old. Steeped in his mother's Pentecostal faith, young Mark spent hours, it is written, at an altar he built in the attic of his home. Later his mother's religious fundamentalism gave way to studies in the metaphysical Unity School of Christianity.

Little is known of Mark Prophet's early life. A handsome, square-jawed, muscular man, Prophet worked as a railway track worker and a traveling salesman. During World War II he served as a clerk for the Army Air Corps. His divine call, Prophet would later say, came at age eighteen when he was working on the Soo Line Railroad and was contacted by the ascended master El Morya.

Mark Prophet was by no means the first spiritual seeker to claim a cosmic encounter with El Morya. This turbaned Eastern adept, pictured in church portraits with a dark beard and intense stare, had been immortalized by Blavatsky, the founder of the Theosophy movement. Six decades before Mark Prophet claimed his encounter with El Morya on the Soo Line Railroad, Blavatsky had brought this ascended master into worldly focus in *The Secret Doctrine*. Often referred to as simply "M" by Blavatsky and later Theosophists, Morya would return again and again as a mythic hero of occultists struggling to personify their dreams, visions, or psychosis. His constant resurfacing has been attributed to plagiarism, archetypal psychology, Satan, and the invisible hand of God. Whatever the cause, El Morya was here to stay.

Blavatsky likewise popularized Saint-Germain, the inspiration behind Elizabeth Clare Prophet's divine call. Spiritualists across the century would also claim messages from this ascended master, but none so central to this story as Guy and Edna Ballard.

Guy Ballard, born in rural Kansas in 1878, had an early interest in fortune-telling and used that skill after moving to Chicago to ply the spiritualist trade. In 1916 Guy married Edna Wheeler, a concert harpist who shared his interest in the occult. They moved out to northern California, where Guy took a job as a government surveyor, an occupation that allowed him to explore the slopes of Mount Shasta, a snowcapped, 12,336-foot peak, and home, Ballard believed, of the ascended masters. By 1935 the Ballards were attracting thousands of devotees to large auditoriums in cities across the nation.

Like a half century later in Montana, apocalyptic predictions were used to inspire believers. In 1934 Edna Ballard began talking about horrible catastrophes that could culminate in cataclysm in September 1936. America, already in the midst of an economic crisis, was about to be physically devastated. The entire Atlantic seaboard was doomed to slide into the sea, an event that would have occurred already if not for the cosmic influence of I AM decrees. Devotees were encouraged to cash in their insurance policies before the coming apocalypse. "Love offerings," as the financial contributions were called, flowed into the Ballards' church.

Guy Ballard, who many followers assumed would achieve cosmic ascension without physical death, died on December 29, 1939. Six months later a federal grand jury indicted two dozen leaders of the I AM Foundation, including Edna and her son, on sixteen counts of fraudulent use of the mails. For several years there had been rumors about financial chicanery, shady backgrounds, and authoritarian leadership in the movement. The government alleged that the Ballards knew their religion was a fabrication and fraudulently used the U.S. mail to bilk believers. The U.S. District Court in southern California convicted them, but in a landmark 1944 ruling the Supreme Court threw out the case against the Ballards. The court acknowledged that the Ballards' religious views "may seem incredible, if not preposterous, to most people. But if those doctrines are subject to trial before a jury charged with finding their truth or falsity, then the same can be done with the religious beliefs of any sect."[17]

From her new base in Santa Fe, Edna Ballard pushed on as the acknowledged leader and divine messenger of the ascended masters until her death in Chicago in 1971. Later in the 1970s, many of those who discovered the Ballards' teachings went to another pair of divine messengers, Mark and Elizabeth Prophet.

According to his widow, Mark Prophet was never a formal member of the I AM movement, although he did join the Rosicrucians and the Self-Realization

Fellowship, founded in Los Angeles in the 1920s by the late Paramahansa Yogananda.

"Mark became a student of Eastern mysticism as a young man and would lecture on how Eastern mysticism relates to Christianity," Elizabeth Prophet said. "He was doing that for some time, and then he became the *amanuensis*, which means scribe or secretary, to El Morya."

Prophet acknowledged she read the I AM books five years before she met Mark Prophet, calling them "one of my main introductions to the teachings of the Masters." But she bristled at the suggestion she and her husband plagiarized Blavatsky's Theosophy teachings or the precepts of the Ballards' movement. Guy and Edna Ballard did not begin the I AM movement, Prophet said.

"It began with Moses," she told me. "Moses saw the bush that burned but was not consumed. And God spoke to him out of the bush and said his name was 'I Am That I Am.' That's where the Mighty I AM Presence comes from."

There is little doubt Elizabeth Clare Wulf felt Mark Prophet's mighty presence when the couple first met at that Boston discussion group in 1961. Elizabeth sat in rapt attention in the front row as Mark delivered his dictation from the ascended masters. She remembers "sitting in front of Mark, him taking me up in meditation, seeing, seeing the whole world and all the souls of the people of the world as these daisies of the field, like stars." Mark Prophet, she recalled later, "was a man of the Holy Spirit. I mean, when Mark Prophet walked into the room the Holy Spirit walked in with him. He always had that presence."[18]

Unfortunately, Prophet and Wulf were already married when they had that cosmic encounter. Elizabeth, twenty-two, had recently wedded her Norwegian husband. Mark, forty-two, had a wife and children who did not understand his spiritual quest. "Mark's wife did not believe in his religion and had not believed for fifteen years," Elizabeth said. "She had turned his children against him in ridicule."

Both marriages soon ended in divorce, and Mark took Elizabeth back to Washington, D.C. During the next three years Mark turned young Elizabeth "inside out and upside down" with intense psychic and esoteric training to transform her into a purified messenger of the ascended masters. Meek and unskilled at first, Elizabeth Clare Prophet gradually learned the technique of putting herself in a trance while remaining conscious, switching back and forth from herself to a channeled entity during lectures.

In 1966 the couple moved to Colorado Springs. Their move coincided with the blossoming of the Sixties counterculture and rising interest in Eastern mysticism among those of the new generation. Younger converts joined the fold, and the growing church bought the old Broadmoor mansion in Colorado Springs, renaming it La Tourelle, or the Tower.

Within a few years the Prophets were looking to head farther west, to California. Keeping their headquarters in Colorado Springs, the Prophets founded Summit University in Santa Barbara in 1971, where they offered spiritual retreats and courses in the teachings of the ascended masters.

Meanwhile, a survivalist mentality was starting to infiltrate the sect. Mark Prophet saw the early signs of the Arab oil crisis and began receiving messages about Arab control of the world economy. Decrees, the same buzzing chants used by the I AM movement, were employed to change the course of history. In the midst of this fervor, Mark Prophet had his own personal apocalypse. He died suddenly, in bed, of a stroke, on February 26, 1973.

As with Guy Ballard's death thirty-four years earlier, Mark's passing threw the sect in disarray. Some devotees left while others remained in a power struggle with Elizabeth, who immediately declared Mark Prophet had ascended and she was now the only living messenger of the ascended masters. Elizabeth seized control of the organization, and only nine days after Mark's death she secretly married her third husband, a young sect member named Randall Kosp. "We became intimate before Mark died," Kosp told the press in 1985, after a falling-out with Prophet. "I think Mark knew. Just before he died, he sat me down and said, 'Now, take good care of Elizabeth. Take care of all her needs.'"

At Elizabeth's request, Randall changed his name from Kosp to King. Explained one former member, "Elizabeth had a thing about being the Prophet and the King."

Prophet and her growing sect bought the 218-acre Saint Thomas Aquinas College near Malibu for $5.6 million. The estate, originally the home of razor blade millionaire King Gillette, was renamed Camelot. During the 1970s spiritual seekers flocked to the pastoral campus nestled in coastal hills outside Malibu. They attended retreats and took classes in meditation. They found an eclectic universe where angels sang, Arthurian legend came alive, and the latest prophecy was but a weekend away.

During the early 1980s information about the darker side of Camelot was revealed in legal proceedings brought by Gregory Mull, a San Francisco architect who posthumously won a $1.5 million settlement against the church in April 1989. Randall King told of an "investment club" in the church where po-

tential donors were brought into a room and told that Saint-Germain had a secret alchemical project and needed their financial help. Intense pressure was
put on wealthy believers to turn their assets over to the church. Promissory
notes that were allegedly covered over so only the signature line was visible
were presented to members, who signed the documents firm in the belief that
their assistance was needed for the good of the church. Mull, introduced to
church teachings at a study group in 1973, mortgaged his home to make contributions. Prophet, he testified, seduced him with grand visions of Mull design-
ing $33 million worth of construction projects at Camelot. They would build
the "New Jerusalem."[19]

Mull's lawsuit and Randall King's defection unleashed a wave of negative
publicity in southern California. Zoning restrictions in the hills of Malibu
stood in the way of the New Jerusalem, and Prophet redirected her attention to
the Northwest. There had already been several failed attempts to establish a
survivalist stronghold in Idaho, but another opportunity was about to appear.
Malcolm Forbes was looking to sell off most of his vast hunting retreat in
southern Montana. It was time for another exodus, a new Promised Land, and
the fulfillment of a new prophecy.

"Our calling," Elizabeth Clare Prophet told me a few years later in Montana,
"the calling of Mark and Elizabeth Prophet, is to fulfill the teachings of Jesus
because people need them to go into the New Age."

Prophet prophesied that October 2, 1989, would mark the beginning of an
eleven-year period of turmoil before the dawning of the New Age. Thousands
of her followers believed her and fled to Montana. They invested millions in
her Royal Teton Ranch, but before those eleven years passed most of those
New Age pioneers had left Paradise Valley. Prophet's sect sold off huge chunks
of the Montana property, and she went into seclusion. In late 1998 Elizabeth
told her flock she was deteriorating with Alzheimer's disease. Two years later
there were rumblings of another lawsuit against the Church Universal and Triumphant by former members who felt Prophet had enriched herself and de-
frauded them.[20]

Meanwhile, up in heaven, Saint-Germain, El Morya, and the ascended
masters waited patiently for another prophet to announce the coming of the
New Age.

They're still waiting. Elizabeth Clare Prophet, J. Z. Knight, and Sun
Myung Moon all announced the dawning of the New Age. But at the time of

this writing, in the spring of 2003, it's hard to see a new era of equality, harmony, and world peace. The religions of the world are not coming together. They seem to be tearing the world apart in an apocalyptic eruption of tribalism and hate. We're not sharing the wealth of the world. We're grabbing at the leftovers.

But let's not end on that note. Let's get back to the bliss. Remember the hippies? Remember the idealism? Remember the children? Remember the dream?

CHAPTER 12

Communes and Hippie Kids: Down on the Farm

Talk about your plenty, talk about your ills
One man gathers what another man spills.

"ST. STEPHEN"[21]

ROBERT HUNTER, THE GRATEFUL DEAD, 1971

Louie Kachinsky was in seventh grade when he suddenly realized he had not been living in the real world. The revelation came on a school playground in Lewis County, Tennessee, where his classmates were giving him funny looks. It didn't take long for them to realize that Louie was one of those hippie kids, born and raised on the Farm, that commune out by Summertown full of longhairs and dope smokers from San Francisco.

It was Louie's first day at public school. Everyone seemed to be looking at his shoes. For some reason they were snickering. "It was a shock," he said. "I didn't realize that shoes were anything but something you put on your feet to stop them from getting injured. My shoes were ratty and didn't say Nike on them."

Then there was lunch. Most of the kids bought school lunches, but Louie didn't have any money. His parents were against money. They were also strict vegans who didn't eat meat, fish, cheese, or dairy products. "They were serving pizza at school with this cheese layer with some kind of meat on it, and I had a

225

paper bag with weird stuff like tofu and purple corn chips. You're in some red-neck school, and you got purple corn chips!"

Louie came back the next day wearing the same shoes and the same clothes. "People came up to me and said, 'Didn't you wear that yesterday?' I was like, 'Yeah? Does it matter?' I mean, I couldn't believe it. People actually cared what I wore and shit. That was foreign to me. We were dirt-poor, but I didn't really get it until then."

His dad, Joel Kachinsky, didn't think of it as poor. He thought of it as politi-cal. "We came here to decondition ourselves from our capitalist conditioning and recondition ourselves for a better society," he told me. "If it was just us, if we were monks and nuns without kids, we might have stayed doing it. But we were so poor that a lot of us just said, 'Enough!' The level of deprivation that we were putting our kids through just wasn't fair."

It was 1983 and the Farm, the largest hippie commune of the 1960s and 1970s, was falling apart—and a major reason for it was the kids.

Once again, the visions of the Sixties collided with the bonds of parenthood. Hundreds of hippies from San Francisco and across America had come to the Tennessee backwoods for a grand communal experiment. They would create a sustainable, self-sufficient community—a model for another way of living. They would reject the nuclear family and form group marriages of four adults or six adults and a growing number of hippie children. They would farm. They would start small collective businesses. They would last ten years, then sud-denly collapse. Few of the Farmies like to admit it, but capitalism would con-quer this commune, just as in the larger world. And the nuclear family would rise from the communal ashes.

"As the kids got older, it was obvious that there wasn't the money living communally that we needed for braces or college or other things you need when kids get older," said Barbara Bloomfield, one of the surviving members. "We just weren't earning enough money. We were so busy being in commu-nity. But that wasn't generating any money, and we needed money to pay the bank for the land."

To understand what happened at the Farm, you have to understand Stephen Gaskin, the university lecturer and freelance philosopher who in-spired it all. Born in Denver in 1935, Gaskin enlisted in the U.S. Marine Corps when he was still a teenager. He served in Korea and was discharged in 1955. He then enrolled in San Bernardino Valley Union College in southern Califor-nia, where he ran a coffeehouse, became a beatnik, and spent six years getting a two-year degree. His first marriage, in 1959, lasted two years. His second, in 1961, produced a daughter named Dana but ended in 1964, the same year Gaskin earned his master's degree at San Francisco State College and began teaching creative writing to undergraduates.

In 1966 the hippie scene was blossoming in the cool gray city of love, and Stephen was flowering with it. He grew his hair and beard long and took to wearing tight jeans and colorful vests over his long, thin frame. His lectures wandered off into mysticism, politics, alternative lifestyles, and the ongoing psychedelic revolution, a subject that many of his students chose for their creative writing assignments. Some were starting to see Gaskin less as a lecturer and more as a guru. One of his assignments was for them to write an essay on "what a world redeemer needed to be like to be effective today," and a few students wondered if Stephen was doing research for his next gig.

Perhaps he was. "My teaching contract expired after two years," Gaskin recalled, years later, "and I was too weird to be rehired. I'd fallen in love with the hippie realization."

His lectures continued off campus and became known as the Monday Night Class, or Saint Stephen's "tripping instructions." They moved to various venues. Hundreds of stoned seekers followed Gaskin to the Straight Theater on Haight Street, the Oddfellows Hall, and finally out to Playland at the Beach.

Stephen married his third wife, Margaret Nofziger, in 1967. After that he stopped bothering to get divorced before "marrying" again. Like Joseph Smith, the polygamous founder of the Mormon Church, Stephen took on Ina May and her lover in a "four-marriage," which grew into a "six-marriage" before the grand experiment collapsed on the other side of the continent, in a very different decade.

That all seemed like ancient history when I sat around the lunch table with Stephen and Ina May. It was the autumn of 2002, and they were still together and still living in their funky house on a quiet corner of the Farm. These prophets of the Sixties were in *their* sixties now, and the days of the four-marriages were long gone.

"We consider ourselves as having been together since the summer solstice of 1968," Stephen said, flashing a loving smile Ina May's way. "We've been through a lot of changes, but we always knew it was us."

Their odyssey to Tennessee began thirty-two years ago, on Columbus Day, 1970, when Stephen and Ina May headed out on a national lecture tour of colleges and liberal churches, joined by a long caravan of two hundred hippies crammed into old school buses, dune buggies, banged-up trucks, and make-shift campers. They headed north from San Francisco on October 12 and were greeted at the Oregon border by twenty state police and Josephine County sheriff's deputies. It was not a friendly greeting. Three members of the road show were held on drug charges, and the cops confiscated quantities of marijuana, mescaline, and a live peyote plant.

Undaunted, the caravan wandered across the country, stopping traffic as the old school buses, brightly painted in psychedelic patterns, moved from town to town. They reached Washington, D.C., in January 1971, where two dozen of the buses parked in a drab downtown parking lot. Children romped around the encampment while the men went out seeking day jobs and donations of food. Inside one of the vehicles, an old 1954 Ford school bus equipped with a woodburning stove and bunk beds for the kids, a four-marriage family of seven sat down with a newspaper reporter and tried to explain what the hell was going on inside these buses and inside these hippies' heads. Peter and Kay Marie Schweitzer and Gerald and Priscilla Wheeler sat holding their three children, Gabriel, Ruth, and John, in their communal laps. Peter pulled his long, straight hair out of his face and told how the nation was "ripe for a spiritual renaissance." As for his unusual marital arrangement, Schweitzer said the quartet lived without rancor or jealousy. "It's our way of life," he said. "Our four-marriage is a lifetime contract that has more meaning than most conventional ones."[22]

Gaskin and his growing hippie family spent four months on the road. By the time they got back to San Francisco, three babies had been born—one in a parking lot at Northwestern University, another in a Michigan state park, and the third during a rest stop in Riple, New York. They returned to San Francisco looking for a place to park their ragtag fleet and wondering what to do next. They soon decided to pool their money, buy a thousand acres of cheap land in central Tennessee, and start a commune. Within in month they were on the road again, a band of hippies headed for the land of the hillbillies.

Gaskin's gang was a fertile bunch, but that's what happens when you bring together hundreds of happy, healthy, and horny hippies and decide that most forms of birth control are unnatural. Abortion was not allowed, and there was a baby boom.

"Suddenly, there were all these single moms," recalls Ina May, the midwife who delivered many of those hippie babies. "It was a huge problem. You could see why it was happening. Women didn't know how to say no, and they often forget to say no when they were most fertile, and then the guy is off some-where else. One of my criticisms of the hippie movement was that it seemed like the women were getting screwed, so to speak.

"When we got to the Farm, we tried to slow things down. We said the women had the say-so. When we made up our own culture here, part of it was to slow down courtship and make it a little old-fashioned—but without the pu-ritanical part that sex is nasty. It was good that the hippies got rid of that, but they went too far the other way. You had all these kids who didn't have dads, and you could see how much they wanted one."

They got to the Farm in the spring of 1971, landing in the poorest county in rural Tennessee, just thirty-five miles from the birthplace of the Ku Klux Klan. They were 278 strong and arrived in sixty-three converted buses, which many of the new settlers continued to call home. Buses and army tents provided shelter while salvage crews fixed up old tobacco barns and long-condemned houses. They wanted to be farmers, and they started out with a pair of Belgian mares and an old plow. They began by growing sorghum and making mo-lasses, selling it as Old Beatnik Pure Lewis County Sorghum. But there was an-other crop under cultivation—at least until Gaskin and three other Farmies were busted for growing marijuana. They appealed all the way to the United States Supreme Court but lost the case and wound up spending about a year in the Tennessee state prison.

Meanwhile, back on the Farm, there were some very lean, very cold winters. But by 1977 the commune had grown in to a functioning experimental com-munity of a thousand men, women, and children. They had their own school, flour mill, cannery, medical clinic, publishing business, and even their own telephone system, Beatnik Bell. They all contributed to a communal treasury, giving them the same tax status as a Catholic monastery. Nobody had to file for taxes until everyone was up to a taxable level.

But the Farm was not just an economic and ecological experiment. It was a spiritual community, forged in many cases by the bond of shared psychedelic experiences. "We were water brothers," Stephen told me. "We were collective in a spiritual sense." He said the same connection inspired some of the four-marriages and other group living arrangements. "Some of the double couples were sort of a fallout from LSD. People who tripped together bonded. Then we'd say, 'Let's just get a house together.'"

Stephen became a licensed Tennessee cleric, married many Farm couples, and led Sunday morning services. They'd meet in a meadow on the commune or inside the schoolhouse. Gaskin would draw from the mystical teachings of various world religions, a synthesis he called "the psychedelic testimony of the saints" or the "totality of the manifestation." Here's how one visitor described a Sunday service in 1977:

> At first, there was no talking: all that was heard was the shuffling of feet, a cough here and there, the sound of a creaking screen door or a baby gurgling in its mother's arms. People sat on the floor, adjusting themselves to get stoned on Stephen. Then, as if by prearrangement and a synchronization of watches, the Om began. The chant started in Stephen's corner and spread across the room like the tide rolling onto the beach. The m of the Om continued for thirty minutes without interruption, the constant hum rose and fell in intensity, and you could begin to pick out unintentional harmonies within the monotonous vibration. Then, again as if prearranged, the m trailed off gently into silence. It was time for Stephen.[23]

On this morning Gaskin talked about some "bad vibes" he was feeling on the Farm. It seemed some folks resented the freewheeling lifestyle of the commune's rock 'n' roll band, which toured the country recruiting new members. "Not enough people on the Farm personally in their private heart of hearts are being good yogis with good integrity and keeping their minds together," he told a crowd of three hundred Farmies gathered in the schoolhouse. "This ship is for all crew and no passengers."

At that stage in the Farm's history, Stephen was the undisputed captain of the ship. Media accounts routinely called him the "guru" and the commune members his "followers," a description Gaskin now hates and insists was never true. "I never let anybody call me guru," he told me. "I had people try to scatter flower petals at my feet back in San Francisco, and I said, 'Don't do that to me!' I never let anybody call me guru."

When we met in 2002, no one at the Farm was calling Gaskin a guru. Fewer and fewer had since the early 1980s, when the population peaked with fifteen hundred members, then suddenly collapsed. Faced with too much debt, radical poverty, and too many mouths to feed, the Farm stopped being a true commune, where everything was jointly owned. It reorganized as a collective, in which members had to pay monthly dues, and only the Farm's seventeen hundred acres were held in common.

Most people here call those bitter days in 1983 "the changeover." Gaskin calls it "a coup d'état followed by a downsizing." Many members wandered off, unable to make it in a community in which they suddenly needed real money to survive. Large households and group marriages dissolved, and Gaskin now concedes that the four-marriages and six-marriages were a failure.

"We discovered it was very complicated," he said. "Adding more people to a marriage is not an arithmetic progression but a geometric progression. A three-people marriage is not 50 percent harder to keep together than two people. It's *nine times* harder. Living with four people is *sixteen times* harder. Some families were arguing so much that they wouldn't show up for work."

Most of the hippies drifted off, but those who remained paid off the debt on the land. By 2002 there were only eighty to ninety voting members in this land-rich, cash-poor enterprise. Except for the publishing house, which prints books on vegetarian cooking, midwifery, and other subjects close to the hippie heart, most of the collective businesses on the Farm, like Ice Bean, the soy milk ice cream operation, went into private hands or collapsed. Twenty-seven large multifamily homes were built between 1974 and 1978. Once crowded with couples in group marriages and lots of children, some of the spacious homes have been taken over by the older couples who stuck around and rode it out.

Bloomfield admits she'd had enough communal living by the 1980s. "We ended up with just two families in a big house, and then we duplexed it," she said. "We ended up being a nuclear family with all my kids. In a way it was a big relief to just be able to have dinner with my family and not have to deal with everyone."

Melissa Meltzer, born on the Farm in 1974, took part in the 1983 exodus. Her earliest memories are waiting for meals in a specially built high chair that held fifteen toddlers. Melissa would gaze down the line, looking for her sister. "We always lived communally, with between fifteen and sixty people in the house. My memories are really positive—running around the woods with a bunch of other kids, being outside a lot. We were surrounded by a lot of love."

Leaving the Farm, moving to California, and making the transition to a public school was not easy. But Melissa's family moved out West with three other families, taking a little bit of the Farm with them and softening the changes.

When we spoke, Melissa was a twenty-eight-year-old artist living in a town just south of San Francisco. She thought she and her boyfriend would get married in a few years and have children of their own. She wants to be part of a community but has no interest in recreating the commune of her childhood. "I see a traditional family," she says. "I don't like this idea of both parents working and having a stranger taking care of their children."

Three of Melissa's friends had just told her that they were moving back to the Farm, partly for financial reasons. It's hard enough for young people to buy into the American dream, but many of the kids who grew up on the Farm have little interest in that dream. Leaving the Farm, they were quick to find the ultimate emptiness in the consumer lifestyle. "People in my generation are starting to plan to have kids and are trying to rekindle that sense of community. One way to do it is go home, go back to where it still exists. We feel like we have that birthright."

Many of these returnees will be surprised when they return. Three decades since its founding, the former commune feels like a ghost town. Some of the old-timers, like Joel Kachinsky, wonder why it still exists. "When we were communal, our level of trust put us in an extraordinary state of consciousness," he said. "There are about four thousand members of our tribe—folks who took the vow of poverty and were seriously doing this thing. That body is our church, or group soul. Since the changeover we've been in a dysfunctional state and back in ordinary consciousness."

Now that the Farm is no longer a commune, all kinds of questions arise about why it exists, who really owns it, and who can come back or join up. Today, Kachinsky says, the Farm even has its own version of NIMBYs, those rigid "not in my backyard" suburbanites who oppose any new development. "We have to deal with that before we hand this over to the next generation. If we don't, it could be a real mess here in another thirty years."

And the next generation is coming back. His son, Louie, the seventh-grader who got laughed at for his tattered shoes, had just returned from Boston, where he went to music school but found it difficult to survive financially. He was back sharing a house on the Farm with two other guys from his generation, wondering how he'd fit in to this formerly communal equation.

Louie, twenty-seven, leaned back in a chair outside his house as three dogs raced around the wooded land. "The only reason I came back is my parents live here," he said. "I was having trouble making ends meet in Boston. I didn't have any urban skills or have a degree, and I wasn't feeling the whole musician thing. It was a real shock being away from the Farm and that support group for the first time."

Of course, many young adults have a hard time making it on their own these days, and it's not hard to find adult children returning to the parental nest. But the Farm is different. Leaving here can seem like leaving the planet. This community is like one extended family, for better or worse, function or dysfunction.

I asked Louie to describe his memories growing up in a house with three or four other families. "I don't have any painful memories from back then, like being treated wrong," he said. "I just remember being disciplined one time by somebody other than my parents, where I didn't like it at all. My parents were off at a service, meditating in the meadow, and they gave me a spanking and I was like, 'No way.' But mostly I really enjoyed those years."

What about the spiritual side of the Farm? What values have you taken away?

It's not an easy question, and Louie balks at first.

"They tried to instill hippie values, which I guess I have."

What values are hippie values?

"I'm not sure what they are," he replies, pausing to think. "They try to take the good out of each religion and leave all the bullshit. It doesn't have to have anything to do with God. It's having respect and doing what you believe is good and respecting other people when they tell you that you're not doing good—trying not to use more than your share. Don't hoard ridiculous amounts of energy and money. Try not to be egocentric, meaning that you're the only people who matter. Don't think you can go to another country and dump all your nuclear waste."

I put the same question to Melissa Meltzer out in California. What spiritual values did she take with her from the Farm? "Mostly it's understanding that we are all one," she answered, "from the same creator and the same love. It's a deep understanding of compassionate love—with no strings attached."

Parents of the Farm kids watch their children come and go, wondering how their unusual upbringing will play out in their lives. Neal and Barbara Bloomfield once lived in a house with thirty other men, women, and children. "A lot of those kids are still very close," Barbara said. "A lot of them have left the Farm and are starting to raise their own families, but they are still connected up."

At the same time, the second-generation Farm families are not embracing group marriages or large communal households. The nuclear family won out—on the Farm and in the next generation of Farmies. The Bloomfields' oldest son, Reuben, lives in Asheville, North Carolina, with his wife and their new baby.

"We weren't focused on material things for our babies, but these kids want that for their children," Barbara said. "We got by with hand-me-downs."

Many of the kids born on the Farm are now older than their parents were when they renounced consumerism and established their Tennessee commune. But very few of the second generation show the zeal or utopian ideals of their hippie parents. And that's okay, says Neal. "They may not be out to save the world, but they're kind people."

Meanwhile, at sixty-seven, Stephen Gaskin keeps on keepin' on. Stephen is no longer seen as the leader of the tribe, but he's still got one vote, lots of energy, and even more ideas. In 1996 he published a book titled *Cannabis Spirituality*, an ode to wonders of getting high on pot. Then he took the politics of pot national. He ran for president of the United States against Ralph Nader in an unsuccessful bid for the Green Party nomination.

That didn't work out, so now Gaskin is promoting Rocinante, a retirement encampment for aging hippies. For his retirement village, Gaskin bought a hundred acres of land adjacent to the Farm. He has plans (but no money) to build an octagonal community center with a clinic, kitchen, Laundromat, and media room with computers and Internet access. "I wasn't quite done running something," he says, his eyes twinkling behind his spectacles.

Gaskin predicts that many of yesterday's counterculture activists—all those folks who "sold out" in the eighties and dropped back into the system—are about ready to drop out again. And they're going to need somewhere to live. "When we first started talking about Rocinante, collectivity was not interesting to people. They were in their peak earning years," he said. "When they get a little older, collectivity will get interesting again."

Thousands of communes formed in the 1960s and 1970s, and the Farm is one of the relatively few that survived, albeit in an altered economic arrangement. In many ways the hippie movement seems like a distant memory, a quaint chapter in the story of a generation that went on to run the country and embrace consumerism like never before. Nevertheless, Gaskin thinks the hippie legacy can be seen today in many forms—holistic health, environmentalism, mysticism, and natural childbirth. "When they write the sixties history centuries from now, the hippies will have a name like the Renaissance or the

Reformation," Gaskin said. "We did change the world, and we're not finished changing the world."

Gaskin's latest dream, Rocinante, is named after Don Quixote's horse, and it is a perfect name. Rocinante may never be more than a collection of cabins built by a spaced-out band of aging, unrepentant hippies. It may also be an indication that this quixotic rebel has learned something about himself over his thirty years on the Farm. *Rocinante* is an inside joke to those who've watched Gaskin's rise and fall. *Webster's* defines *quixotic* as "foolishly impractical, especially in the pursuit of ideals . . . marked by rash lofty romantic ideas or extravagantly chivalrous action." That's Stephen Gaskin.

Today there is no farming on the Farm. It's a famous commune that hasn't been a commune for twenty years. It's an expression of Sixties ideals and a place where only the well-off have health insurance. It's a place where group marriage was tried but the nuclear family prevailed. Its utopia interrupted— paradise lost. It's a place where dreams took form and were recycled back into dreams. Was it ultimately a failure? Perhaps, but someone has to dream.

CONCLUSION

W e didn't save the world, and judging from the first few years of the new millennium, we've got a long way to go. Religious fundamentalism, zealous nationalism, and unfettered capitalism are on the rise at home and abroad.

We didn't transform ourselves, but many of us are still working on it.

Perhaps the miracle of the Sixties is that we truly believed we could save the world and transform ourselves. Some of us still believe that, and the world still needs changing.

Cosmic consciousness turned out to be an elusive state of mind. Nevertheless, we did go through some changes along the way. In fact, the spiritual, social, and sexual legacies of the Sixties are so pervasive that we often fail to see them. Let's look again.

The liberation movements of the 1960s and 1970s changed society as they reshaped our own lives. Feminism put women in the Senate and behind mainline Protestant pulpits while the sexual revolution and the gay rights movement shook church and family to their foundations. A new awareness of the connections between mind and body, the values of meditation, and the benefits of more natural and wholesome foods began on the New Age fringe but spread to medical centers and supermarkets across America. That changed everything from the food we eat and the clothes we wear to the way we heal ourselves and the way we die.

Millions of Americans turned away from Jewish and Christian traditions to explore the mystical and meditative paths of Eastern religion. Many of them stayed away. Others sought to transform themselves through self-help therapies, psychedelic drugs, and the various consciousness-raising techniques that blossomed in the West. Few were transformed, but millions were never the same again.

Powerful spirits moved the religious revolution of the Sixties: idealism, innovation, empowerment, and the search for authentic experience. They remain the hallmarks of the era.

There was a thirst for authenticity, for telling it like it is. There was a turning away from materialism and greed and old roles. Many of us replayed Dustin Hoffman's role in the 1967 film *The Graduate,* searching for our own life and our own set of values. Benjamin was right. You *don't* have to go into plastics. You can follow your bliss.

There was a feeling of hope in the Sixties that's hard for young people to imagine today. There was an almost embarrassing innocence among the hippies. We would learn that real change—changing ourselves *or* society—is much harder than we thought. Marianne Williamson, the popularizer of *A Course in Miracles,* now sees that the New Age will not come without grassroots political organizing across three generations. Buddhist leader Jack Kornfield says enlightenment is not all it was cracked up to be. "You might be more compassionate or wiser or more awake, but you're still the same person. The spiritual life turns out to be less about some spiritual state and more about the life you lead."

What was good and what was bad about the spirituality born of the Sixties? What stayed with us, and how has it altered the American religious landscape? What have we learned about the promises and the pitfalls of this spiritual path?

Here are six aspects of Sixties spirituality, good *and* bad:

1. It is *liberating,* but it can also be divisive. We needed women's liberation, gay liberation, and sexual liberation. But those movements spawned lots of separation along with all that liberation. Families were divided. Society was divided. Feminism fueled the battle of the sexes. Gay liberation divided mainstream religion into opposing camps of tolerance and tradition. Sexual liberation could become sexual exploitation. On the other hand, the child abuse scandals in the Roman Catholic Church show us that the repression of desire can just as easily lead us into temptation.

2. It is *experiential.* It is felt. It cares little about doctrine or tradition. Pentecostalism and New Age spirituality both blossomed in the Sixties, and both put a premium on personal experience. It's not about believing in God as much as experiencing the power of the divine. Both movements emphasize faith healing, prophecy, and altered states of consciousness, whether through speaking in tongues or reliving past lives. At the same time, the lack of tradition and oversight allows both charismatic Christians and explorers of consciousness to be swept away by charlatans or silly fads—everything from aura photography to holy laughter.

3. It is *antiauthoritarian*, with deep distrust for religious hierarchies. Nevertheless, some seekers are easily duped by authoritarian leaders from adopted traditions. Lapsed Christians and Jews leave the perceived oppression of their parents' faith only to follow Indian gurus or Tibetan lamas who abuse *their* spiritual authority. So many people in my generation too easily dropped their defenses and lost their minds in the glow of *spiritus exotica*.

4. It is *eclectic*, sampling the buffet of world religion. But this can also make Sixties spirituality rootless. It's the religious version of fusion cooking—mixing California cuisine with Asian flavors or Mexican spice. Eclectic is fine, but not forever. Read a little Zen, whirl like a dervish, and chant "Hare Krishna," but you eventually need to decide if you're Buddhist, Sufi, or Hindu. Or just go back to being a Catholic or a Jew.

5. It is *unifying*. Nothing wrong with oneness, but it can be so ephemeral. At its best, this path unifies mind, body, and spirit and helps us understand the real connections between that essential trinity. It is universalistic, seeking the common wisdom in all religions, the mystical core, the perennial philosophy sought by Aldous Huxley. But this formless faith can be a slippery sort of spirituality. Ask a seeker what she means by spiritual "energy," and you may hear the sounds of silence.

6. It is *therapeutic*. It's about stress reduction, not salvation. It seeks to make us feel good, not be good. It's practical, not pious. Yoga becomes a lifestyle choice, more like going to the gym than to the ashram. In the West Buddhist converts often take a psychological view of meditation, turning their Zen master or Tibetan lama into a kind of East-meets-West therapist. Again, there's nothing necessarily wrong with that. There are real connections between yoga and physical health or Buddhist mindfulness and psychological health. But this self-focus can easily lead to the spiritual narcissism of the "worried well."

There's the list, but I don't pretend to define the decade, and neither do I intend to bash it. My mission was to tell the stories of parents and children who lived inside the spiritual upheaval of the Sixties and to show how those polarizing changes played out in actual lives. These were not typical families. The parents were trying to transform themselves and the world. While their children do not carry the fervor of the Sixties, they tend to be good people who care for matters beyond their personal affairs and the kinds of cars they drive. They have inherited their parents' distrust of organized religion but not their rejection of the nuclear family. If there is one theme that runs through nearly all these stories, from David Price's Esalen upbringing to the "blessed" childhood of Donna Collins, it is the feeling that Mom and Dad just weren't around enough. This, of course, is not confined to pilgrims of the spirit. My father wasn't around much either. But he wasn't out saving the world. He was a traveling businessman on the road to divorce.

Many of these parents were more concerned about changing the world than raising their families. The world needed changing. It still does. Today the family has been raised up as the most sacred and sovereign unit of society. Many of the families profiled in this book paid less attention to the kids than the children wanted, but the neglect was mostly benign, the by-product of social idealism or a life a bit too centered on self-improvement.

Of course, the vast majority of hippie kids were *not* living in intense new religious movements like the Unification Church or the Hare Krishnas. Others who have studied children raised in less authoritarian Sixties communes seem to like what they have found. One researcher, for example, reported that communal kids in the 1970s "demonstrated a high degree of maturity, self-confidence, and self-reliance."[1]

Another scholar, Professor Thomas Weisner, an anthropologist at the University of California at Los Angeles, followed up on more than two hundred families with hippie parents. "These families were performing social experiments," he said. "There were concerns they might have health problems because of different diets, not do well in school because of different lifestyles of their parents, or they might be stigmatized." But after conducting IQ tests and other surveys, Weisner found most of the commune kids to be exceedingly normal and doing well in school.[2]

Timothy Miller, a professor of religious studies at the University of Kansas, also has done extensive follow-up research on Sixties communes. He found that those who grew up in alternative communities "generally had rosy memories of their halcyon years in the cultural vanguard, with plenty of playmates, exposure to slices of the culture that most children never got to see, and adventures. Many have gone on to advanced education and successful careers."[3]

Daniel Greenberg didn't grow up in a commune, but sometimes he wishes he did. Today he lives with his family at Sirius Community is Massachusetts, one of thousands of small intentional communities that still flourish in city and countryside across the United States. "I grew up in suburbia and always felt there was a veil between myself and the adult world," he writes.

My father was a mechanical engineer, but until I was six or seven I thought he drove trains. I didn't know what my father did when he left the house, didn't know where supermarket food came from, didn't know where pee went when I flushed the toilet, and didn't know how adults worked, played and loved together.

Community children, on the other hand, are exposed to and learn from many aspects of adult life that tend to remain "behind the scenes" for mainstream children. They see adults building houses, building relationships, building political structures.[4]

Greenberg's observation reminds me of the last person I interviewed for this book. So here's one final story, this one about the childhood of Nicholas van Aelstyn, who as a boy took a magical mystery tour through the social and spiritual changes of the Sixties.

Nico's parents were devout Catholics when he was born in the early Sixties. Then in 1968 they moved to northern California. His father got a job teaching at San Francisco State College. He threw himself into New Left politics and avant-garde theater. In the 1970s Nico's family moved to Boulder, Colorado, where his parents studied Tibetan Buddhism.

Nico grew up in an assortment of communal homes in Boulder and around the San Francisco Bay Area. When he was very young, his parents insisted that he call them by their first names. "We had discussions about it," Nico recalled. "They didn't want to glorify the status of mom or dad. They were just other people, along with all these other people living in the house."

Dad never took Nico to baseball games. There was no Little League. "We had a certain scorn," he says, "for normal family activities."

Today Nico and his wife, Sarah, have their own children, ages five and three. They don't live in a commune. Their kids call them Mommy and Daddy. Nico doesn't meditate. He and his wife are not Buddhists. But they are lay leaders of the Episcopal church in their San Francisco neighborhood.

Nevertheless, Nico appreciates his unorthodox upbringing and the values his parents instilled in him. "I was treated with more respect than many of my peers. My opinions were taken seriously. I had a vote in house meetings about things. I was taken seriously as a member of the community."

While they don't live in a commune, Nico and Sarah do want to expose their children to the larger world. "The phrase that's popular today is 'it takes a village to raise kids.' I liked the vitality of having lots of people around and the engagement my parents had in the community. They were a bridge to the larger world."

Today Nico sees other parents organizing their lives around their children, ferrying the kids to soccer, play dates, music classes. "One of the illnesses of the American nuclear family is that children are raised thinking they are the center of the universe, and the only other planets are Mom and Dad. That is unhealthy for the child, but it's also unhealthy for the adults. We love our children very much. They are the most important things in our lives. But for their sake and ours we want more people to be involved in their lives than just us."

His children interact with other adults at their church and are brought along to various political activities. The weekend before we spoke, Nico and his two kids were among a hundred thousand protesters marching up Market Street in San Francisco in opposition to the invasion and occupation of Iraq.

"What drew me to Christianity is the incarnation, the notion that the divine is here with us in the world," he said. "We need to be more engaged in the world and not run away from it. Our understanding is that Jesus stands with the broken of the world. We are here to stand up to injustice and in solidarity with those who are suffering.

"What I most appreciate about the counterculture upbringing that I had is that it gave me a critical stance. We learned to think critically. We were taught to ask questions about how society was run."

Sixties bashing is facile. In the 1990s those titillating times were subject to endless sniping by the talking heads of television, apostles of the ordinary, and neoconservative pundits. For many Christian commentators the Sixties became the metaphor for the fall from grace. It was more convenient to blame drug addiction, poverty, teen pregnancy, and the breakdown of the family on a past period of permissiveness. Criticism of the excesses of the Sixties shifted attention from the undoing of the vital social gains of the decade. It was easier to preach a narrow and regressive sexual morality than to look at other forces threatening poor and middle-class families in the late twentieth century, such as the desperate shortage of affordable housing and the grinding necessity for both parents to hold jobs. It wasn't until the corporate accounting scandals of 2002 and the plundering of people's pensions that the general public began to question, once again, if the business of America was just business and to realize that when it comes to national well-being, corporate responsibility is as big a factor as personal morality.

Our appraisal of the 1960s flows from our ideas about the 1950s, and many of those ideas are wrong. Sixties bashers claim that America's moral, religious, and familial life reached shining heights in the 1950s, then collapsed into a cacophony of selfishness and sin. America's "greatest generation," we are told, saved the world in the 1940s, then moved to the suburbs and set us on the path of peace and prosperity. In this fantasy, all began to unravel in the 1960s, when a rebellious generation tore society apart and couldn't put it back together again. Our most grievous loss was said to be traditional family values, three words that became the political battle cry of reactionary, post-Sixties politics and religion.

In reality, there wasn't much about the faith and families of the fifties that was traditional. If anything, the fifties, not the sixties and seventies, were the aberrant years. The post–World War II era saw an abnormal emphasis on piety, patriotism, and the nuclear family. In fact, the decade was just an aberrant blip on the long-term charts of public piety. Our religious "revival" had more to do with demographics and politics than the hand of God. The baby boomers reached their Sunday school years. This is when many families traditionally—and often temporarily—reconnect with church or synagogue.

Enough about "the greatest generation." It had its greatness, to be sure, but it was also the generation that built the Japanese internment camps, saluted McCarthyism, and mostly turned its face away from racism and anti-Semitism. Many of the problems we blame on the Sixties—child abuse, domestic violence, substance abuse—were no less prevalent in the fifties. We just didn't talk about them then. It was much easier to hide all that behind the walls of our now-separate homes out in the suburbs.

Sociologist Stephanie Coontz points out in *The Way We Never Were: American Families and the Nostalgia Trap* that the rise of the nuclear family came at the expense of other old-fashioned values, like the *extended* family's inclusion of grandparents and aunts and uncles in children's lives along with the social ties of truly interdependent communities.

Don't get me wrong. Being a child of the Sixties was not easy. Divorce is hard on families, and from 1960 to the mid-1980s, the divorce rate tripled and the number of children in one-parent homes doubled. Meanwhile, the percentage of teenage mothers who were unwed jumped from 15 percent to 61 percent.[5] None of those are healthy trends, but it's too easy to blame the bogeymen of the counterculture and Sixties permissiveness. Most people who divorce remarry and form new and extended kinship networks. Back in the fifties, pregnant girls got married, but they produced a lot of unhappy marriages and unloved children. Bad marriages are not necessarily better than good single-parent homes.

If you need some sixties to bash, try the 1860s. The Victorian model of the family was revived as the 1950s ideal. In Victorian times nurseries and nannies kept children away from their parents. Husbands kept their wives away by retiring to their private quarters, smoking room, study, or billiard parlors. In 1869 a leading Congregational minister, the Reverend Horace Bushnell, opposed women's suffrage as "the reform against nature."[6]

Like the churchmen of 1860s, the leaders of today's Christian Right respond to the 1960s and women's liberation with fire-and-brimstone rhetoric. Pat Robertson, the televangelist and former GOP presidential candidate, proclaimed in a fund-raising letter in the 1990s that feminism was inspiring women to "leave their husbands, kill their children, practice witchcraft, destroy capitalism and become lesbians."[7]

It's hard to decide which part of Robertson's rant is more shocking, especially from a man who claims to be a follower of Jesus, but let's just consider the parts about leaving husbands and destroying capitalism. According to the Bible, Jesus said that his true disciple must reject his earthly life to follow the Master; he must "hate his own father and mother and wife and children and brothers and sisters." As for capitalism, the Savior advises the rich man to "sell what you own, and give the money to the poor, and you will have treasure in heaven; then come follow me."[8] So much for family values and capitalism.

So what would Jesus do? What would he find good and bad about the spiritual legacy of the Sixties? Search the Bible for clues about the Savior's worries about sex, wine, and celebration, and you won't find much. The Nazarene does not appear to have been a great advocate of traditional religion or traditional families. He inveighed against the accumulation of wealth and talked instead about voluntary simplicity, peace, justice, love, and communal living. He was much more interesting in saving the world than raising a family.

Sound familiar?

Now, more than ever, we need to remember that the Sixties was about keeping hope in the world and faith in ourselves. We also need to remember that the Sixties was not about the culture. It was about the counterculture. Today the new world disorder seems a long way from the Age of Aquarius. Terrorists kill innocent people in the name of God. Our nation, under God, flexes its military might in a vain effort to win the hearts and minds of poor people on the other side of the world. Those people don't seem to be buying. Meanwhile, hundreds of thousands of demonstrators take to the streets and demand peace and justice for all. Millions have lost faith in the free market but hope to reclaim at least a degree of empowerment in their own lives and local communities.

Sound familiar?

Perhaps the children of the Sixties—young and old—can help us find another way or at least help us find our way back to what was best about that extraordinary era.

INTRODUCTION

1. Peter Coyote, *Sleeping Where I Fall* (Washington, D.C.: Counterpoint, 1998), 69.
2. Joe Queenan, *Balsamic Dreams: A Short but Self-Important History of the Baby Boomer Generation* (New York: Henry Holt, 2001); David Brooks, *Bobos in Paradise: The New Upper Class and How They Got There* (New York: Simon & Schuster, 2000).
3. See "The Me Decade and the Third Great Awakening," first published in *New York Magazine* and *New West Magazine* on August 23, 1976. That piece is also included in a Tom Wolfe reader, *The Purple Decades* (New York: Farrar, Straus, Giroux, 1982).
4. Alice Echols, *Shaky Ground: The Sixties and Its Aftershocks* (New York: Columbia University Press, 2002), 48.
5. George Gallup, "Americans' Spiritual Searches Turn Inward," *Religion and Values,* Feb. 11, 2003.
6. Jackson W. Carroll and Wade Clark Roof, *Bridging Divided Worlds: Generational Cultures in Congregations* (San Francisco: Jossey-Bass, 2002), 228.
7. Joseph Campbell, *The Power of Myth* with Bill Moyers (New York: Doubleday, 1988), 5.
8. Campbell, *Power of Myth*, 120.
9. Wes "Scoop" Nisker, *The Big Bang, the Buddha, and the Baby Boom: The Spiritual Experiments of My Generation* (San Francisco: Harper-SanFrancisco, 2003), xi.
10. Roger Finke and Rodney Stark, *The Churching of America, 1776–1990: Winners and Losers in Our Religious Economy* (New Brunswick, NJ: Rutgers University Press, 1992), 15.
11. Robert Fuller, *Spiritual but Not Religious* (Oxford and New York: Oxford University Press, 2001), 20–21.

12. William James, *The Varieties of Religious Experience* (New York: American Penguin Library, 1982), 115.

PART 1

1. Walter Truett Anderson, *The Upstart Spring: Esalen and the American Awakening* (Reading, MA: Addison-Wesley, 1983), 20.
2. Anderson, *Upstart Spring*, 100.
3. Anderson, *Upstart Spring*, 92.
4. Tom Wolfe, *Purple Decades*, 279.
5. Quoted in Don Lattin, "After 25 Years, Esalen Institute at a Turning Point," *San Francisco Examiner*, Feb. 17, 1987.
6. James Redfield, Michael Murphy, and Sylvia Timbers, *God and the Evolving Universe: The Next Step in Personal Evolution* (New York: Tarcher/Putnam, 2002), 58.
7. Quoted in Don Lattin, "Divine Tension Between Science, Mysticism," *San Francisco Chronicle Sunday Review*, May 3, 1992, 9.
8. Thomas Merton, *The Intimate Merton: His Life from His Journals* (San Francisco: HarperSanFrancisco, 1999), 167.
9. Joseph Ratzinger, *Homosexualitas problema*, Congregation for the Doctrine of the Faith, 1986.
10. Thomas Moore, *Care of the Soul* (New York: HarperCollins, 1992), xv, vxii.
11. William D'Antonio, James Davidson, Dean Hoge, and Katherine Meyer, *American Catholics: Gender, Generation, and Commitment* (Walnut Creek, CA: AltaMira Press, 2001), 78.
12. Don Lattin, "Religious Turmoil—Idealistic Young Priests Who Lost the Church Calling," *San Francisco Chronicle*, Oct. 29, 1990.
13. Quoted in Don Lattin, "Fathers and Sins," *San Francisco Chronicle*, April 14, 2002.
14. D'Antonio et al., *American Catholics*, 11.
15. Larry Stammer, "Organized Religion Slips in Survey," *Los Angeles Times*, January 11, 2003.
16. Gary Smith, "Peace Warriors," *Washington Post Magazine*, June 5, 1988, 22.
17. Quoted in Don Lattin, "A Course in Miracles Touches Thousands," *San Francisco Examiner*, February 10, 1985.
18. D. Patrick Miller, *The Complete Story of the Course* (Berkeley, CA: Fearless Books, 1997), 33–34.

19. D. Patrick Miller, "Rights and Miracles: An Interview with Jonathan Kirsch," posted Aug. 11, 1999, at www.fearlessbooks.com.
20. Miller, *Complete Story*, 58.
21. Quoted in Leslie Bennetts, "Marianne's Faithful," *Vanity Fair*, June 1991.
22. Robert Bellah et al., *Habits of the Heart: Individualism and Commitment in American Life* (Berkeley and Los Angeles: University of California Press, 1985), 221.
23. Quoted in Don Lattin, "Alternative Religion—Going to Church the 12-Step Way," *San Francisco Chronicle*, Dec. 17, 1990.
24. Quoted in Lattin, "Alternative Religion."
25. Quoted in Lattin, "Alternative Religion."
26. For more on the small group movement, see Robert Wuthnow's book *Sharing the Journey* (New York: Free Press, 1994).
27. Quoted in David Crumm, "Rift in Church Is Blamed for Departure," *Detroit Free Press*, Sept. 4, 2002.

PART 2

1. Byron Thomas, trans., *The Dhammapada* (New York: Bell Tower, 2001), 38.
2. Quoted in Don Lattin, "Transgenerational Meditation: Parents Confront the Challenges of Raising Kids Buddhist," *San Francisco Chronicle*, April 14, 2002.
3. Quoted in Don Lattin, "A Buddhist Shangri-La in Marin: 400-Acre Meditation Retreat," *San Francisco Chronicle*, Jan. 30, 1991.
4. Quoted in Richard Hughes Seager, *Buddhism in America* (New York: Columbia University Press, 1999), 41.
5. Quoted in Don Lattin, "Dalai Lama in Marin to Shape Future of American Buddhism," *San Francisco Chronicle*, June 24, 2000.
6. Stephen Levine, *Turning Toward the Mystery: A Seeker's Journey* (San Francisco: HarperSanFrancisco, 2002), 126.
7. Noah Levine, *Dharma Punx* (San Francisco: HarperSanFrancisco, 2003).
8. Noah Levine, "Confessions of a Dharma Punk," *Tricycle: A Buddhist Review* (Winter 2000), 71–72.
9. Donald Lopez, *The Story of Buddhism: A Concise Guide to Its History and Teachings* (San Francisco: HarperSanFrancisco, 2001), 22–23.
10. S. Levine, *Turning Toward the Mystery*, 16, 18.
11. S. Levine, *Turning Toward the Mystery*, 24.
12. S. Levine, *Turning Toward the Mystery*, 63, 64.

13. N. Levine, "Confessions of a Dharma Punk," 76.

14. Quoted in Don Lattin, "A Smorgasbord of Spirituality: Baby Boomers Eschew Name-Brand Religion to Create New Rituals," *San Francisco Chronicle*, June 28, 1993.

15. "Jesus Christ, the Bearer of the Water of Life: A Christian Reflection on the 'New Age,'" cited by Thomas Ryan in "Christ and/or Aquarius?" *America*, March 24, 2003, 12–15.

16. Alistair Shearer and Peter Russell, trans., *The Upanishads* (New York: Bell Tower, 2003), 119.

17. E. Burke Rochford Jr., "Child Abuse in the Hare Krishna Movement, 1971–1986" (unpublished paper, Middlebury College, n.d.), 5.

18. George Harrison, "Awaiting on You All," *All Things Must Pass*, Capitol/EMI Records, 1970.

19. John Hubner and Lindsey Gruson, *Monkey on a Stick: Murder, Madness, and the Hare Krishnas* (San Diego: Harcourt Brace Jovanovich, 1988), 49.

20. Rochford, "Child Abuse," 13.

21. Hubner and Gruson, *Monkey on a Stick*, 252.

22. Quoted in Don Lattin, "A Test of Faith: Allegations of Past Child Abuse Threaten Hare Krishnas' Existence," *San Francisco Chronicle*, Feb. 13, 2001.

23. Rochford, "Child Abuse," 11.

24. Quoted in Don Lattin, "Growing Up in the Hare Krishnas," *San Francisco Chronicle*, Feb. 13, 2001.

25. For more, see Mary McCormick Maaga, *Hearing the Voices of Jonestown* (Syracuse, NY: Syracuse University Press, 1998).

26. Susan Palmer and Charlotte Hardman, eds., *Children in New Religions* (New Brunswick, NJ: Rutgers University Press, 1999), 7.

27. Bhagwan Shree Rajneesh. *The Book*. Rajneesh Fou

ndation International, Rajneeshpuram, 1984. P. 115.

28. Don Lattin, "Rajneesh City Arms Against Outside World," *San Francisco Sunday Examiner and Chronicle*, July 1, 1984.

29. Quoted in Don Lattin, "Controversy Follows the 'Sex Guru' West," *San Francisco Examiner*, Oct. 13, 1982.

30. Bhagwan Shree Rajneesh, *The Book: An Introduction to the Teachings of Bhagwan Shree Rajneesh* (Rajneeshpuram, OR: Rajneesh Foundation International, 1984), ser. 3, pp. 181, 191.

31. *Osho Times International*, Nov. 16, 1992, 15.

32. Satya Bharti Franklin, *The Promise of Paradise: A Woman's Intimate Story of the Perils of Life with Rajneesh* (Barrytown, NY: Station Hill Press, 1992), 18.

33. Franklin, *Promise of Paradise*, 40.

34. Franklin, *Promise of Paradise*, 54–57.

35. Ma Satya Bharti, *Death Comes Dancing* (London: Routledge & Kegan Paul, 1981); Satya Bharti, *The Ultimate Risk* (London: Wildwood House, 1980); Satya Bharti, *Drunk on the Divine* (New York: Grove, 1980).

36. Osho, *Autobiography of a Spiritually Incorrect Mystic* (New York: St. Martin's Press, 2000), 254–55.

37. Franklin, *Promise of Paradise*, 209.

38. Franklin, *Promise of Paradise*, 336.

39. Rajneesh, *Book*, ser. 1, pp. 508, 505.

PART 3

1. Quoted in Don Lattin, "Americans Search for New Sexual Ethic," *San Francisco Chronicle*, Nov. 29, 1994.

2. Mark 10:9.

3. Quoted in Lattin, "Americans Search."

4. *What Is Burning Man Page*, viewed May 21, 2003, www.burningman.com/whatisburningman/about_burningman/faq_what _is.html.

5. Quoted in John Heidenry, *What Wild Ecstasy: The Rise and Fall of the Sexual Revolution* (New York: Simon & Schuster, 1997), 35.

6. Richard McBrien, ed., *The HarperCollins Encyclopedia of Catholicism* (San Francisco: HarperSanFrancisco, 1995), s.v. "Birth Control."

7. Quoted in Don Lattin, "General Assembly of Presbyterians Draws Protesters: Christians Stump for Gay Rights," *San Francisco Chronicle*, June 26, 2000.

8. Quoted in Don Lattin, "Presbyterians Back Ban on Gay Unions: Ministers Would Be Barred from Officiating at Church Ceremonies," *San Francisco Chronicle*, July 1, 2000.

9. John Boswell, *Christianity, Social Tolerance, and Homosexuality: Gay People in Western Europe from the Beginning of the Christian Era to the Fourteenth Century* (Chicago: University of Chicago Press, 1980), 117.

10. Boswell, *Christianity*, 7.

11. Boswell, *Christianity*, 73.

12. Clement of Alexandria, *Paedagogus* 2.10, cited in Boswell, *Christianity*, 146.

13. Augustine, *Soliloquai* 1.40, cited in Boswell, *Christianity*, 164; Augustine, *Contra mendacium* 7.10, cited in Boswell, *Christianity*, 157.

14. Boswell, *Christianity*, 293.

15. Boswell, *Christianity*, 329.

16. *San Francisco Chronicle*, September 11, 1976.

17. Mark Jordan, *The Silence of Sodom: Homosexuality in Modern Catholicism* (Chicago: University of Chicago Press, 2000), 34, 89.

18. Jordan, *Silence of Sodom*, 190.

19. Carl Jung, *The Collected Works*, vol. 9 (New York: Pantheon, 1959), pt. 1, pp. 86–87.

20. Quoted in Don Lattin, "Escaping a Free Love Legacy," *San Francisco Chronicle*, Feb. 14, 2001.

21. For more on Williams's story, see Miriam Williams, *Heaven's Harlots: My Fifteen Years as a Sacred Prostitute in the Children of God Cult* (New York: Eagle Brook, 1998).

22. All of the Berg quotations are taken from these "Mo letters."

23. The Judgment of Lord Justice Alan Ward, 26 May 1995, W 42 1992 in the High Court of Justice, Family Division.

24. Peter Amsterdam, "2003, Here We Come" ("Family" newsletter sent out in early 2003).

25. Rita Nakashima Brock and Rebecca Ann Parker, *Proverbs of Ashes: Violence, Redemptive Suffering, and the Search for What Saves Us* (Boston: Beacon Press, 2001).

26. Quoted in Don Lattin, "Religion Expert Has Had a Long, Strange Trip," *San Francisco Chronicle*, Jan. 20, 2002.

27. Quoted in Robert Forte, ed., *Timothy Leary: Outside Looking In* (Rochester, VT: Parker Street Press, 1999), 50.

28. Quoted in Don Lattin, "Stroke Teaches Ram Dass Anew to 'Be Here Now,'" *San Francisco Chronicle*, May 26, 1997.

29. Quoted in Robert Forte and Nina Graboi, "Ram Dass Remembers Tim," in *Timothy Leary*, ed. Forte, 57, 64.

30. Don Lattin, "From Rhythm to Blues: Fight over Dances and Drugs Tearing S.F. Church Apart," *San Francisco Chronicle*, Feb. 4. 2003.

31. Quoted in Don Lattin, "Inside a Peyote Tepee: A Psychedelic Prayer Meeting," *San Francisco Chronicle*, June 19, 1989.

32. For the whole story, see Joel Selvin, *Summer of Love: The Inside Story of LSD, Rock & Roll, Free Love, and High Times in the Wild West* (New York: Dutton, 1994).

33. Quoted in Don Lattin, "Rock (Music) of Ages: Monterey Crowd Testament to Growth of Christian Sound," *San Francisco Chronicle*, Aug. 2, 1997.

34. Quoted in Don Lattin, "Superman of the Cloth," *San Francisco Chronicle*, Sept 21, 1997.

35. Vicki Haddock, "Son of a Preacher Man: How John Ashcroft's Religion Shapes His Public Service," *San Francisco Chronicle*, Aug. 4, 2002.

36. Quoted in Don Lattin, "Growing Flock Who Ask Guidance in All Things," *San Francisco Examiner-Chronicle*, Feb. 19, 1984.

37. Quoted in Don Lattin, "Boomers Abandoning Mainline Churches," *San Francisco Chronicle*, Jan. 14, 1995.

38. Quoted in Don Lattin, "Revival Fever Rising: Apocalyptic Notions Fuel Pentecostal Movement," *San Francisco Chronicle*, Sept. 18, 1999.

39. Quoted in Don Lattin, "Two Faces of Spiritual Revival," *San Francisco Chronicle*, Dec. 1, 1989.

PART 4

1. Quoted in Michael Inglis, ed., *40 Years in America: An Intimate History of the Unification Movement* (New York: HAS Publications, 2000), xv.

2. Massimo Introvigne, *The Unification Church* (Salt Lake City: Signature Books, 2000), 65.

3. Gil Ja Sa Eu, "My Testimony," photocopied essay in Unification Theological Seminary Library, Barrytown, New York, cited in Mose Durst, *To Bigotry, No Sanction* (Chicago: Regnery Gateway, 1984), 74.

4. Durst, *To Bigotry, No Sanction*, 26.

5. Durst, *To Bigotry, No Sanction*, 34.

6. Durst, *To Bigotry, No Sanction*, 50.

7. Quoted in Don Lattin, "Some Moonie Parents Now Converts Too," *San Francisco Examiner*, Nov. 8, 1977.

8. "Moon's Japanese Profits Bolster Efforts in U.S.," *Washington Post*, Sept. 16, 1984.

9. Quoted in Marc Fischer and Jeff Leen, "Stymied in U.S., Moon's Church Sounds a Retreat," *Washington Post*, Nov. 24, 1997.

10. Sun Myung Moon, Address to the Family Federal for World Peace, Aug. 1,

1996; remarks on women quoted in Don Lattin, "In Oakland, Moon Stresses Family, Criticizes Childless Women," *San Francisco Chronicle*, Mar. 13, 2001.

11. Quoted in Don Lattin, "Cruising the Spiritual Marketplace: Spirituality Is for Sale as Never Before: Americans Are Changing Faiths like They Change Web Browsers," *San Francisco Chronicle*, Nov. 29, 1998.

12. Quoted in Lattin, "Cruising the Spiritual Marketplace."

13. For more on this, see Richard Cimino and Don Lattin, *Shopping for Faith: American Religion in the New Millennium* (San Francisco: Jossey-Bass, 1998).

14. Quoted in Don Lattin, "New Age Hucksterism on Small Screen," *San Francisco Chronicle*, Nov. 25, 2001.

15. Quoted in Don Lattin, "Ramtha Changes Channels, but He's Up to His Old Tricks," *San Francisco Chronicle*, Sept 2, 2001.

16. Elizabeth Clare Prophet, "I'm Stumping for the Coming Revolution in Higher Consciousness" (taped lecture, Summit University, 1979).

17. Robert Ellwood, "The Mighty 'I AM,'" *History Today*, June 1988, 21.

18. Quoted in *Los Angeles Herald Examiner*, Jan. 29, 1985.

19. For more details, see *Church Universal and Triumphant, Inc., v Gregory Mull*, 1981, "Cross Complaint for Damages," Superior Court of the State of California, Los Angeles County, no. C358191 (May 11), 1–12; *Church Universal and Triumphant, Inc., and Elizabeth Clare Prophet v Linda Witt*, 1989, "Appeal from a Judgement of the Los Angeles County Superior Court, Alfred J. Margolis, Judge," Court Appeal of the State of California, Second Appellate District, Division Five, Superior Court no. C358191 (April 10), 1–32.

20. Associated Press, "Religious Sect Leader Has Alzheimer's," *San Francisco Chronicle*, Nov. 27, 1998; Associated Press. "Lawyers Testing Sentiment for a Class-Action Suit Against Church," *San Francisco Chronicle*, July 21, 2001.

21. Some believe this song was actually written about Stephen Gaskin, but the lyricist, Robert Hunter, has publicly debunked that theory.

22. Times-Post Service, "Caravan's Search for Beauty," *San Francisco Chronicle*, Jan. 12, 1971.

23. James Robison, "San Francisco Guru and His Million-Dollar Farm," *San Francisco Sunday Examiner and Chronicle*, Nov. 6, 1977; reprinted from the *Chicago Tribune*.

CONCLUSION

1. Charley M. Johnson and Robert W. Deisher, "Contemporary Communal Child Rearing: A First Analysis," *Pediatrics* 52, no. 3 (Sept. 1973): 323–24, 326, cited in Timothy Miller, *The '60s Communes: Hippies and Beyond* (Syracuse, NY: Syracuse University Press, 1999), 185.
2. "Children of Hippies Doing OK," *Los Angeles Daily News,* reprinted in *San Francisco Chronicle,* Dec. 5, 1991.
3. Miller, *'60s Communes,* 185.
4. Daniel Greenberg, "A Place in the Tribe," *Communities: Journal of Cooperative Living* (Spring 2002), 22–23.
5. Stephanie Coontz, *The Way We Never Were: American Families and the Nostalgia Trap* (New York: Basic Books, 1992), 3.
6. Quoted in Rosemary Radford Ruether, *Christianity and the Making of the Modern Family* (Boston: Beacon Press, Boston, 2000), 104.
7. Quoted in Maralee Schwartz and Kenneth J. Cooper, "Equal Rights Initiative in Iowa Attacked," *Washington Post,* Aug. 23, 1992.
8. Luke 14:26; Mark 10:21.

CREDITS AND PERMISSIONS